Weeds Like Us

a memoir by Janiva Magness

Fathead Records 2019
Los Angeles

The events and conversations in this book have been set down to the best of the author's ability, although some names and details have been changed to protect the privacy of individuals.

First paperback edition June 2019
Second paperback edition July 2019

Editing by Deborah Block and Deb Lubin
Cover concept by Janiva Magness
Cover art by Brie Darling, Dan Navarro, Ant Morgan
Cover photo by Bill C. Magness
Book design by www.bookclaw.com

Printed in the United States of America by Steuben Press
Longmont, CO 80501

ISBN 978-1-7330652-0-7 (autographed, numbered paperback)
ISBN 978-1-7330652-1-4 (paperback)
ISBN 978-1-7330652-2-1 (ebook)
ISBN 978-1-7330652-3-8 (2nd edition paperback)
ISBN 978-1-7330652-4-5 (2nd edition ebook)

Published by Fathead Records
P.O. Box 251511, Los Angeles, CA 90025

www.janivamagness.com

Grace —
xox
Thank you —
Lauren Magness

For Carsa Mia and us all...

Contents

A Note From The Author

I have long believed everyone has a story. This is simply mine. I say "simply," but writing down these bones has been a difficult process for me – difficult, but a compelling and healing one, too.

I am compelled by the idea that in some way, my telling of these experiences might help someone else survive their own struggles with their lives and histories. Mental illness, major dysfunction, tragedy, and violence: I'm comforted if the telling helps someone else. I'm comforted, too, because the telling helps me make better sense of my own chaotic history. (I find it funny and revealing that the first word I ever spoke was not "mama" or "dada," but "why?")

I want you to know that I resisted giving these experiences voice for most of my life. I agreed to the idea of this book very slowly, and started it with great trepidation. It has come out in fits and starts, with long periods of procrastination — which, of course, caused the actual writing to take far longer than I'd wanted, which, of course, I also resented.

But hell, anything worth doing is worth doing right – right? (Who said that anyway, besides my dad?) And in doing this right, I now understand something that has taken me years to recognize: Hidden away, powerful experiences like the ones I've had become a kind of time-released poison. They hold the power to stifle and do irreparable damage to body, mind and spirit for generations to come if left untold. Deep sorrow, rage, and tremendous grief are entirely different beasts than self-pity. They are feelings that require air and light in order not to become a rotting pile of dung inside of us. Left to fester, they can ruin a person's life, and the lives of those near them.

As it turns out, I have also found that same deep sorrow; grief and rage hold within them the intense power to heal when they are handled with patience and love. Mind you, neither patience with myself nor self-love is the usual first choice for me. I have had to learn those, too. And therein has come an unexpected healing and a beautiful freedom for me.

So I invite you into this series of experiences and hope you will find in the telling of my tale some relief, some release, and even some collateral beauty for yourself or a loved one. Even the smallest morsel will do.

Like the famous bluesman Louisiana Red once said, "I'm gonna tell you a story. . . Now this one is true."

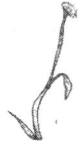

Weeds Like Us
Introduction — B.B. and Bonnie

B.B. King looked regal, as he stood tall on the stage of the convention center in downtown Memphis the night of May 7, 2009. The late, great bluesman wore a black satin tuxedo, shiny silver vest and pocket-handkerchief placed just so. His head was covered in pale stubble, the same shade of silver as his pencil-thin mustache. At eighty-four, he still had that trademark sly and adorable look of a seasoned lady-killer.

Standing next to him was Bonnie Raitt. She also looked radiant, wearing a signature blouse with sheer, belled sleeves and a warm, sweet smile on her pretty face. The flag of silver sweeping through her thick red hair seemed to testify to her stature and well-deserved status as a resilient blues superstar who had overcome plenty of her own adversity.

My band and I were at the convention center that night, taking time off from the grind of the road from our spring tour, to attend the thirtieth annual Blues Music Awards. In the blues world, which is where I've been blessed to make my living for about three decades, the BMAs are huge. They are the Grammy Awards and Oscars rolled into one, the most anticipated night of the year for blues artists and the thousands of hardcore fans who watch the nominees perform in a rousing show that lasts more than five hours.

I was fortunate enough to be up for awards in several categories, including the grand prize of B.B. King Entertainer of the Year, so the boys and I would be playing a short set.

As always when I perform, I was dressed to the nines, looking sharp in a tight halter and low-cut black jumpsuit slit high up the legs. It was the kind of revealing outfit that Bruce Iglauer, whose Alligator Records signed me a year earlier, used to scold me for wearing. He told me time and again I needed to dress "more appropriately" for a singer my age, but I couldn't give a shit. I'd been around too long and been through too much to have someone else dictate how I dress or behave. Besides, I'd loved playing dress-up since I was a little girl and still do. My fans dig it, too, so case closed.

As I walked into the packed convention center hall with Pearl, my 33-year-old daughter by my side, my insides were shaking. Pearl and I being together after everything that had happened between us was a miracle all by itself. I was also nervous because so many of the big blues stars I loved were attending the show or would be honored that night. B.B. and Bonnie, Buddy Guy, Taj Mahal, Bettye LaVette, Irma Thomas, Koko Taylor. Just being in the same room with legends like that was a mind-blower for this Detroit girl. To be nominated for multiple awards, including the crown jewel B.B. King Entertainer of the Year, well, that was off the charts.

Not that I expected to win anything. I'm not the person who goes into a situation like that anticipating that anything good will happen. There's too much bad history rattling around my head that tells me, "Don't expect too much. Who the hell do you think you are, anyway?" Losing is what I know how to do. In my family, where I come from, that's familiar territory. The idea of winning is like winning the Lottery. It's going to happen to someone, and that's cool, but it sure as hell ain't gonna be me.

Entertainer of the Year was for legends. Icons like Buddy Guy and B.B. King won it again and again. In fact, B took home the prize so many years in a row, the Blues Foundation finally renamed it in his honor. Before he started racking up the awards, it had always been just "Blues Entertainer of the Year." The only woman ever to win it was Koko Taylor, a Goddess in the blues world. She was known for decades as the "Queen of the Blues" and that was no exaggeration. I didn't believe I even belonged in the same room with any of these people. Being on the short list of nominees for an award they spent a lifetime earning was too much for my brain to handle. But I loved being there and tried to soak up the music and all the good vibes in the hall. Simply put, the sense of being accepted in this community was more than I could resist.

When it was time for my band to go on, I was more nervous than usual, but with so many heavyweights in the house, I was determined to let it rip. We played the racy Little Milton hit, That's What Love Will Make You Do, which was the title tune on the CD I had released a few months earlier. You always want to showcase your most recent stuff, even at a quick show like this. While Zach Zunis, my guitar player of many years, ripped through his solo, I moved and grooved behind him as if I didn't have a care in the world. And I guess I didn't. No matter what I was feeling or how much pain might have been breaking my heart, playing and singing always took me to another place. At least for a while. That's the whole purpose of the blues in the first place. Sing about the pain. The joy. The rage. Connect with other people through the universal experience of music, and look what happens: You feel better. Funny how that works. It's some of the best medicine there is. For me anyway. Always has been.

We were treated to some ass-kicking performances by other nominated acts, and after more than four hours of being washed clean by the music that speaks to me like no other, it was finally time for B and Bonnie to hand out the big prize.

You have to realize, B.B. King IS a god in my world. The man Eric Clapton correctly called "without a doubt, the most important artist the Blues has ever produced," had been a hero of mine since 1971. That's when I first saw him perform at the old Met Sports Center in Minneapolis. I will always remember it: He opened for Quicksilver Messenger Service, a 1960s-style psychedelic band from San Francisco, but in my world, it was all about B. There are a lot of reasons the whole world came to know Mississippi-born Riley B. King as "King of the Blues." He took B.B. as his stage name after cutting his first record in Nashville when he was in his early 20s, shortening it from "The Beale Street Blues Boy," as he was known on the radio when he was starting out.

By the time I first saw him perform in Minneapolis, he was international blues royalty. He tore up that hall and burned the headliner by playing such a ferocious show. I was a lost and depressed fourteen-year-old at the time. I didn't want to be alive. But even then, deep down in my soul, I understood that he was sending out something powerful. His deep, gospel-rich voice — a voice that always seemed to speak the truth — cut through the air and carried me away. He played and sang from the depth of his soul, as if he had nothing to lose.

With that trademark guitar vibrato of his, the unique phrasing and that tight, cutting sound only he could coax out of the guitar, the King went for blood on that stage in Minneapolis. He got it all, too. I can still see him in my mind's eye from that magical night. Big old B in his loud plaid suit, hair perfect in a beautiful natural, sweat running off him as he bent the strings on his beloved Lucille. He was working his ass off. Something inside me came to life when I saw him play like that. I didn't feel alive at all very often in those days, so you know he really spoke to me when he played and sang.

And here he was on the stage in Memphis for the 2009 Blues Music Awards with me sitting in the audience, nominated for the Entertainer of the Year prize that bears his name. It seems kind of crazy to me even now. B was tearing at the envelope, as he got ready to announce the winner. The stage lights seemed to reflect off his glasses. He had a hard time reading what was written on the card, stumbling a bit before the words finally came out.

"Ladies and gentlemen," the one and only King of the Blues declared, "the B.B. King Entertainer of the Year is . . . Miss . . . Janiva . . . Magness."

Holy shit. Several of my cousins were in the audience and I heard them scream, "Janiva! Janiva!" My heart swelled in my chest. I gasped at Pearl, put my arms around her and pulled her close as I stood up, wobbly as a newborn lamb. Pearl was already weeping, which made me even more of an emotional mess.

"Come on," I managed to say, grabbing her by the hand. There were years when I hadn't known if my only child was dead or alive. I wasn't going up on that stage without her.

My legs were rubber, a problem because the stage seemed a mile away. When we finally got there, I took a deep breath to keep from passing out. I could feel my face flush. My cheeks were red and hot. Bonnie, it seemed, tried to reassure me by shooting me a big smile, but I had a hard time taking it all in. Absorbing good news has always been tough for me. I can only take it in through a tiny cocktail straw, unable to accept more than a small amount at a time. It's an obvious character trait to the few who really know me.

About 25 years ago, a woman from Texas who was my close friend — her name was Lila — sized me up pretty accurately after knowing me for just a little while. "Yeah, honey," she said to me one day. "We know you're tough. We know we can tie your hands and your feet and gag you and you will scale that brick wall with your teeth. Not a problem. You got that. We know that. Nobody's worried about that. But let's untie your hands and your feet. Let's ungag you. Let's give you a really good life and then let's see what you got. Let's see how you handle that. Let's see what you're made of then, when life gets good."

Lila was dead on. Fear has always been next to me, but at times I wondered if I feared success more than failure. I'm still working on it, but my dear friend had me pegged. I know what the rules are and how I'm supposed to act when life is a nightmare and everything feels like shit. Success or peace of mind, love or peace in my heart — not familiar or comfortable territory for me. Like I said, I'm working on it.

And here was some of the best news I had ever received in my life. I had just been crowned B.B. King Entertainer of the Year, an award others might have killed for but I could never truly have imagined for myself. "Surprise," Bonnie said to me with a happy twinkle in her eye. She made a two-thumbs-up gesture that signaled her approval. With B.B. King standing next to her and the hall erupting in applause, it was a scene I will always remember and cherish, even more so now that the great King of the Blues is no longer with us. His music lives on forever, of course, as does the memory of that night with me.

For most of my life, no matter how much people have complimented me on my singing, I never really believed I had enough talent to make a career out of music. Putting myself down was part of what I've always called the Magness Curse, a family history where the default position is despair, depression and addiction. With suicide as the ultimate end. There is a certain stubborn streak and unwillingness to give up mixed in there, too, so it's all kind of messy and complicated at times. When I was younger, and especially before I got clean and sober, the negativity and depression always seemed to win out. I spent more time plotting my demise than I did fighting to stay alive and following my heart. I know I always had music in me. I always wanted to sing and did whenever I was alone. But for the longest time it was impossible for me to acknowledge it. I never believed I was good enough to do anything more than sing in private, around the house or in the shower. A career? You gotta be kidding me.

So I did everything else instead. I was a waitress, a hotel maid. I bussed dishes. I worked as a receptionist. Hell, I even interned as a juvenile probation officer when I was shooting dope and living with a violent sociopath who sold drugs, which I also did. I worked at a Dairy Queen, was a grocery store clerk, a house painter, an office manager, a night manager at a health food store, a cashier, a bookkeeper, and an intake counselor at an extended care facility that helps women with addiction and mental illness. I was a music production manager, musician contractor, delivery driver, extra in movies, an office temp, a maid in private homes and a motel, a limo driver and God knows what else. And that's just the legal activities. The list goes on and on. But all the while, there was one thing that kept eating at me. Music. Blues music to be precise. I loved it, I needed it, and I wanted to sing, for the longest time it was a dream for someone else, but not for me.

And now, as I stood on stage next to these musical giants, in my trembling hands was a bronze award statuette that proclaimed me blues "Entertainer of the Year." B.B. King and Bonnie Raitt are telling me this? Are you fucking kidding me? It was impossible to hold back the tears. I didn't feel like trying so I just let 'em flow.

B, ever the true Southern gentleman and flirt that he was, gently took my hand, greeting me with a sweet kiss on the cheek. It felt wonderful. All I could think was to ask him for "a little more sugar" because that's how sweet it felt. I got two extra smacks before Bonnie gently escorted him off stage. With my daughter nearby, I stood at that podium and struggled to breathe. Time seemed to come to a standstill as I searched for the right words. Any words. It was impossible to think straight. The crowd grew silent—listening, waiting for me to say or do something. Needless to say, I had not prepared a speech for an award I didn't believe I could win.

When I'm asked in interviews why my music of choice is the blues, I always say the same thing: because the blues is the music of the American people. I believe it to my core. It's the music of working people who get up, go to the job every day and suffer some difficult and painful shit but find a way to get through it. People who come out the other side no matter how many times life kicks their ass. The blues can be filled with hot rage and heartbreak, but at its core, it is about persevering and surviving. It always has been for me. We celebrate that in the blues. We proclaim to the world that life might be a motherfucker kicking our ass, but we ain't giving up. This shit will not defeat me. It's the blues, not the end of life. I'll get through it. I'm not sure I always believed that, but I loved the feeling it gave me nonetheless. I relied on it.

The truth is, the blues is a lot more than my vocation. It's been my salvation. There is no doubt in my mind I would have been cold in the ground a long time ago were it not for my love affair with the genre. I wouldn't have found my daughter, that's for sure. I wouldn't have any of the joys or wonder I now have in my life.

This rich music that helped save my life has been called many things. Three chords and the truth. The devil's music. Nothing but a bad woman feeling good. The mother of American music. It was born in the pain-filled work songs, chants and spirituals of African slaves, but I don't think music that celebrates triumph over suffering knows what color any of us are. I am a white woman, a grandmother proud to say, and from the very first time I heard it, the blues got to me in a way that nothing else has ever touched me. As B.B. himself once said, "The blues was bleeding the same blood as me."

I was nowhere near that articulate in the moments after I accepted the award bearing his name. "I don't even know what to say about this," I stuttered from the stage after winning the B.B. King award, my mouth frozen in a grin so wide my face hurt. "This is like off the hook for me. I'm so, so grateful to be here. I'm so grateful to God Almighty for keeping me around this long."

Apparently artists often say that kind of thing when they win something at awards show, but I was not exaggerating. There were so many reasons I should not have been standing on that stage and taking in the waves of applause and love coming my way.

Have you seen the movie Shawshank Redemption? Some people say I could be Andy, the Tim Robbins character who finally won his freedom by crawling out of prison through the sewers. The Morgan Freeman character characterized Andy's escape route as "five hundred yards of shit-smelling foulness I can't even imagine." I can relate to that. The escape route I took to be on that Memphis stage was well, a bit longer than five hundred yards. My escape route snaked through and around a lifetime - a lifetime at times, I still can't believe actually happened or that I was able to survive.

One - Pixie Girl

I was a four-year-old shy, skinny little girl with a pixie haircut when I tried to kill myself for the first time. That might seem impossible to believe, but like everything else you're about to read in these pages, it's absolutely true. I'm not the kind of person to sugarcoat things or pretend they didn't happen. When I finally decided to write this book, believing my story might help someone else who ever felt overwhelmed by life and the pain it can sometimes bring, I made a commitment to myself that I would tell it all faithfully, the good, the bad and the ugly. I have changed a few of the names to protect the innocent and even the guilty in a few instances, but every single other word of the story is true. For me, there can be no other way. At this point in my life, the truth and being able to live with it, are really all I know.

Psychiatrists will tell you it's rare for anyone as young as four to try to take her life, but it does happen. There are recorded cases of children as young as six actually succeeding in killing themselves, but I guess for me—thankfully—I was too young to pull it off. Even so, I was always precocious and more grown up for my years, so maybe that explains my early pre-occupation with suicide. It stood out in my mind as a solution to a problem, the only idea that really made sense. Before I understood much of anything about life, I had a powerful, all-consuming desire for my life to be over. I had an overwhelming desire to escape from my family and remove myself from this world. I was certain I didn't belong here, convinced even at that early age that my parents and siblings were not the least bit interested in me. I was sure that I would be better off dead, whatever I thought dead was. It was not anything I could have understood at 4 years old, but I recognized enough about my circumstances to make the calculation that it was the best way out. It was my ideal option, the only logical way of ending the suffocating sadness that took up residence deep inside me

17

no matter what I was doing, where I was or who I was with. This was a single truth for me back then and for many years to come.

It was 1961, the year the Soviet Union erected the Berlin Wall, when the U.S. invaded Cuba and a lot of people were convinced the Cold War was about to go nuclear and destroy the world. As a small child, I knew none of this. But I can look back and see this was not exactly the best year for the rest of the world either.

My family and I were living in Omaha, Nebraska. Dad had moved us there from Detroit, where he had been a patrolman for the First Precinct downtown for about fifteen years. He finally changed jobs at my mother's insistent urging he find safer work, eventually winding up as a salesman for the John Hancock Mutual Life Insurance Company. It was a career that caused us to move a lot as my smart, capable father climbed his way up the company ladder.

Mom and Dad were drinkers. They battled depression. But they functioned well, at least in the daytime. My dad had a good job. We lived in nice houses, where things were clean, orderly and in their place. Mom cooked great meals from scratch. We took summer vacations and looked perfectly fine to the outside world. You would never know just by looking at us that darkness and the Magness Curse were always lurking just below the surface.

I got the old home movies a few years back and put them on a CD so they would be preserved. If you were to watch them, you'd think we were the all-American family—loving, happy and full of fun. There is shot after shot of smiling little kids frolicking on the lawn, playing cowboys and Indians, throwing a ball, shooting baskets, riding bikes, running after our adorable little dogs as they gleefully wagged their tails. You'd see a lovely house on a big lake, the lawn looking as wide as a golf course. Kids and dogs were everywhere. There's a sporty boat out for a summer cruise around the lake in suburban Detroit. You'd see my tall, handsome dad packing up the car to take us on a family vacation, a contented grin on his rugged face. My brothers and some neighbor boys are horsing around having a great old time, shirtless in the summer breeze, mugging for the camera. There are scenes of precious little boys in sailor suits or cute little sport coats and bow ties, dressed up for some special outing. Little girls, me included, are chasing after them in perfect cotton dresses or pants suits. We look so happy and well-appointed. We were adorable. Pay close attention and you'll see my mother, when she's not hiding from the camera in an innocent display of female vanity. In one scene where my dad must have caught her unaware, it's a summer afternoon. She looks stunning in a white cotton dress festooned with giant polka dots. A pair of large silver earrings frames her face. Her shoulders are bare save for two thin straps on the dress. Her dark, curly hair is pulled back, away from her high cheekbones and angel's face. She is gorgeous. But even in these idyllic-looking moments, frozen in time, there is a telltale sign something is off. I can see it in her beautiful green eyes, framed precisely by eyeliner that was always perfectly applied. In the few shots she's in, when she's not bending at the waist to straighten one of the kids' clothes, her eyes are looking somewhere else. They search for a horizon she can't seem to see with all the cheery chaos unfolding around her.

When I watch those movies now, they trigger some sadness, of course, because my parents are no longer around and all that has been missed. But they also bring up sweet memories that I still cherish. Summers when Dad made homemade root beer that was insanely good. And ice cream. Homemade vanilla, rich and perfectly sweet. My job was to sit on top of the baby blue bucket to hold it down while he would churn the thing with a big handle. I was about six; young enough—and that bucket was big enough that my feet would dangle down the side. I remember that as clearly as if it were last week. I would proudly sit up there and be so happy to play such an important role in my dad's creation. It made him happy, too.

Or so I liked to think. There was nothing better than my dad when he was happy. Nothing and no one, at least to me. He was always happy when he was cooking barbeque or making root beer and bottling it. He made the best corn on the cob, too—showing me the only way to smoke it on the grill without burning the corn. And I had better listen. Make no mistake about it. This was VERY important information he was imparting to me. My job was to listen closely to the wisdom being handed down. I can see now these were treasures of tradition to him; generations-old traditions he'd probably learned growing up in rural Oklahoma.

He would soak the corn overnight in a big laundry tub filled with water and hickory chips. He'd keep the husk on and then throw the corn, husk intact, straight on the grill. I can still hear that loud sizzle because it was soaking wet with hickory water and that grill was hot enough to brand a bull's hide. The barbecue grill was homemade, too, something he concocted from a big fifty-gallon drum of some kind. He took a welding torch and cut it in half. Put a hole in the bottom for the charcoal dust to fall through. Stuck a few bolts to hold it up and put a grate over it. He welded two chains to hold the lid up when it was open, and stuck a handle and four legs on that bad boy. It was a work of art, really. He was so proud of that grill; he seemed proud of his family and the whole scene we were enjoying. I loved watching him do all that. Even as a young girl, I could tell the other dads in the neighborhood were envious that my dad had the know-how and skill to make something so cool and functional. He just seemed to be in control, with all contingencies figured out and bases covered.

I'm sure the pearls of wisdom he gave me were things he would have preferred to tell his sons, but my brothers simply were not interested or were busy doing other boy things and not around the house. I somehow became the chosen one, at least by my dad, and when he was in that fatherly frame of mind — gentle, funny, warm, instructive and loving — I was in heaven.

The trouble with my dad was that there was another side to him; a dark, angry side that could crush my spirit and make me hate him.

At the time of my first suicide attempt, I remember feeling terribly and painfully alone. I was the fourth of what would ultimately be five kids. By the time I came around, my mother had pretty much checked out. She hardly ever paid attention to me. My dad would play around with me, but he was so stern I was already pulling away from him. Whenever I did anything to set off his temper—believe me, it didn't take much—he'd whip my behind with a vengeance. I would eventually become close with my brother Jimmie, who was nine years older than me and the oldest of three brothers, but Jimmie and I wouldn't bond like that for several years. My older sister, Sara, never wanted much to do with me. Joe, another brother, loved to torment me. Carson, the baby of the family, was not born yet. From as early as I can remember, I just felt like I was in the way. Unwanted and disconnected from the rest of the family.

Even then, I loved to sing. Most of my time was spent watching television and putting on musical performances for our pets or my stable of imaginary friends and stuffed animals. I learned the words to nearly every television commercial and all the songs in the old movies and TV shows I loved: Captain Kangaroo, 77 Sunset Strip, Bonanza, Dobie Gillis, Batman, Superman, The Musketeers, Bewitched, and this classic from the Wonderful World of Disney: When you wish upon a star, makes no difference who you are. Anything your heart desires will come to you. If your heart is in your dream, no request is too extreme. When you wish upon a star, as dreamers do. I didn't really understand what the words meant, but I loved singing them.

I was a dreamer, dressing up in whatever fancy clothes I could find in the house and performing. My mom loved Siamese cats, so we always had a couple in the house and consequently in my audience. We also had collies that we named Lassie. Dad liked beagles, too, which he used for hunting. He named them all Si, short for Simon. I have no idea why, and they seemed to come and go when I was a kid. But they were attentive for my concerts in the bedroom, our garage or anywhere else around the house. I was a sponge, soaking up all the music I heard. I didn't know it at the time, but I was woodshedding. That's what musicians call practicing a song over and over until they get it right, get deep inside the song.

Truthfully and sadly most of the time, I just felt neglected and abandoned. If I wished upon a star, it was for those awful feelings of isolation and sadness to go away. To my mind, there seemed only one way to make that happen.

The idea of tying a noose around my neck was something I suspect I picked up from all those Westerns my dad watched on TV. Someone was always being hanged. They tie a rope around some cowboy's neck and the next thing you know, he's dead. I was a smart little kid. It was easy to put two and two together.

As I remember it, mom was in the kitchen making supper. Dad sat in the living room, his face buried in the newspaper. The TV was blaring. Joe and Sara were engrossed in a game of Pick-Up Sticks or Tiddlywinks, the only games we played in the house back then. I took the cord from the drape and made the noose—I remember very clearly having learned to tie a slipknot, which I had practiced—and climbed up on the end table next to the sofa. I put the cord around my neck and jumped.

I don't know what I expected. It seemed like I hung there choking for eternity, but I know it could not have been long. My mom must have heard something was wrong as I gasped for air and my feet dangled above the floor. Rushing into the room, she screamed at my father the instant she saw me. Dropping his newspaper, he cursed a blue streak and cut me down with scissors a few moments later. I can't remember if I was crying during any of it.

For years, my neck had a red scar on it from where the rope burned into my flesh. Ever one for putting on a good facade, Mom did a fine job hiding it beneath my hair, cutting it just so to make sure the wound didn't show. Or she put shirts on me with high collars. It was important in my family to keep up appearances. We would never let anyone know we were screwed up or suffering. "Dysfunctional" was not a word in anyone's vocabulary back then, even though that's what we already were in spades.

What's amazing to me even now is that we never spent a moment talking about what I did. Not once did my parents ask me why I would want to hang myself. They never took me to a psychiatrist or anyone else who might be able to help. You really didn't do that back then anyway. In true Bill Magness fashion, and most importantly because Magnesses don't need help, everyone pretended it never happened. Like the scar on my neck, it was covered up and made invisible so no one saw it. Like so many other dark secrets in my family, we put it in a box, hid the box in a closet and never looked inside.

After this first brush with death, my young brain began to fixate on a different sort of getaway. At this time, I enlisted God as my partner, praying for him to take me away from there forever. I probably had no clearer idea of God than I did of death, but I knew people asked Him to fix problems in their lives. So I started talking to Him. I would run off to the flowerbed of Lilies of the Valley that my mother had meticulously planted outside our house, hiding in those terraced flowerbeds and asking God to rescue me. It was like running away inside a dream. The delicate white flowers looked like tiny bells. Their scent permeated everything. It was a prime fantasy zone for me. I could lose myself in there for hours and hours, imagining forever that I was somewhere completely different. I conjured up make-believe friends and fairies that did care about me and would play with me. In my little girl's imagination, I created a whole other life. I pleaded regularly with God to make it permanent.

Later, as I grew a few years older, I have vivid memories of regularly emptying my Barbie Doll suitcase, stuffing some clothes inside, pushing out the screen from my bedroom window and running off. I could never shake the feeling of needing to be somewhere else. To be anywhere other than inside that house. I would perform this little ritual at night, getting no farther than the edge of the front yard before Mom or Dad might see me and haul me back inside. I'd get scolded. Dad might hit me. But no one ever tried to find out what was wrong with me. No one wanted to know why I was so unhappy or seemed to care. I was never asked about my brooding. I'm sure they wouldn't know how to deal with any answer I gave them, if I even could come up with one. No one, in fact, would ask about my forever-sullen moods until I was thirteen, in seventh grade. A kindly English teacher by the name of Gary Strauch stopped me in the hallway while I was ditching class one day. I was sobbing when he saw me. He asked why I was so distraught. wanting to know why I always looked so sad. He was the hall monitor that day and my favorite person in the whole school. He had a Rod Stewart haircut and a picture of the British soul singer hanging on the chalkboard in his classroom. He seemed pretty cool. He could see I was having a meltdown and pulled me into an empty classroom and talked to me for fifteen minutes. He knew I had run away from home; everyone in my class knew that much. The whole school did, for God's sakes. When he asked what was wrong with me, all I could do was mumble something unintelligible.

"Hang in there," was all he said. "Things will get better. You'll be okay."

I'm sure I didn't believe him, but I remember feeling in that instant he spoke to me that at least I wasn't invisible. Someone had noticed me. My eyes were swollen and red from crying. My nose was running. I'm sure I looked like shit. The feeling I had when I was four and tried to hang myself was choking me again. Why was I in this world? I saw no reason to be alive. I desperately wanted that feeling to end. I wanted me to end.

During those early childhood runaway episodes, I would cry myself into a tizzy and soon give up on the idea of leaving home. Then I would feel worse, more trapped than ever. It's not as if I had a plan. Who knows where I was headed? One of our dogs always followed me out the window, making me feel a tiny bit better. At least she seemed to actually give a shit and know I shouldn't be alone. She would sit with me while I bawled my eyes out. I'm pretty sure that was the beginning of the deep connection with animals I have had my entire life. I have always joked that I get along with critters far better than I do with humans.

"Please God," I would beg. "I don't belong here. I'm not part of this family. Why won't you help me? They don't want me here anyway. Please get me out of here."

At other fucked-up points in my life, I believe God actually did hear me. But as a lost and sad little girl, I was pretty sure He didn't care about my pain or me. I just wanted it to stop. Suicide, I would learn a number of years later, was always a reliable ally in my family. It's where you turned when life became too much to bear. Ending your life seemed easier and made more sense than trying to fix it. That "fixing it" thing? I would come to understand many years later, takes tons of hard work and honest self-assessment. Who wants to deal with all that?

Two - Both Hellfire and Brimstone

Much of the hard edge and sickness in my family traces right back to my paternal grandfather, a tough-as-nails, closed-minded man named C.A. Magness. Charles Arthur Magness was a towering, stoical Scotsman. In old photos, which is the closest I ever got to laying eyes on him, his thick white hair stands straight up on his head. His eyes are cold and unforgiving. There are times even today, when my stubborn nature gets me into trouble, that I still curse his name out loud. "C.A., you fucking S.O.B.!" I know I have some of his craziness in me. He did so much damage. He's doing it still. When I say he left a wide trail of emotional debris through multiple generations of my daddy's side of the family, I'm being kind. The way I see it, he was more like one of those midwestern twisters that tear through the countryside and leave damage and destruction in their wake, making it nearly impossible for people to regroup and put their lives back together. But, of course, things are more complicated than that. They almost always are.

C.A. was a barber and a hellfire-and-brimstone preacher in rural Oklahoma. That whole side of my family was populated with preachers, drunks, barbers and beauty operators. He belonged to the Church of Christ, which makes Southern Baptists look like bleeding-heart liberals. According to family lore, he regarded his wife and kids as members of his congregation. If you didn't follow C.A.'s teachings and his version of God's word, you were excommunicated—banished forever from his unforgiving little corner of the world. Disobey him, and C.A disowned you right back. Life was black and white for old C.A. Magness. I suppose that is simpler. No shades of gray in his world.

He and his wife, Jessie, had two daughters and seven sons. Louise was the oldest girl. She wanted to date a local boy named Jim Cox, but grandpa didn't approve

25

because Jim liked a drink now and then. They lived in a dry county in Atoka, Oklahoma, just outside of Coalgate. My grandpa warned her not to date that boy. Louise ignored him and eventually became Jim's wife. The line had been crossed. From then on, C.A.'s own daughter, Louise, was dead to him.

You've made your bed," he is said to have told her. "Now you're going to have to lie in it."

Louise and Jim went on to have a son and four daughters of their own. They lived about a mile down the road, yet those kids never would know their grandmother until after C.A. died. That's when his family finally began to break free, and it was safe to delicately try to mend some of the damage. There would be family reunions while C.A. was alive, but Louise and her brood were never invited. That's who my grandfather was. A rigid, by-the-book, unforgiving son of a bitch. A mule that stands in the road and refuses to budge would be considered accommodating by comparison.

Like a lot of sanctimonious people, C.A. had his own secrets. Living in a dry county, he had to be creative to get a drink medicine when he needed it. According to a story my brother, Jimmie told me, C.A. had a "prescription" for Hadacol, an alleged cure-all marketed back then as a vitamin supplement. It was popular in the dry counties of the South because it contained twelve percent alcohol and hydrochloric acid. Seems old God-fearing C.A. always had a bottle of the stuff in his inside coat pocket, sipping from it throughout the day. Seems he was toasted day and night. Another reason, I am sure, my dad wanted to get the hell out of there as soon as he could.

My uncle Bob, another of C.A's kids, was disowned by C.A. because he married a Catholic girl named Marguerite. She wasn't Church of Christ, so C.A. didn't approve. He went on to make life miserable for Bob and his entire family.

My cousin, Tim, who was one of their children said C.A. was often mean to him. When Tim was a kid, C.A. told him he was worthless and would never amount to anything. He still remembers that C.A. used to pinch him black and blue when no one was looking. He often told Tim—and I'm sure the other grandkids, too—that children should never talk, only listen. Tim, a great guy who had a successful career as an aerospace engineer in Southern California after serving multiple tours during the Vietnam War, hated to be alone with C.A. Tim grew up hating his grandfather, with good reason. Still does.

With C.A. at the helm, dead or alive, the entire Magness family felt toxic and dangerous for me. That's why I didn't have much contact with any of them until around the year 2000. Keeping them out of my life seemed like the only way I could survive. When my parents died, we only heard from a few of them. My aunt Eleanor, dad's youngest sister, Uncle Floyd and Aunt Mamie, and Uncle Leroy, came to Dad's funeral. That was it for the most part. Out of sight out of mind I guessed. But in 1991, Eleanor reached out to me while I was on a coast to coast tour with Jimmy Buffett. She and my uncle Martin and their daughter, Toy, came to one of our shows. It was incredible to be with them and very emotional. My aunt had my dad's eyes and similar sharp features. It blew me away to see her and the other family members. We had a tearful, intense reunion and I slowly felt a weight lift from me as the gulf between us began to evaporate.

A short time later, my sweet uncle Martin, Aunt Eleanor's husband died. For his funeral I was asked to sing and as difficult as that was, I felt strongly that I wanted to do as much as I could for my newly restored relationships with Aunt Eleanor and her daughter Toy. Especially in this time of great need.

I saw more of my cousins there, which made me feel nervous but ultimately good. My Uncle P.D., who had rebelled against C.A. in his own way and by becoming a Baptist preacher, even took a moment to apologize to me for not reaching out to us kids when our parents died. He apologized on behalf of his whole family as well. Truth is, most of them didn't even show up at the funerals. Uncle Leroy and Aunt Eleanor. That was it of my dad's eight siblings. That was confusing for us kids and created a true bitterness towards them in our hearts for a long time.

Slowly, I started to want them back in my life. I feel fortunate today to be close with several of them. Some come to see me perform when I'm in their vicinity. Toy, for instance, lives in the San Francisco Bay Area, and we've kept in touch throughout the years. She's often in the audience whenever we're playing anywhere nearby. It's a huge blessing to me that she and other cousins are in my life today after so many years without contact. An awful lot of personal healing had to occur for me to get to that point, but I am grateful it did. Grateful even more that they were willing to accept me into their lives.

You know how people's strengths can also sometimes be a weakness, too? Well, that's how it seems things are for me. When I consider everywhere I've been and all I've been through and experienced, I see that the stubborn part of my temperament passed on from C.A. and my father has been a blessing and a curse. On the blessing side, there have been many times in my career when I felt like I had my back against the wall. My default position of fear kicked in and took over. Fear has always been my close friend. I suspect a lot of people are like that but don't want to admit or dwell on it. Fear and worry have been constant companions for me and often still are. To this day, I worry about being broke and not being able to pay my rent or my bills. I worry about what I don't have. I worry about losing what I think belongs to me. I worry about losing my ability to sing, which I came very close to doing just a few years ago. I worry about whether I will always have to work as hard as I do or will life ever get easier? I have spent a lot of time worrying about living and dying alone. This is not me making a conscious choice or decision to fret and obsess about these things. It's hardwired into my brain. It's what I wake up with every morning. I open my eyes and this big gorilla of fear is on top of the bed staring down at me. It is a monster that bears down on my chest. I look up, and there it is. Doesn't matter what else might be happening in the world or my life. Things can be going great, and that motherfucker will press down and grab me by the throat and squeeze until I can barely breathe or move.

Even to this day, I do my best to stay as far away from scary shit as I possibly can get. I see it coming; I lace up my sneakers and run the other way. Movies, TV shows, violent stories on the news. They freak me out. I remember watching the movie Poltergeist shortly after it came out in 1982. That shit gave me terrible nightmares for years. The scene where the guy is in his kitchen and all of a sudden a steak moves across the counter. It explodes with maggots and then he's hallucinating and thinks his face is hamburger. He starts to tear into his own bloody skin. Oh my God. I am done right there. Seriously. Over-done. It seemed real as a heart attack to me. For weeks after, I could not get those images out of my head. I'm sure it goes back to my history and the violence I experienced from my dad's beatings, my brother Joe's particular cruelty, and two extremely abusive boyfriends I hooked up with. I have always scared very easily.

The good news, what's beautiful today about all this, is that the fear doesn't stop me in life like it used to. Through a lot of hard work and therapy, when I'm in this fearful state of mind, I know I have ways to fight that monster and put him back in his cage. I know how to grab him and lock him up, which I could not do before. Certainly not when I was getting loaded or high rather than face him. By using these tools for more than thirty years now, I believe that I have created new wiring in my brain. The old wiring is still there. It's not going away. It still takes over at times.

But there is new circuitry and information inside me now. And believe me when I tell you, this did not happen by accident. I have had to work at it every single day of my life. I still do.

I might be singularly responsible for the destruction of an entire rain forest for all the paper I have gone through writing about this merde is part of my morning rituals. No matter where I am, in my own bed or in some roadside hotel after a night performing, every morning I take out a pad of paper, a pen and I purge. It's like emotional bulimia. I write and write and write. I do it so I am not weighed down by the poison and dark thoughts that rattle around my brain in every conscious moment. I also do yoga. I meditate. I go to therapy. I suppose all this work is not necessary for most people and God bless them for it, but I know I have to work at my recovery. I have to face this shit and stare it down emotionally or I will not be able to stay clean and sober, which I have been now for more than twenty-eight years. It helps immensely. But I'll be on the road in some creepy motel and when I turn on the TV late at night because I'm too tired to do anything else, and if there's something the least bit scary or violent on, I turn that shit off in a flash. My mind can still play tricks on me. I am happy to say that I have learned over the years to not give it any extra material to work with.

Thanks to that stubborn part of me that is also hard-wired into my brain, I have been able to put the fear and anxiety aside to get through a number of tough spots during my career when the easiest thing—what I really wanted to do more than anything—was lie down and give up. That's what both my parents did when life got too overwhelming for them. It is an impulse I understand to my core. It's what made me put that drapery cord around my neck when I was only 4. But there was always an opposite impulse deep inside me, too. Some strange reservoir of inner fortitude that, at times, was the only thing that made me press on. I don't understand it. It just seems to rise up and keep me from quitting. That was not always the case; I hope you will come to understand as this story moves on. But for a long time now, when I've been up against it I could step back, reload and come out swinging harder than before. Whether it was a showdown with some band members I played with early in my career or a dispute with my husband or record company that led me to take a plunge and go out on my own, I found some way to learn what I had to and take things in a new direction that seemed to make all the difference in the world.

That stubborn do-it-myself attitude has also caused me a shitload of trouble and pain over the years. Especially in my personal relationships, when the best thing I could have done was give up and walk away. Learning to let go of people, ideas and desired outcomes has been brutally painful for me. Being stubborn cuts both ways. It has taken me so many years to learn how to recognize unsolvable problems, cut my losses and walk away from destructive relationships or the kind of negativity that drains all your energy. It has taken a lifetime to learn how to move toward the light and love that's in my world now. To focus my eyes and my heart on that place where joy and beauty can be found instead of locking in on fear, worry and self-destructive behavior. It has probably been the toughest lesson of my life, something I know I will forever need to work on. Far too often, I stayed too long or worked too hard to change other people and circumstances, only to fail at it and make things worse.

As you can imagine, I have dissected these twists and turns with my therapist for a long time. Only recently, she helped me get some clarity about the one thing that has puzzled me more than anything else. How exactly have I survived? How have I made it this far? Why am I still alive when others in my family couldn't get through the tough stuff, lost that battle with their own demons and monsters, and chose suicide because it seemed to much easier than life?

This is not survivor's guilt talking here. That is a difficult and understandable consequence for people who have survived extreme setbacks while witnessing others suffer great loss, brutality or even lose their own lives. This is just me trying to figure out something that has always confused and confounded me. I have never seen myself as more deserving than anyone else, so it's not that. The way I have come to understand it, the 'x' factor of my having survived all the bullshit I've been through, is probably that same dog-headed stubbornness I got from C.A. The refusal to accept the unacceptable in spite of all odds and circumstances. It has both cursed me and saved me. It was never something I felt was coming from me. But I can see now that it's always been there to one degree or another. I suppose it's the Magness Way. It didn't save my father. It skipped out on me on a number of occasions, too. The same determination and steel that Charles Arthur Magness had to do things his way no matter what anyone thought— that has saved me on more than a few occasions. You admit nothing, deny everything, shut the fuck up and just figure your life out. It has taken my entire lifetime to recognize where it came from, accept that it's mine and even feel grateful that I have some of the same qualities as my dreadful, unforgiving grandfather. Instead of cursing his memory, maybe I should thank him. As it turns out, I would not have survived without that inner strength and resolve. Like I suggested at the start of this chapter, strengths and weaknesses—sometimes it's hard to tell them apart.

Three – Siblings

My relationship with my other siblings was nothing like the bond I would eventually forge with Jimmie almost nine years older than me but the only one in the family I really felt close to. At times it seemed he was the only child my mother really seemed to care about. Must have been all that natural charm he was born with. My mother doted on Jimmie constantly. She was forever interested in anything he was doing, good or bad. My sister, Sara, who is three years older than me, seemed to hate me when we were kids, though she did bail my ass out a few times when I was older and in trouble with no place to go by letting me crash at her house. She also got a license to be a Foster Care parent at one point so she could be compensated for some of her costs while I stayed with her. Our early rifts were mostly sibling rivalry I guess, but our relationship was always strained.

I'm not sure how old I was, but I do remember my father talking to Jimmie and me and telling my brother, "Your job is to take care of your little sister and I don't care what it takes. You take care of her. If someone's mean to her, you take care of it." Meaning, you kick their ass. It was an edict from on high and Jimmie was glad to honor it.

That didn't stop Jimmie from being tough on me occasionally, like the time he offered to teach me how to swim when I was about five. We were living in a house on a lake in Mahtomedi, Minnesota. He picked me up, put me over his shoulder, walked down to the end of the dock, and threw me in. I knew I was in trouble as soon as he picked me up, but there was no stopping him. I was flailing around, swallowing water and screaming. All he could say was, "I promised mom I would teach you how to swim."

Jimmie had a big, boisterous laugh and I remember seeing him doubled over in hysterics as I went under the water. "Swim," he yelled at me. Somehow I did. It wasn't the way I would have done it, but it worked.

Jimmie would go from my protector to the guy who first got me high and offered to put a syringe in my arm. The guy who gave me my first drugs and alcohol and the only person whose murder I would ever plot and come within moments of carrying out.

Of all five kids, Sara, to her credit, was the only one who didn't wind up getting strung out on drugs and alcohol. She chose the Bible and religion as her way of life. For the most part, it seems to have worked for her. She was an angry and rebellious kid. She ran away from home when she was sixteen after my dad threatened to beat the crap out of a young black boy who came to pick her up for her first date. Sara dating a black kid was not something my dad would tolerate; he chased the boy away from our house with a baseball bat.

Carson, seven years my junior, was the youngest. He was what we now call unplanned, conceived after Mom and Dad went out for a night of cocktails. As soon as my mom was done breast-feeding him, she literally handed Carson to me and said, "I'm done. You take care of him. He's your charge now." I was eight. At the time, this made me happy, at least for a little while. It felt as if I finally had a reason to be in the world. I had a job and I loved my baby brother. Like the rest of us, the Magness Curse would get Carson in his clutches with some hellish years where he battled multiple demons and drug and alcohol addiction. Poor sweet soul, he did this for the majority of his life.

Then there was Joe, my other older brother who seemed to have been put on this earth for the sole purpose of tormenting me. Joe was five years older than me and my constant nemesis. He was cruel. He loved to hit, slap, and trip, push, intimidate, threaten and in general bully me. He seemed to be on a constant terror campaign. Jimmie, who was a few years older than Joe, would protect me when he was around. He was big and strong like my dad, with curly, sometimes longish hair and an abbreviated Fu-Manchu mustache when he was in his 20s. But most of the time, Jimmie was off in his own world, oblivious to what was going on, as was the rest of my family.

I do remember very fondly one time Jimmie enlisted me to mess with Joe and we had the best fun doing it. Joe was really scared of the Mummy and the Werewolf.

He was scared of Dracula and Frankenstein. Whenever he saw them in a movie or anything having to do with them, he would tremble in fear. So Jimmie asked me one day to help push Joe over the edge after he was already a nervous wreck from seeing the movie Psycho. I must have been about six at the time.

We were going to lie under Joe's bed before he went in his room to go to sleep for the night, wait for Mom to tuck him in and then scare the living crap out of him. I didn't need to be convinced. You know what they say about payback! By the time Joe got into bed, it seemed like we had been under there forever, but our patience paid off. Finally, the lights were out and Jimmie and I were dying. We could barely contain ourselves, had to hold our breath to keep from laughing. After a good amount of time had passed, we put our hands up on the bed from each side and Jimmie started making deep, guttural growling sounds. Joe literally pissed the bed and jumped up, screaming for Mom before running into the bathroom and locking the door. Jimmie and I laughed our asses off. We lost it. But I was so happy because most of the time I was Joe's personal punching bag. It felt good to get back at him a little.

Eventually, Joe's habit of dishing out physical abuse and intimidation turned into something worse. He started molesting me that same year, when I was six. I didn't really understand what was happening, but it felt awful. When he began to force me down and rub up against my body until he ejaculated, it seemed like a variation on his same daily abuse. I just couldn't stop him. He didn't abuse anyone else, as far as I know. But he tortured me; the molesting was just another sick part of who he was.

Joe threatened to kill me if I told anyone, so, of course, I kept quiet. Sara knew, but — classically — she blamed me. She even came into my room one time when Joe had me down and was doing his thing. Instead of going after him and protecting me, she hit me, pulled my hair and yelled at me as if I was the problem. That crushed me. It also doubled down on the feeling I had of being alone in the world, all by myself in a house filled with people who really didn't care about me.

Sara ordered me not to tell a soul. "I will handle this," she insisted. I begged her to tell Mom, but Sara kept it to herself. Silence in the face of crisis has always been part of the Magness family's unspoken credo: If you got a problem, shut the hell up and deal with it. You don't whine, you don't complain. And you don't ask for special attention, 'cause you ain't special. And you sure as hell don't rat anyone out. If things get too hard, you figure out how to fix it. There is always a way out, always an end to the suffering. Shut your pie hole and handle your business. More or less, it's what every member of my family was inclined to do in the face of adversity. I suppose there was some kind of mind set that made it seem easier to handle bad shit that way rather than trying to deal with things forthright. But I would learn over time that this thinking was not only wrong, it was dangerous and completely self-destructive.

Eventually, about fifteen years later, after burying the memories for so long I got some help. Then I found the courage to confront Joe about what he did to me. Eventually I even came to make peace with him. But let's not get ahead of the story. I would lose everything and more before Joe and I were able to resolve anything.

Four - Jimmie

After Joe began molesting me, I withdrew even deeper into myself, shutting out as much of the world as possible. The rest of the family was spinning faster into its own doom at the same time as me. The poet Mary Karr has said her definition of a dysfunctional family is any family with more than one person in it. There were seven in my immediate family, so do the math. When everyone is sick in their own way, that's a lot of insanity to live with.

I didn't talk to anyone if I didn't have to, other than to the cat and dog, of course. They were my friends and seemed to love me no matter how screwed up I felt. The only time I was animated or lively was when I was putting on my little shows for the pets and singing the songs I learned from the radio or TV.

Maybe I picked up my sense of isolation and being withdrawn from watching my mom. When I was a little girl, I remember her sitting alone in the kitchen at night, smoking her Pall Malls, nursing a drink and writing, writing, writing. Turns out she was working on solitary poems and sad little vignettes that were I suppose a release for her and also windows into her despair. I still have copies of a lot of them I found in the house one day. They are pretty bleak.

I still get sad when I read them. But later on, they were also a map of sorts to the source of her dampened spirits, providing clues she would never offer to her children when she was alive. One that I still have was titled On Wisdom. Happy it ain't. "I look down and up the street tonight and I see the lighted windows and people moving about inside and I ask myself: Are they like me? Do they have the problems I face today? Do they understand? Do they sit and cry? Do they drink too much? Do they want to die?" Not much left to mystery there. Breaks my heart to realize how much pain she was in to put down on paper words so devoid of hope or any kind of support in her world. Very, very alone.

My dad was less remote, bouncing me on his knee and letting me sit in his lap when I was small. That kind of delightful horseplay came to an abrupt halt as I started to approach puberty. He must not have known how to handle or react to my development and changing body. For whatever reasons, he became more cruel and mean. It took less to set off his temper, not as much to provoke a wicked beating from him that would leave me sore and brokenhearted for days on end.

Young girls always want to own a bra before they're ready. I was no exception. One afternoon when I was eight, Dad barged into my room as I was trying one on and teased me unmercifully after that. The father-daughter relationship is always complicated by puberty and the daughter's budding sexuality, but so-called normal families seem to find ways of dealing with these rites of passage. In my family, everything just got weirder. The love I had for my father as a little girl, even though he whipped me often for little or no reason, began to wither. It hardened into resentments. We certainly no longer had fun together. It was all tension, terror and terrible beatings. Eventually my feelings turned into hatred. I didn't want to be anywhere near him. What a sad state of affairs. It was as if there wasn't anything we could do to stop that downward spiral even if he had wanted to.

Our relationship seemed to sour for good when I was nine and I pissed him off about something I can't remember. When he went to the closet to grab the wooden paddle he used for "disciplining" the kids, I slipped a thin book into my pants to cushion the blows I knew were coming. The padding must have made me feel a little cocky because suddenly I was on my feet as he had a grip on my left arm so I couldn't run off.

My dad was a big man, about six feet, three inches tall. In college, he refereed basketball and football games. Despite always having trouble with his back, he was strong and in pretty good shape. When he hit one of us kids, we felt it. Plus, that leather belt hurt like hell and the piece of wood he spanked us with had a handle he carved in it for extra leverage. So when I knew I was in store for it, I'd be terrified.

But this time, when he wound up and started in on me, I barely flinch. There were no tears or screams. My stoicism set him off more. He began to hit me harder. I took his best shots without breaking down. He had a sort of crazed look in his eyes. Then he discovered the book in my pants and lost the last remnants of control, barking at me to remove it.

"Go ahead," I said to him like I was Clint Eastwood in the Dirty Harry movies. "But this is the last time you are ever gonna hit me."

I was looking deep into his brown eyes when I said it. Standing my ground like that must have unnerved him. That was the last time he did that to me. He would backhand me across the face again a few years later, but in that moment when I was nine, I think he realized the days of me just sitting there and taking his beatings were over. My dad demanded to be in control. It meant everything to him. He was losing dominance over me, just as he had lost it over my mother and those of my siblings who were old enough to rebel.

Until that final showdown, it was always the same story when he got mad at me. I would run and hide in my familiar place — as far back into the closet in my bedroom or in the hallway, on the left side where the long coats were kept. I'd try to make myself as small as a mouse, crawling back in there, sitting on top of the shoes and boots, hoping that this time, somehow, he would not be able to find me, holding my breath forever, wondering how long it would be before I turned blue.

Of course, he knew exactly where to find me. As he stood outside the closed closest door, I'd see the shadow of his shoes. I wonder where she is, he'd say, cracking that leather belt of his. Snap! Snap! I can still hear that awful sound. I'd flinch, trying not to breathe. I'd pray to be a mouse so I could chew through the wall and escape. Those prayers were never answered.

This ritual would go on for what always seemed like forever, but it was probably no more than a minute. Then the door would fly open and he'd tear into my hide for who knew what offense I might have committed or been blamed for. Maybe I hadn't put my clothes away and cleaned up my room. Or I hadn't made my bed just so. Maybe I hadn't finished dinner. Not exactly capital offenses, but it never took much to make my dad fly off the handle and take his anger out on me. As a child, the dance back and forth between affection and intermittent terror confused the hell out of me.

My dad and Jimmie were knocking heads more and more, too. They were a lot alike. Dad was having no more success getting Jimmie to bow to his wishes than he was with me. More control was gone, compounding my dad's frustration and rage. Jimmie could be a violent hothead like my dad, depending on whether my brother was high or not. When Jimmie was clean, he was a sweetheart, larger than life: full of charisma, energy, charm and wit. There was nobody better. But by his own admission, Jimmie, like the rest of us except for Sara, got loaded a lot. He was stubborn, hell-bent on going his own way and doing what he pleased. A little C.A. Magness was surely inside him, too. In a 1988 letter Jimmie wrote to a lawyer in a family dispute I'll get to later in this story, Jimmie summed up the dynamic inside our house, particularly our relationship with Dad, rather concisely.

"I became a teenager in the early '60s," he wrote, "and although I was taught right from wrong and had a good moral upbringing, I chose to become a hippie and a drug addict and a criminal. I guess that's because it's illegal to be a drug addict. Anyway, this caused bitter strife between us. Our dad thought I rejected society's role and adopted a different philosophy. I thought I could help change the world, maybe I did. It seems to have changed. My younger siblings followed suit. We were all dropouts and runaways. All his friends knew of his family problems."

Years later, when he was in his mid-30s, Jimmie began working as a logger, cutting down and hauling trees in Minnesota. He was big and strong like my dad. Twice, he had his back broken because—with typical Magness bravado—he violated the logger's rule of never doing the job alone in the woods. He couldn't stand working with anyone. On two occasions, he was cutting down trees and they fell on him. Once after he was hurt, he managed to drag himself to a dirt road. A farmer came along and put him in the back of his truck. Jimmie wound up in intensive care, doped up. The doctors told him he would never walk again. He was in the hospital for about two weeks and he finally just got up one day, said "Screw you people," and left.

Later in his life, he went back to school and got his license to become a nurse. That blew our minds because Jimmie was the same guy who was escorted to the border in handcuffs and shackles by authorities in three different states, let out of the car, unshackled and ordered to never to come back. He was a hell raiser of monumental proportions. And he could be fearless. Jimmie was the only other person I ever saw stand up to my dad. When he was about seventeen, they had a big, noisy fight about something. Jimmie hauled off and punched my dad in the head, knocking him out cold. My brother knew he better disappear after that. Disappear he did. We didn't see a trace of him for months until his photo was on the front page of the Minneapolis Star & Tribune.

He was not in the newspaper because he won the Minnesota Lottery. Jimmie was into the drug scene pretty heavily by then and he was busted for manufacturing and selling amphetamines. It was probably a good thing he got locked up. Jimmie routinely ripped off drug dealers and sold their stash to other stoners and freaks. There were more than a few people in Minneapolis eager to get rid of him.

When Jimmie was on the lam, my mom missed him so much she made up a story to tell my father about how she wanted to visit a former neighbor and took me along. She always seemed to have time and love for Jimmie. No matter what. We snuck off to see him like that a couple times; I always had to swear not to say a word to my dad. He had disowned Jimmie after their brawl and would have gone ballistic.

One time, when Jimmie was living in a rundown apartment in south Minneapolis with his girlfriend Sam, he charmed my mom into believing he was doing okay, so she let me spend some time at their apartment. She knew I missed my big brother and thought it would be good for both of us to spend some time together. Big mistake.

Jimmie took me up to the apartment, where he proceeded to fix some dope and shoot up. I didn't know what he was putting into his arm. It was probably morphine, Jimmie's drug of choice in that moment, but it repulsed me. Laughing like a crazy man, he offered me some. I knew it was flat-out evil, even if it was some sort of sick joke on his part. I ran into the other room and started bawling my eyes out. I thought I was gonna puke.

I think I was 9 at the time. I demanded to go home, swearing to myself there was no way I would ever stick a needle in my arm. Sadly, later in life I broke that promise.

Sadly, too, going home didn't solve much for me. That scene in Jimmie's apartment was emblematic of everything in my house and in my life. Everything seemed crazy and terrifying, totally uncertain and precarious; I felt like my whole world could go up in smoke without a moment's notice. Nothing was right or easy. No place felt safe or comfortable. I had no one to trust or confide in. My family was dissolving in the worst way, before my very eyes. When you're a kid of 9 you can't articulate what's wrong with your environment, but I knew none of it was good. I walked around sure that something terrible could descend on us at any time, and it often did. Something bad always seemed to be happening to me or around me and I had no clue how to make it stop.

Like the day when I was 12 and my dad came home and announced to my mother that we had to move. He had been having more problems at work, not getting along with his boss, and John Hancock began to demote him; now he was being transferred to the company office in St. Louis.

I had never seen much happiness in my mother, but somehow she was keeping her life together inside our old house in the little township of Afton, fifteen miles southeast of St. Paul. The place was nothing fancy, an old farmhouse, but it was on a big piece of land with a chicken coop and a barn that my mom loved. She put in a large garden and relished being able to dig around in that dirt. The property had lots of big, overgrown trees and a small apple orchard. It was a sanctuary for her. Now, because my dad was losing his grip on things, she had to give that up, too. The sense of defeat that came with my dad's proclamation was like one of those earthquakes we experience every once in a while in Los Angeles, where I live now. It rumbled through us like a shock wave, while we held our breath and waited to assess the damage.

If anyplace symbolized the state my family was in at the time, it might have been the home we moved into just outside St. Louis after my dad's transfer from work. It was a small, 1950s-style ranch house, decent enough, but it didn't have many windows. Inside, it was always dark and cold, a perfect metaphor for my mom's state of mind and for the light that seemed to grow dimmer in our family by the day.

"My life is cold and dark and dreary," she wrote in one of her late-night kitchen ramblings. "It rains and the wind is never weary. My hope still clings to the moldering wall. But with every gust, dead leaves fall. Yes, my life is dark and dreary."

Her words were a premonition. It was in that house in suburban St. Louis where my family entered its final stages of collapse. It happened quickly, in the span of just a few months, sending me into a spiral of the worst and most terrifying years of my life. My family barely had a fragile and tenuous grip on things when we moved into that place. Now, we were about to lose that, too.

Five - Bill and Billie

Our move from the Minnesota farmhouse to that dreary place outside St. Louis was the beginning of the end for my mother, who was known to everyone as Billie. Her real name was Wilhelmlna. Dad's name was Billy Clark Magness. They were Bill and Billie. She was a beautiful brunette, half-Irish and half-French. She was bright and strong-willed, but at several points her life became unbearable.

Billie and Bill met during summer vacation one year when she was a student at the University of Michigan in Ann Arbor. Her roommate and best friend, Jane, had a radio show in Texas called "GI Jane on the Air." Jane had asked Mom to come to the station during her summer break to help answer phones. Dad, who always had a beautiful singing voice, was in a vocal group and they were at the station for an interview when Mom was there.

By the time they got married, Mom was a young homemaker and a functioning alcoholic. We lived in decent places, dressed well and had just about everything material that we needed as kids. Mom was like a lot of smart, creative women of that era who got swept up in the American Dream, getting married and having a bunch of kids. Other than the stories and journal entries she wrote in the kitchen late at night with her drink and cigarettes, she had no real outlet for her creativity. Nor did she have the wherewithal to follow any dreams she might have had for herself. I never gave it a moment's thought when my mom was alive, but sometimes when I think of her now, I wonder when in her life she realized that any of the personal ambitions she might have had would go unfulfilled. She loved literature, poetry and music. She could have been a writer or an actress. Having five kids and a husband to care for left little time for anything else. That seemed to wear her down over time, sucking the life right out of her.

We didn't have much time together, but most of what I recall about her — what I saw — was a sad, distant woman who didn't have much spark for life. I know there was more to her than that. I just rarely saw it. It fills me with sadness to know her life was so much less than she might have imagined for herself.

Dad was different. He was a proud, charming, Southern man. Macho, strict, and part of the generation that believed men work and women stay home with the children. He craved control and order. They were everything to him. Eventually, life became too much for both of them to handle.

But for a long time, we looked like a perfect family, that's what mattered most. Appearances. Mom cooked three meals a day from scratch. She sewed almost all our clothes. The house was never dirty. Dishes were not stacked up in the sink. The latest issues of Better Homes and Gardens and Family Circle magazines were always properly displayed on a coffee table in the living room. It was so orderly. So perfect.

I don't think she wanted to be a mother to five kids, but she still managed to be an exceptional homemaker. She was a devout Catholic. I know that she loved my dad very much, but by the time I came around - child number four, Mom was pretty much checked out. She and I never really bonded. It wasn't something that interested her, which I suppose means that I did not interest her. She almost never seemed to pay me much mind. Even at a young age, I was sure she didn't want me around. She was not physically abusive to me, just passive and disinterested, which I now know is its own form of abuse when you have a child. Some people say it can be worse than physical abuse. I don't know. Neglect like hers means you don't even care enough to discipline your daughter. At least I never doubted that my dad cared about me.

I still have a small Kodak snapshot of her that is dated December 1957 in the white border surrounding the image. I was almost a year old when the photo was taken. Her hair is pulled back, her green eyes and red lips perfectly made up. She appears to be holding something, maybe a coin, in her small, delicate hands. There is a big, warm smile on her face, her mouth open slightly so you can see her perfectly white teeth. She looks happy in the photo, as if she's laughing at a joke or is pleased to see someone she knows. I'm glad to have that image of her, frozen as it is in time, because she truly was a stranger to me, indifferent and off in her own world. I never had any idea what she was about, deep down in her soul. I now know a girl should know that about her mother.

But families create their own definition of normal. It didn't seem unusual to my siblings and me that she was brooding and quiet, always nursing a drink in the kitchen after dinner. We had no other frame of reference. We also had no idea that during the day she took prescription methamphetamine pills known as black beauties. At night, she took Phenobarbital to sleep. That was standard treatment for depression at the time. Up in the day, down at night.

By the time we were settled into the house near St. Louis, Mom and Dad had stopped communicating altogether. Jimmie was gone, Sara had run away, Joe was in the Air Force. It was just me and my little brother, Carson, living at home with mom and dad. That December, Sara called home after being away about a month to say she was okay, back in Minneapolis with friends. She also informed my mother that she was getting married. "Over my dead body," was my mother's response. Turns out Sara had been hanging out with a friend of Jimmie's and thought she was in love. Mom didn't buy it. Funny thing, Sara is still married to that man. They went on to have five kids. But I suppose Mom and Dad didn't have much reason to feel happy by that time. They never danced or clowned around like they did when they were first married. Whatever spark mom once possessed had grown cold. Her eyes had a dull, far-away look. I rarely saw her laugh.

During the holidays in 1969, just before I turned 13, she was crocheting a caftan for my grandmother. It was supposed to be a Christmas gift, but the holidays came and went. She was unable to finish it. She worked on it furiously all through January. It still wasn't done when February 1st came around. To miss a holiday deadline like that — to miss any kind of deadline — was not like my mom. She was organized and orderly. Something was really amiss.

On the night of February 7, 1970, Mom and Dad were arguing about something. This was odd, too, as we almost never heard them exchange harsh words. Or any words, for that matter. The tension between them was palpable as she sat in the family room watching TV, making slow progress on the caftan. Dad came into the room while I was leaving to go upstairs into my bedroom. I overheard their conversation as I stood in the hallway. He must not have known I was there. He never said anything cross to her when I was within earshot. It was part of the facade they kept of pretending everything was normal.

"Billie, come to bed!" he told her. I remember the words as if I heard them yesterday or had them on tape and could play them again and again. The scene unfolds in my mind to this day.

Without looking up, she said, "No, Bill."

When he told her to do something, she either obeyed, ignored him, or said yes and did what she wanted anyway. For her to openly defy him out loud like this was huge. "Come to bed!" he told her again, his voice harder and sterner.

"I'll be there when I'm ready," she told him, shooting a hostile glare his way as she turned back to the TV and her crocheting.

Holy shit, I thought to myself. Something bad is coming. I feel it.

He must have been worried about her. I know he loved her, but they had stopped being good for one another years earlier. She'd been drinking heavily all week. That night was no exception, as she labored over that almost-finished, shell-pattern caftan. I eventually went up to my room with a sense of dread that something was going to happen, though I didn't know what.

I had school the next morning, but I was determined to stay up late. Three Dog Night was on Hugh Hefner's Playboy After Dark. With their mullets, lean good looks and deep harmonies, they were one of the most popular groups around, and I loved them. There was no way I was going to miss that show.

I had moved into the only upstairs bedroom we had in the new house. It had been Sara's before she split when Dad chased off her date with a baseball bat. My new room looked out over the backyard, which had a swimming pool in it. I had a TV. Mom kept yelling at me to turn it off and get to bed.

I ignored her and continued watching. At one point, when I went downstairs to get something to drink, she was in her usual perch at the kitchen table writing, drinking and smoking.

Why was I still up? she demanded. "Didn't I tell you to go to bed?"

"I'm watching my show," I said.

"Go to bed," she snapped again.

And I told her, "Go to hell!" I still see us in that dark kitchen, a grainy black and white movie playing forever in my mind. "Go to hell" turned out to be the last words I ever spoke to my mother. The final conversation my sister Sara had with her consisted of my mom telling Sara she could get married "over my dead body." For the rest of our lives, we both have lugged around the bones from those final, sad encounters with our mother. I cringe today when I think of my last words to her.

She was told to go to hell, and I went back upstairs. Three Dog Night was lip-synching their song, Find Someone to Love.

You better find yourself someone to love, Life's so short, sweet and groovin,' And brother I ain't foolin,' You better find someone to love.

When the song ended, I turned off the TV and tried to sleep. Tossing and turning all night, I woke up again and again with a sick feeling something was not right. I felt it in the pit of my stomach. I kept looking out at the garage, telling myself I needed to go down there and see what was happening. I needed to make sure everything was all right. I never did. I was too frightened.

I dozed off for a few short hours. When it was time to get up for school, I could barely move. I knew something terrible had happened. Mom usually woke me up. Dad came into my room that morning instead.

"Where's Mom?" I asked him.

"Put your clothes on and come downstairs," he said with no trace of emotion.

I sat up and saw my sleepy reflection in an antique mirror on top of my new dresser. I knew with one hundred percent certainty that my mother was dead. I didn't have to be told she was gone, but I did not want to believe it. I stared at myself in that mirror, muttering, no, no, no.

A neighbor was sitting in the living room with Dad when I got downstairs. With a grim face, Dad told me to sit down.

"Your mother is dead," he announced.

"Where?" It was the only question I had.

"In the garage."

He offered no details or explanation. No condolences or regrets. Just the barest of facts. Your mother is dead. End of story. I found out later she had been drinking and took a bunch of pills. She pulled Dad's Cadillac out of the garage, drove her car in, closed the garage door and cranked up the engine. Ever precise and on task, she lay down under the exhaust pipe so nothing would go wrong. She removed herself from the world — from all of us — forever.

Later, we learned that she left several suicide notes, beautifully handwritten letters in pencil. On her favorite light green stationery. In big letters on a chalkboard kept in the hallway off the kitchen, she also wrote the words "Goodbye Bill."

The suicide notes were more revealing. I took them out and read them again when I started to work on this book. They open a cold, hollow ache in my heart to this day, nearly fifty years after her death.

It was the dead of winter when she wrote them and died. My mom wanted to make sure Carson and I had new jackets. She left explicit instructions for my father about what to buy.

"There is one at Famous Barr she really liked," Mom wrote about me. For Carson, she told my dad to "Get brown or gold to go with that hat I made him."

In another note she wrote, "My dearest Bill: I know you think I don't love you. Not so, not so. The only problem is I love you in a different way than you want me to. I hope God will look on you with favor and you will find someone to love you in the physical sense you need—indeed, require".

"I'm sorry, but I cannot give you or rather fulfill this need anymore. Love the children and they will reward you with more than you ever dreamed possible . . . Sorry I messed up 23 years, but that's the way it goes I guess. No sad songs for me baby. Just get out of this house and you'll make it fine. . . I hope I succeed this time and you don't have to go through any more of these idiotic letters."

She also sent several "final" letters to her mother, who she loved dearly, including a long one dated Feb. 7, 1970, the night of her death. It hurts to think how much pain she was feeling. How hopeless and desperate she had to feel to leave her mother and all of us as she did. To sit in the dark kitchen, consumed with guilt and disappointment, determined to die, but not before writing a nine-page, handwritten letter to her mother, trying to explain why her life was finished.

"Please forgive me," it begins. "I am just weak. I can't go on any more. For the past year I have tried to tell myself I had to go on for Carson and Lisa, but I know now they would be better off with someone who can follow some accepted norm." Lisa was my given name, but years later, in another story I will tell later, I went down to the courthouse and had it changed, thinking it would help me, help my mind, and help my life, too.

"Mother, you have been more than anyone could ask for in a mother," her letter went on. "Love all my children for me, no matter how difficult they may seem, and remember it is my fault they are so ornery. . . I love you and am sorry to bring more grief to your weary shoulders. Look upon it as release."

"I hope I succeed this time." Obviously, this was not my mother's first attempt at suicide. None of us kids knew it then, but she had tried to kill herself at least nine times before, always the same way: alcohol, pills and carbon monoxide poisoning. Somehow, she and Dad had hidden this from us. Keeping secrets was another Magness tradition. Maybe you've heard the expression, "You're only as sick as your secrets." We had a lot of them in my family, and we were very sick.

I realized later that these earlier attempts were the reason Mom disappeared so often when I was a little girl. She was admitted to the hospital many times and we were fed cover stories about a collapsed lung or some other supposed malady. We were never allowed to visit her. In a few days, she would be back home as if nothing happened. Once when we were living in the big house on White Bear Lake in Mahtomedi, Minnesota, it was getting dark and we had no idea where mom was. We searched high and low for her, inside and out, finally finding her hiding under a bed. She made a joke about it, how she was playing a game with us, but she was seeking refuge from whatever had become too much to bear.

My sister, Sara, tells a story about mom once pouring out her heart to her when she was sixteen. We were in St. Louis by this time. I would have been 12 and never had that kind of conversation with mom. My parents had come home surprisingly early from a party at a neighbor's house. Mom was drunk. Sara was in her room, distraught because her cat had eaten a baby white rat she also kept as a pet. When mom came upstairs to comfort her, she began telling Sara how sad she — Mom — was feeling. She stunned Sara by telling her that she had an abortion years earlier, before she met my dad. She could never forgive herself for it. Worse, the father of the baby was a married man with whom she had an affair, compounding her Catholic guilt and self-loathing. Sara could not believe my mother was suddenly bearing her soul and confessing in this way. I am sure it was all too much for her. A few weeks later, Sara was gone, back with friends in Minneapolis. She no longer could live with my dad's strict rules and constant badgering.

When I was a small girl, I was convinced Mom didn't love or care about me, but I eventually came to understand her distance wasn't about me at all. She was severely depressed, suffering in silence, unable or unwilling to let any of us in on what she was going through. The truth is she was spent and saw only one way to end her misery. She was 44 when she died.

Although we were never close, when she died something died inside of me, too. I was still pretty innocent at 13, a naive little girl in so many ways. But the little girl was gone now. I was just starting to discover my body and my mind. But I had no idea who I was or the impact her absence would have on my life. With my mother out of the picture, I tried to convince myself nothing mattered anymore. Within days, I was acting out accordingly.

On the day of her funeral and burial, we were all at my Grandma Pearl's house doing what families do after someone dies. We were eating, the adults were getting drunk. All of us were locked in a stupor from sadness and grief. Snow was coming down in big, fat flakes. Typical February weather in Michigan. Someone knocked on the door. The mailman had a delivery. He handed my grandmother a medium-sized box. She sat down with the package in her double rocking chair and slowly started to paw at it. Because I was worried about her and watching her closely, I sat right next to her.

Grandma opened the box: folded neatly inside was the caftan Mom had been struggling to get done by the holidays. Underneath was a handwritten card from my mother. "By the time you get this, I will be gone," it read. "It is better this way. . . Please forgive me, Mother." She was tying up loose ends, making sure she finished what she started.

Grandma pushed her face into the fabric, sobbing uncontrollably. It was terrifying to see this strong woman so distraught. We both cried for a long time while she rocked back and forth. No one said a word. How could they? We were all too numb to speak.

After a while, Dad reached over and tried pulling the caftan from grandma's grip. He must have thought it would stop her loud, deep crying, but she was not about to let go of all she had left of her daughter. Clutching it close to her wet cheek, she tightened her grip and continued sobbing. The caftan smelled like Chanel Number Five, the perfume my mom wore.

I will always be able to see the look of horror and sorrow on my grandmother's face in the days following Mom's suicide. I was just a kid, but I remember telling myself: This can never happen to me. I could not bear to bury my own child. I would never survive it. Having my own child die is still my greatest nightmare.

I'm sure I feel that way because of witnessing my grandmother breaking down so completely. Certain things you never forget, no matter how hard you try. To this day, I cannot comprehend how someone gets through a tragedy like that. Mom's death shattered my Grandma Pearl beyond repair.

It shattered me too, but in a different way. For years, I was convinced that if only I had been a better person—a better daughter, less troublesome and rebellious—my mother would have found a way or a reason to hang on. She would not have left us. I tortured myself for not going to the garage that night when my gut told me I should. I looked out into the murky backyard darkness three times that night, overcome by the premonition that something was wrong. I didn't act on my instincts. I beat myself up relentlessly for that, even worse for having told her to go to hell. For a long time, I hated my mom for leaving. I despised myself more for letting it happen.

That is a hell of a load for someone to carry, which is why I always say and still believe that during all those years I was getting loaded, I needed every drink I poured and every drug I took. What else could I do? What else did I know how to do? A long time went by before I understood that drugs and alcohol were only a tool, bad ones at that. That in the end, they actually made me feel worse. More helpless. More depressed. That would take years to figure out and I learned the hard way that it's not something you can figure out when you're drunk or loaded.

It was in those immediate weeks after my mother's funeral, consumed with shame and sorrow, that I began my career as a drunk and drug addict. Only thirteen, I started out slowly, not graduating to shooting cocaine until years later. But getting halfway high was never for me. What's the point? Years later one of my boyfriends called me "garbage head" because I would take just about anything, and a lot of it, to get fucked up. I wasn't into a few puffs on a joint or a couple of drinks. I wanted to alter my consciousness as completely as possible. My mom's death opened the floodgates for me. I didn't get clean for good until more than two decades later.

I spent years hating and resenting my parents. It took even longer before I could realize they weren't bad people, they were sick. That they were in so much pain, it was impossible for them to be more loving or supportive of us kids. They only knew one way and believe me when I say that change was not on the family menu. My mom and dad did not know how to do that. There was no one to help guide them or try to figure out a way forward. Eventually, neither of them could find enough hope to hold, or any reason to keep pushing through it all.

As messed up as my relationship was with my mom and dad, I also came to realize and appreciate that I inherited so much more from them than simply their depression and mental illness. Today, after years of hard work in recovery programs and therapy, I understand that they loved me. I have no doubts about it. Today I feel deep and abiding love and sorrow for them and what they endured and all they determined they could endure no longer. I feel grateful for a lot of what they gave me.

I have my dad's off-beat sense of humor and head for business. I absorbed his love for music, though when I was a kid I hated those country and western records he played, particularly on Sundays, when he'd blast them loud enough for the whole neighborhood to hear. Buck Owens and the Buckaroos. Hank Williams. Dad loved Hank's tearjerker, I'm So Lonesome I Could Cry, as well as Just In Time and Honky Tonk Blues. I heard Tex Ritter moan his slow, mournful hit, Blood on the Saddle, so many times I can sing it word for word fifty years later. There was blood on the saddle, and blood all around. And a great big puddle of blood on the ground. A cowboy lay in it, all covered with gore. And he never will ride no broncos no more. Pretty gruesome stuff.

Dad loved Patsy Cline. Bob Wills and His Texas Playboys. Marty Robbins. That's all he heard growing up in rural Oklahoma. He liked other music, too. One of his favorite songs was Mona Lisa by Nat King Cole. I heard that one a million times. Once in a while, some blues would sneak in there. One song I'll never forget was Bull Moose Jackson's Big Ten Inch. I wonder what the neighbors thought when they heard Bull's lyrics, which were more than a little suggestive. I gave my love a little pinch. She said, 'Now stop that jivin.' Now whip out your big ten-inch. No matter what it was, the music was always played loud. I think about it today, and have to laugh. It's pretty fucking funny.

Dad liked to sing along with his favorites. Sometimes he'd lay in a hammock stretched out in the backyard, singing or playing his harmonica. He was pretty good on that thing. Luckily, if I did not inherit his particular taste in music, I did inherit his ability to sing. It has given me a life, a career and the gift of being able to make a living doing what I love. It's also given me a way to survive and maintain my sanity. Those are pretty sweet blessings it took me a long time to understand and appreciate.

From Mom, I inherited a lot, too. Her stubbornness, no doubt. Both Mom and Dad were very headstrong. When she made up her mind about something, that was it. I probably got some of my creative side from her.

I can bake, crochet, sew my own clothes and clean house like nobody's business. I know how to make a bed and bounce a quarter off it. It used to drive my first husband Jeff, crazy because he never knew how to make a bed. "Get out of here," I'd tell him, and then I would go ahead and do it like Martha Stewart. Only faster.

Once in a while when I was a little girl, my mother would let me come into the kitchen and help her cook and bake. Especially around the holidays, when she produced hundreds of gorgeous Christmas cookies, pies, cakes and sweet breads. She gave them to neighbors and people we knew. Not a lot of words passed between us. She'd tell me to stir something really well, put this or that in the blender. Practical, instructional stuff, mostly. She taught me how to separate an egg without screwing up the yoke, which is really important. Studying her every move, I loved being in there with her, wearing an apron, participating, and contributing.

To this day, if I feel depression coming on, I get an urge to go into the kitchen and bake a chicken and I don't even eat chicken. I love baking a pie, making my own crust. It makes me feel better to be in there and get my hands all messy while producing something beautiful and good-tasting. I can feel her with me when I'm in the middle of it. Cooking and baking give me comfort, a warm sense of satisfaction. That comes from Mom.

My mom also gave me something that might seem surprising, given all the gloom that surrounded her when I was alive. No matter what else was going on in our house or in the world, my mother was an impeccable homemaker. Me, too. I can make a Christmas Angel out of a National Geographic magazine, a Styrofoam ball and a can of spray paint. They make great doorstops, too, because they're heavier than shit.

I also inherited her quiet, brooding depression. I picked up both parents' habit of drinking too much, trying to get and stay numb rather than face life on its own terms. By osmosis, I suppose, I absorbed the idea that suicide is what you do when being alive in this world seems too much. As all the evidence suggests they did, I saw it as a perfect and sensible solution to pain that felt suffocating and never-ending.

Even though she was a distant figure to me most of the time she was alive, losing her for good hurt more than I could have imagined. What I didn't understand was that once she was gone, things were about to get much worse. For my family and for me.

Six - Breakdown

After my mother's suicide, Dad shut down completely, like a house too weak to withstand the battering of a bad storm. The combination of her death and his emotional collapse ushered in a stretch of about nine years when I could scarcely think about anything other than how to end my own life.

My father was a tall man with Clark Gable good looks and a magnetic personality. My now ex-husband, Jeff, who writes brilliant songs, had more than a passing resemblance to him.

I loved my father dearly. Even though he often beat the hell out of me when I was a little girl with his thick leather strap or that wooden board of his, I know he loved me, too.

Dad managed to escape C.A. and his Grapes of Wrath upbringing in rural Oklahoma after answering a Help Wanted newspaper ad for police officers in Detroit. His professional accomplishments, gorgeous wife and adorable children transformed Bill Magness into someone the rest of the family admired and respected. He was the shining success of the Magness clan. Until things began to implode.

Dad was a policeman in downtown Detroit for fifteen years, a job he loved. Under pressure from Mom - who had said repeatedly that she didn't want to be a policeman's widow. He left the police force and got a job selling baby books door to door. With his Southern accent and sharp business sense, he could charm the skin off a snake. He soon switched to life insurance, moving us first to Omaha, and then to the Minneapolis-St. Paul suburbs, where he eventually became District Manager for John Hancock Mutual Life Insurance Company.

When I was in first grade, he enlisted me in the cause of "helping him out" to sell life insurance. Here's what we're going to do, he said one afternoon. He told me to ask my teacher if he ever thought about life insurance and what he would do if something happened to him. Who'd take care of his wife and children, I was instructed to ask. I now know it was ridiculous, but at that time I didn't mind because I loved my daddy and craved his attention.

"You got it?" he asked.

I assured him I did. "Can I go out and play?"

I was on the job the next day, my first cold call. Me, a seven-year-old asking my teacher whether he had thought about protecting his family in case something terrible happened.

My dad was dead serious about it. I was instructed to give my teacher Dad's business card and he would follow up with a call to my teacher, sharing the commission with me if there was a sale. Of course, I never saw any money, but I was glad to be his partner. He was a consummate salesman. Charming, convincing, witty and determined. Sometimes during my music career, whether I was negotiating with a record company or in the middle of some other business proposition, I have felt his presence. I have always had his knack for sales and a head for business. Thank you for that, Dad.

I probably got some of my sense of humor from my father, too. He was quick to anger and even more easily provoked as I got older. But he was also an inveterate jokester who loved to clown around and do outrageous things that would make everyone shake their heads even as they laughed.

You never said pass the butter to my dad, for example. Even when we were growing up, you learned real fast it was not smart to say that to my dad because he would pick up the butter and stick it in your hand. You were literally in the butter. He was that guy, and then he'd break up laughing. He would embarrass us in front of our friends. He was the guy at the company Christmas party who showed up in a giant diaper with a nipple strapped to his head. He was goofball funny, trying almost anything for a laugh. But he was also the guy who beat the shit out of us with a leather strap and a board. Hard to reconcile both in one person, but people are rarely all one thing or another, and my dad was no exception.

Dad made good money in insurance, and, even though there were bumps in the road at work that none of us kids understood until much later, he had a solid career. I also know that he dearly missed being a policeman. That was obvious to all of us. Walking the precinct and doing his best to keep people safe must have made him feel useful and important. It was the job he loved most. He took tremendous pride in it.

Even though Mom and Dad didn't have much of a marriage by the time she took her life, once she was gone my father was completely lost in his own day-to-day existence. He didn't know what to do without her. His pride had always made it important that we showed the rest of the world that we were a fine, upstanding family on the rise. Handsome kids, beautiful wife. Big house, rewarding career. When my mother took her life, that charade became impossible. The facade crashed. People would know his wife was so forlorn she chose death over staying alive and caring for her five children. People would start to see his kids were rebellious, out of control, getting loaded. Hardly the picture of familial success we had carefully crafted over time. That perfect picture was suddenly deeply flawed and broken. Even if their relationship had cooled to the point of being frozen, without my mom at his side, life became more than he could handle. He could go through the motions no longer.

It was shocking to see him fall apart so completely after her suicide, fumbling and flailing around with even the simplest tasks. I barely recognized him. For years after her death, those memories of him melting down were lodged firmly in the front of my brain. That's no longer the case, thank goodness. But I can still conjure up the picture of Dad collapsing in grief on the frozen cemetery ground as my mother's casket was lowered slowly into her grave back in Detroit.

"Please, Billie, no, please no," he wailed. "Please forgive me. Please, dear God. No . . . "

My big, strong, smart, ex-policeman dad who always seemed to be in control could not stop shrieking. His cries haunted us all. Once the service ended, everyone left the gravesite as quickly as they could. I stood there alone with him for a long time, freezing in the bitter cold. I watched him sob and shake as he held his head in his hands. My fingers were turning blue, but I waited until he regained enough composure to help him up so we could get out of there. In the crazy swirl of emotions I felt at the time, anger at Dad was at the top of the list. I was enraged over his role in my mother's death. Furious he was so up and down emotionally. Furious he was so distant and strict. I was livid with him for making us move from Minnesota to the

St. Louis suburbs and the house my mother hated so much. I never gave a moment's thought to any of the demons that tormented him. All I knew was he was the head of our family and our family was fucked up. I was furious at him for everything that was wrong with us. But somehow, I still had enough empathy for him in my heart. I wasn't about to leave him alone at the graveside as broken as he was inside and out. I had to make sure he was able to pick himself up and walk away from my mom for the final time.

Once the funeral was behind us and we were back home in Kirkwood, Dad was no better. He lay on the bed for weeks with the curtains closed, crying and moaning. It was like having a sick baby to care for. He wouldn't eat. I had to try to feed him and get him to sit up, take a bath. He was unable to pack up her things, so that task fell to 13 year old me. He ordered me to put everything in boxes and send the whole pile to Goodwill.

I stepped gingerly into their bedroom in the middle of the afternoon to get started. The air was thick with darkness. My father was lying on the bed fully dressed. I drew open one of the blinds to get some light, so I could go through Mom's closet. He protested, so I pulled them tight again, leaving just a crack of light to see what I was doing as I opened the closet.

I had forgotten she had such a stunning collection of cocktail dresses – twenty-five or thirty of them - all lined up perfectly in a row. Several were elegant, flowing chiffon. They were all black with the exception of one sizzling red number. These dresses had fit her like a glove. I could still smell her perfume lingering on the material. There were shoes, gloves, purses and hat boxes galore. Everything was organized neatly, in rows. This was going to be my last goodbye to my mother, a mother I never really knew.

"There's too much cool stuff in here to just give it away," I said to my dad, his face buried in a pillow on the bed.

"Give it to Goodwill," he moaned while barely looking up. "I told you I don't want any of it."

Slowly, I took down each dress from the hanger it was draped on, examined the label to see who made it, drinking in the smell. I knew it would be the last time I'd experience even a trace of my mother's physical presence. I worried about each item, how to fold it just as she would. What a deeply sorrowful exercise, as I carefully placed my mother's dresses, one by one, in a big cardboard box. Folding each one just so, within moments I knew this was a final ritual for her. Such an unfitting burial ground for my mother's elegant clothes. Such an unfitting goodbye for my mother.

It felt like I was dismantling a holy shrine. More than anything, I had an overpowering realization that I never really got to know this woman who had given birth to me thirteen years earlier, cooked my meals, sewed my clothes, lived in the same house I did. My mother was a stranger to me. I knew a few things about her, but I had no idea who she was or what was in her heart. There was barely a connection between us, none of the intimacy or love that should come with raising a child. I saw it between others and her, particularly Jimmie and even Sam, and, of course, with Sara. Never with me.

I put those thoughts aside as best I could and finished emptying her closet. I whispered to her while placing her clothes in the boxes as delicately as possible. I'm not sure I thought I deserved her grace, but I asked her to forgive me for everything I did in my life that caused her pain. I asked her to forgive me for telling her to go to hell. I asked her to forgive me for being so much trouble, for not being a better daughter. My heart was beating rapidly as I did this. My legs and hands trembled; my eyes were wet. Somehow, I managed to finish clearing out her closet.

I was a selfish kid, but with my dad in such desperate shape, I knew he needed my help. He was broken, unable to do anything for himself. I had to get Mom's things out of that house. Maybe then he would start to come to terms with the fact that she was gone. Maybe then he would be able to start putting his own life back together. At least that's what I hoped.

The trouble with suicide, of course, is that it's permanent. There is no taking it back. No apologizing, no fixing it or trying again. It hangs in the air and attaches itself eternally to those left behind. Whatever went on between the two of them was now frozen in time. For-fucking-ever.

Over time, Dad eventually started to show signs of life. He reached out to Jimmie, who was still in Minneapolis. So was Sam; she and Jimmie had married but were separated. The two of them had a toddler son named Artese, the first-born son's first-born. Dad asked Jimmie to bring Sam and Artese to live with us. He figured Jimmie and Sam could help look after me and Carson, who was five at the time. It also seemed like a good opportunity for Jimmie and Dad to patch things up after years of bad blood between them that started even before Jimmie cold-cocked my dad and knocked him out.

Dad knew Sam and Jimmie had split up, but when he pulled Jimmie aside at the funeral, when he first raised the idea of my brother and his estranged family coming to live with us. Now Dad was trying to close the deal as he and Jimmie appealed to Sam about the idea of reconciling the marriage, of putting the family back together. More than anything, my dad always wanted things to be okay. If they were broken, he would come up with some plan to fix things. Now he was doing it again for Jimmie, Sam and the rest of us.

Billie would want it that way, Dad told Sam. He said they both owed it to my mom to give it a try. Dad knew just what to say. He was a top salesman, after all. He also knew Sam loved my mom and had been devoted to her. He was confident Sam could not say no to him; he knew she would feel too guilty. Dad was right about that, but it would turn out to be another terrible and tragic mistake.

Seven - Artese

For months after my mom's death, Dad was still devastated emotionally, but eventually he went back to work, traveling for his job or going out of town with a new girlfriend he didn't want us to see or know he had. Jimmie and Sam had come back as he requested, and whenever Dad had to leave town, which seemed to be more and more often, he apparently felt confident he was leaving Carson and me in good hands. Um, that was a huge mistake for us all.

Jimmie had started drinking again, smoking a little weed, and then came the harder drugs. It got ugly pretty quick. He and Sam threw these huge parties that attracted all kinds of pals from just about everywhere. When the party is happening, and the drugs are good, you make friends fast. It was the early '70s and hippies would come from miles around. Once everyone was high enough, we often got up on the roof of the house and jumped into the pool in the backyard. It was dangerous and more fun than you can imagine. Until it wasn't.

I loved my big brother dearly. That's why it was so confusing to come to hate him. I was 13 and had seen him beat Sam so brutally on more than a few occasions. When he was drunk or high, I no longer recognized him because he had become a monster. When he would start in on her, and I would hear the commotion, I got in between them best I could. I grabbed at him to get him off her, but it was no use. God, he was so strong.

One time, I saw Jimmie beat Sam so bad, he nearly did kill her. He was fucked up from doping and was getting ornerier by the minute. Sam and I were both screaming at Jimmie as he pummeled her again and again. She lay on the floor defenseless as he kicked her in the head and abdomen. Calling her a whore. She

59

finally lost consciousness. Her blood was all over the bedroom floor. It was a horror scene. At one point, as I tried to get him off her, he turned on me and threw me against the wall like I was a dish rag. I didn't care. I kept coming after him. Kicking, hitting, biting, screaming. Anything to get him away from Sam. As he punched me, I became strangely calm. I realized with each blow what had to be done. It was up to me. I had to stop him. I got real clear in those moments of brutality that it was my job to put an end to this insanity. And I knew exactly where dad kept his shotgun and shells.

The whole time, the baby was in his crib in that same small room hysterically screaming "Mama…. Mammmaaaaa." Then just like that, something came over Jimmie and he stopped. But by then I had made up my mind, just as I had when my dad whupped me for the last time, that this would never happen again. To save Sam, I would have to kill my brother. There was no other way out. In my mind at the time, it was either that or watch him beat Sam to death, and I wasn't about to let that happen. I loved her too much. As things turned out, something worse would intervene and scuttle my plan. But I was stone-cold serious about shooting him, even if I was only 13.

About a week after that beating, one Sunday in May late in the afternoon, we were cleaning up the place after another big blowout. Dad was due home any time now with a woman he had just started dating. Sam, who was angry and upset about that, was making dinner. She couldn't believe my dad was hanging out with another woman. "Your mom isn't even cold in the grave, for God sake," she said.

As Sam was getting dinner finished, my job was to watch my eighteen-month-old nephew. Artese was the most beautiful baby boy I'd ever seen. His red hair hung in soft curls like his mama's. Also like his mama, he had the most exquisite, translucent and milky skin. He had Jimmie's gigantic blue eyes, and his smarts, too. Even at eighteen months, you could tell he was wicked bright. Jimmie adored that little boy. We all did.

Artese was mischievous, too, just like his daddy. I was sitting on a chaise lounge chair next to the pool, talking on the phone to my old friend, Tina. Artese was playing near the pool. He loved that water. I was still loaded from all the weed and wine I had the night before. I hung up the phone and walked back inside to the kitchen.

Plopping myself down on a chair at the table, Sam looked at me and asked, "Where's Artese?" Oh my God. I had completely forgotten about the baby. In the instant we made eye contact, we both bolted outside, knocking over the kitchen table with all the dishes and supper on it. There was Artese, floating face down in the pool. Sam started to scream for Jimmie, who flew out of the house and jumped into the deep end of the water. Jimmie pulled his little boy's limp body from the pool and started CPR. Jimmie had been trained in it, but not on babies, who are so small and delicate. Water kept flowing out of Artese's mouth and nose. I could not believe what was unfolding in front of me. I see it still to this day. The whole scene was surreal, as if I was watching someone else's very bad movie.

Sam screamed over and over for Jimmie to be careful. "But don't stop," she said. "Don't stop. Don't stop."

I raced into the house and called an ambulance. Jimmie and Sam weren't about to wait. They carried Artese to the car, peeling rubber out of there and making a frantic dash to save their baby boy's life. As they disappeared down the road, I was frozen where I stood, in total shock and disbelief at what had just happened. At what I had caused to happen because I was such a complete fuckup.

After a few minutes, I went inside the house to find the small metal cross that had been with my mother's casket. I didn't know what else to do. I needed to hold on to something familiar. Back outside, I sat with that crucifix in my hands at the edge of the pool, my feet dangling in the same blue water that Artese had just been floating in. I thought maybe somehow, I could connect to him if I touched the water and pled with God. I held that cross in my hands. My whole body was shaking as I convulsed with tears. I had never cried that hard in my life. I begged God to please let Artese live. I begged him to save the baby and take me instead. How could I have been so fucking careless? I was gasping for breath, unable to take in any air.

Please, God, I kept sputtering. Take me, take me. Don't take the baby. I will go. Just please don't take him. The words and sobs came so fast, I thought I might pass out.

Before that day, I had always been a sad, lonely girl. From my earliest memories, I was deep in self-loathing. That's why I put that cord around my neck and tried to end my life when I was just 4. As time went on, the feeling only increased. It ate away at me. I grew up with that deep depression and sadness the way some kids grow up feeling safe because they have friends and parents who look after them. I had no real friends, just my make-believe playmates, the cat and the dog. I was sure my sister hated me. My mother was checked out and lost in her own mental illness and depression. My father horsed around and played with me when I was little, but I mostly lived in mortal fear of his next punishment. When my brother Joe's constant cruelty escalated to the point that he was molesting me, it made perfect sense to me. Of course, bad things happened to me. If I wasn't worth a damn in the first place, what else should I expect?

Then Artese came into our world. That dear, sweet little redheaded boy we all loved so much. I adored him. He had such a beautiful, happy smile. He was pure innocence and joy. Our household was in desperate need of his bouncy, beautiful baby spirit. We needed something light and sweet to counter the dank, dark vacuum of mental illness and despair that was destroying us all. For eighteen months, that bouncing baby was nothing but light, laughter and sweetness.

I had abandoned him. He was a baby, asking for nothing and expecting only love. I had failed him. It was five months after my mother's suicide. My addled teenage brain was still in a thick fog, made worse, I'm sure, by the fact that my family and I never—not a single solitary time—talked about my mother's death. My father did not do what a parent should in a situation like that: sit us down and discuss what happened. Or at least seek out professional help to face our loss and grief. Pretending it never happened is not an answer. Today there is all kinds of literature and information available about the importance of giving yourself time and space to grieve after the loss of a loved one. That concept was unknown to any of us at the time. Instead, we sat in silence. With our broken hearts, we did nothing but let our pain grow and engulf us.

I became a walking zombie, getting stoned or drunk every chance I could. I took just about anything, so I didn't have to think about my mother and her absence, or about my final hateful words to her.

Now this: my reckless and irresponsible behavior took Artese's life. I stole him from his mother and father. I stole that child from all of us. That sent a powerful shock wave through my family. We were unable to feel because none of us knew how to listen to our hearts or ask for help, but we all felt the full force of this loss. The one good, wholesome thing in our lives was gone. Because of me. Because of my stupid negligence.

I saw with absolute clarity what had to be done. I was a skinny thirteen-year-old with thick glasses, long, wavy brown hair almost to my waist and—since my mom's death— the beginnings of a problem with drugs and alcohol. Now, for the first time in my life, I had a mission. I would carry it out in true Magness fashion, a job that had to be done no matter what. I would quietly go about my business. No whining, no looking for sympathy. Overly dramatic? Maybe. But if you'd put a gun to my head at the time and demanded I come up with a reason that I should be alive, I'd have come up empty. If you'd asked me why I should be dead, I could have offered a dozen reasons. It was as clear to me as the water in a Minnesota lake.

People talk of finding their True North, the absolute right course for their lives. They use it to navigate their way out of the wilderness to a path absolutely right for them. I found my True North that dreadful Sunday afternoon in the backyard of that wretched house in suburban St. Louis where two members of my family had died far too early.

My True North was nothing blissful or beautiful. However, it was revelatory. There was no turning back: I needed to end my life.

When Sam and Jimmie returned to the house a few hours after rushing to the hospital with Artese, their faces were ashen, drained of all color and life. I knew what they were going to say before they spoke.

Artese is dead, Jimmie muttered. D.O.A.

I wanted it to be an awful nightmare, asking God to wake me up and make everything right. I knew it wasn't a dream, though. It made sense in a perverse way because of the path I had been on and the toxic dynamics within my family.

Within days after Artese died, my brother and Sam went back to Minneapolis. Jimmie would tell me years later that the baby's death was not my fault, but I could never believe him. After that, he and I didn't talk for years. I knew what happened that day in the backyard at the pool. I was there, the only living witness. Of course, it was my fault. If not for me, that baby would be alive. I was one hundred percent to blame for his death.

Even today, it blows my mind to think that Sam and I remained close for a number of years after Artese drowned. We still spent a lot of time together. But we never said a single word about the baby or his death until a long time after the fact.

Eight - Deep Shit

Our family was in shambles. Jimmie and Sam were gone. Sara had run away several months earlier and was not communicating with any of us. Joe was in the Air Force, having his own breakdown. Within days of Artese's death, Dad got a letter dated July 24, 1970 from a close friend who was an officer. The friend had been trying to look out for Joe at Randolph Air Force Base in Texas, where Joe was stationed. Punk, my dad's friend's nickname, wrote that Joe was in serious trouble after completing his basic training, with some of the problem tied to the fact he wasn't allowed to pursue a medical training course that interested him.

"Since he was not busy, he got to feeling sorry for himself and thinking about his problems," Punk's letter informed my father, who needed one more family crisis like a man with a broken leg needs a kick in the shin. "This led to about 20 trips to the hospital on sick call and he was in such a poor mental attitude as evidenced by his statements that he might go AWOL or even take his own life, he was committed to the psychiatric ward at the hospital for five days. The doctor concluded that he had a mental problem of significant magnitude to warrant his discharge as unsuitable."

Punk went on to say that Joe had written my dad a number of letters and had not heard back, making Joe even more distraught. "The boy is concerned about your home and I strongly recommend you write to him frequently, if only short notes. He really needs some assurance from you that things are alright at home." Punk closed by telling my dad, "Sorry for the troubles you are having. I hope they will smooth out soon. Joe is basically a fine boy who really needs to grow up and I surely wish him the best."

A short time later, Dad got another letter about Joe from a Captain Skog who informed him that Joe was AWOL, his "whereabouts unknown to military authority."

I wasn't thinking about my dad's troubles or what he was feeling at the time. But when I look back at the chain of events now, and how our family tragedies piled up on him, my heart weeps. I am filled with sadness and empathy. His dark moods and hair-trigger temper set the tone for much of what afflicted us, but no one deserves that much pain. With so much happening that Dad could not control or comprehend, he needed time. My father was unable to take care of himself, let alone look after two kids. Carson and I were sent to live with our grandparents, Pearl and Paul, in Mt. Clemens, a suburb of Detroit.

I loved my grandma and grandpa, but I was so miserable and emotionally remote they didn't know what to do with me. It is hard to remember much from the few months I was with them. I don't even remember going to high school, but I know I did. I do recall sitting at the kitchen table a lot in a daze, playing the radio and weeping. I listened to music cranked up loud as I sat there and cried. It was impossible to get Artese or my mom out of my head. Let It Be, the big Beatles hit, was released in that spring of 1970 and was on the radio constantly. I was pretty sure it was written just for me.

When I find myself in times of trouble, mother Mary comes to me,

Speaking words of wisdom, let it be. And in my hour of darkness she is standing right in front of me, Speaking words of wisdom, let it be.

I was unable to let anything be. I begged God to have Mary appear to me. She never did.

Hearing that beautiful song again and again on the radio sent me deeper into myself and my sorrow, which I was sure would never end. It was during my time with my grandparents that the machinery in my head started working overtime about the exact best way to bring about my own death. I wouldn't act on it right away. I would plan it methodically, another Magness trait. It gave me something to do, like a long-term homework project at school that I was determined to ace. I might get sidetracked by one diversion or another, but my planning and calculating would not stop until I finally had everything in order. Until I knew the plan was solid. Until I knew the time was right.

After a few months feeling miserable at my grandparents' house, I telephoned my dad, telling him I wanted to come home. Like the great Elvis Costello song goes, It was a fine idea at the time, now it's a brilliant mistake.

By the time I arrived home, Dad had already moved to a new townhouse in Mehlville, another suburb of St. Louis. That meant I had to change schools yet again. By this time, though, I was so out of it from everything that had happened, I didn't blink or protest. Not much mattered to me one way or the other. I was glad to get out of that terrible house where Mom and Artese died. I was convinced the place had been cursed. I suspect all the neighbors had some theories of their own. They certainly never spoke with us again.

It wasn't long before Dad and I were back to our old arguments about how late I was staying out, why my grades were going down, why I was so checked out all the time. He told me I was the mom now, in charge of all household responsibilities for me, Dad and Carson. I had better behave myself and get my grades up. We never talked about what happened to Mom or Artese.

To my 13-year-old self, living with my father felt like prison. I was consumed with shame, convinced I had caused the deaths of two people I loved dearly. I was miserable and acting out. I didn't have the foggiest idea how to please my dad or do anything to make myself feel better. All I could do was listen to music amped up loud. It was Hendrix and the Live at Woodstock album and get loaded — I did that every chance I had — and work on my exit strategy.

I started hanging out at a head shop in St. Louis where everyone was stoned and all kinds of drug paraphernalia was sold. I panhandled in front of the place for something to do and to dig up spare cash. Everybody did it, mooching for smokes, a bottle of wine, money for weed. That was how I struck up a friendship with a girl named Marina. One day she said she knew where to get some LSD, was I interested? I had never tried acid before, but I was game for just about anything that would get me out of my head. After hustling enough money for Marina to score a few hits, we were off and running.

I needed a cover story, so I called my dad and told him I was going to a friend's house and would get a ride home from her mom later that night. Before I knew it, I was at Marina's with her and some of the older guys who used to hang around the head shop, tripping my brains out. Suddenly, it was 10 p.m., so I mustered all the clear-headedness I could and called my dad. He demanded to know where I was.

When I said I was at my girlfriend's house, he didn't buy it, telling me he'd called there, and my friend's mom said she hadn't seen me in days. Errr…. Uh- oh.

Now I was in deep shit and asking two longhaired guys from the head shop to drive me home in their 1960s-era Mustang might not have been the smartest move. We pulled into my driveway, and there was my dad waiting for me. He marched out of the house toward the car with a baseball bat in his hand and that familiar look of murder in his eyes. The guys pushed me out of the car and took off for their lives, tires squealing as they burned rubber to get out of my driveway. My dad grabbed my arm and started pulling me toward the house, demanding I go inside. Then he started the interrogation, Magness style.

"Where were you? What were you doing? Are you high? Who were those lowlifes?" I went into my usual lying routine. I don't remember what kind of story I tried selling him, but he was an ex-policeman and he didn't fall for any of it. Sticking his face up against mine, he shouted, "Your eyes are dilated. You're high. What did you take?"

In the kitchen, I told him I wasn't high. "You're crazy," I shrieked. He called me a liar, then backhanded me in the face so hard I flew across the room, my body slamming into the cabinets. It was the first time he'd laid a hand on me since that incident with the book in my pants about four years earlier, when I was nine. I ran from the kitchen into the living room, hell-bent on getting out of the house and away from him. Being high on LSD, angry and in a hurry are not usually compatible. In my haste to escape, instead of opening the glass storm door at the front of the house, I barreled through it, cutting my hands and arms, with glass flying everywhere. Now I was out in the street, bloody, in pain, running full out with no idea where I would go or what I'd do, and peaking on acid.

I made it to a main intersection where if you stood on some railroad tracks off to the side, it seemed as if you could see for miles. There was a pretty good view of the lit-up St. Louis Gateway Arch. I stopped to catch my breath and saw the gleaming silvery landmark off in the distance. But it was no gateway to anywhere for me. I wanted to escape my life and everything in it, but I had no place to go. I quickly realized I was too out in the open for my own good and took off running once more.

Out of nowhere, a cop car suddenly appeared and approached me. The two officers came out of their car and for whatever reason, they seemed to take pity on me. The patrolman who had been driving helped me get into the back of the car. Before long, I was in a hospital emergency room getting treated for cuts on my hands and my knee, where it broke through the glass. The ER doc gave me a couple of injections to bring me down from my high. I was in a daze and lost all sense of time. Next thing I knew, my dad was standing there in front of me, ready to take me home.

The last thing in the world I wanted was to have a conversation or be interrogated again. I staggered up to my room and luckily, he did not come after me. I slept like the dead until the next morning. When I got up, the house was eerily quiet. It felt as if I was alone. But as I headed into the kitchen, I could see my dad in the living room, reclining quietly on the couch, lying in wait for me to appear. He didn't move a muscle as I inched my way into the room; he just kept lying there on the couch, eyeing me intently with a seriousness of purpose that soon became apparent.

"We need to talk," he said in a low whisper. "You can't do any more drugs. This has to stop." I was facing criminal charges for my behavior, he said. Ingestion of an illegal substance. "Tell me exactly what happened, right now."

I felt the hormonal hatred rising in my thirteen-year-old brain and I will always remember what he said to me: "You need to tell the truth. Be truthful. You know the truth will set you free. I want you to tell me the truth and promise me you will never do drugs again. Right now."

I don't know where my nerve came from, but I just stared at my dad and let him have it. I was a smartass and an asshole all at once. The truth? I still remember the words that came tumbling out of my mouth instead.

"You want me to tell you the truth? Are you sure, 'cause I don't really think you do. You want me to tell you what you want to hear. But that ain't the truth. You want me to promise you I will never do drugs again? Okay, I will never do drugs again. But that isn't the truth. The truth is I really don't know. The truth is I like them. I like how I feel when I take them. I can't look you in the eye and promise you that I will never do them again. You want me to lie and tell you that."

I can only imagine how it wounded him to stand there and hear his youngest daughter talk like that to him. If I hadn't hurt him enough, my rant ended with me calling him an old fool.

"Are we done," I said, "because I have places to go and people to see."

I never should have talked to my father that way. It was off-the-wall crazy and cruel, but at that point in my life, I didn't see him as a human being. To me, he was the enemy, just this mean, angry, stupid shithead old man who knew nothing about me. He was ultimately responsible for my mother's death. He was why our family was such a mess. He was the reason there was a giant gulf between us, or so I was convinced. The only option in front of me now was to split for good, find some way to be on my own. I needed to get away from him, and that's what I became determined to do.

I had begun to make friends with some of the other misfit teenagers in the complex where our townhouse was located. I'm not sure how it happened. I felt so apart from everyone and everything, but my radar usually had the ability to hone in on in on the kids who smoked pot and were nursing their own personal wounds. I didn't have much in the way of social skills, but I was drawn to kids like that all the time. They seemed to like me, too. I figured if I left town and got away from my dad, somehow things would be better. Turns out I was wrong about that, too.

My father must have felt like he was out of all options. All of his kids were a mess. I was 13 and trying to destroy myself before his very eyes. Desperate, he called an old neighbor of ours from Birchwood, the St. Paul suburb we lived in before St. Louis. Her name was Martha Funke. She was the middle daughter of our former neighbors, a close family friend who had been my sister's best pal when we lived back in Minnesota. Martha was about 17 at the time. As soon as school was out for the summer, she accepted my dad's offer of a job to come out and help with the house, me and Carson.

Martha was a nice, normal, compassionate girl who genuinely wanted to help our family, but I didn't stick around long enough to connect with her. By the time she arrived, I was hanging out with Carl, a drug dealer who lived across the street from us. He was nine years older than me. He was smitten, and I thought I liked him, too. More than anything, he was a distraction from my life, a way out of living under my father's roof. I was just starting to sense the power I had over men; I could play the conniving Lolita role pretty well when I wanted to. It was easy to get Carl to do just about anything I wanted. As soon as I met him, I knew he was my ticket out.

Before Martha made it to town, Dad came home early from work one day and found me on Carl's lap as we sat on the couch. I could see my dad's blood pressure rise, the vein in the side of his neck bulging. It was the same look he'd had in his eye when those two hippies dropped me off on the front lawn during my acid trip. I was sure he was going to hit Carl, but he just threw him out of the house and said I could never see him again. For good measure, he told me I was grounded for a year and to put on a bra! He didn't know I had already burned it in a late-night ritual with the rest of my girlfriends.

I began to set things in motion the next day, telling Carl we needed to make a plan and split. The day after Martha arrived in St. Louis, we were gone. It wasn't hard to talk Carl into going along with my idea.

Choosing bad guys was familiar to me. For years, I became drawn to what I knew. I don't want to dignify them by calling them relationships, but the men I got involved with affirmed the hatred I had for myself. I liked Carl okay at first, but he didn't really mean much to me except as a way to escape.

Carl's preference was for us to head to Texas. He had some friends there. It was familiar territory for him. I nixed the idea. It wasn't far enough for me. I worried that my dad would find us. My idea was to head out to Berkeley, Ca. Convincing Carl was simple; I told him that's where we should go, and he said, fine.

I had wanted for a long time to be in California, away from the boring Midwest and its harsh winters. Like a lot of young girls I knew, I dreamed about it for years. Here was my chance. Carl was on board, but he needed to get some cash for the trip. He was tight with a lot of shady people, and he soon began breaking into homes and committing burglaries. When I found out what he was up to, I didn't protest. I didn't tell him he was crazy or that it was wrong. Instead, I insisted he let me help. I don't know what motivated me. I think part of it was wanting to contribute and carry my own weight, but I'm sure the adventure and badass behavior appealed to me, too. He resisted at first, but I convinced him by explaining that because I was smaller than him, I could crawl into tight places he couldn't squeeze into. We wound up bankrolling our travels by committing a string of burglaries in the St. Louis area.

Carl would break a window in a basement or at the back of a house. I'd crawl in and open the door. He found out about some people with gun collections, which is what we were after. Carl figured they would fetch the most money fast. He was right, using his connections to sell the guns to some people in the Black Panthers.

This was 1970. A very complicated time politically and socially...The Panthers had started in 1966 as a grassroots organization to monitor police brutality by patrolling city streets. Eventually they launched food programs for children and free community clinics. But they were viewed as an increasingly militant group by F.B.I. Director J. Edgar Hoover, and often finding themselves in confrontations with both police and Federal authorities.

There was nothing cool or romantic about stealing guns. But I was desperate to get as far away from my father as possible, as quickly as possible. The burglaries and gun selling were a means to an end. I never thought about the morality or consequences of what we were doing. What I did feel bad about was the idea of leaving Carson with my dad, but I knew Martha would be there to help when Dad wigged out. Carson would be okay with someone else watching him. Actually, probably better.

I made plans for my best friend to mail a letter from me to my father after Carl and I were gone. I told her to send it from a St. Louis post office across town about a week after we split.

I figured my dad would assume I was hiding somewhere in the vicinity and would be thrown off our trail. But using his police connections, within weeks he had an all-points bulletin issued on me. He enlisted the help of my principal at Mehlville Junior High School, who told him I hadn't been in class for six weeks. "This letter is to inform you of my referral of your daughter to the juvenile court authorities," Principal Harry W. Hadd wrote my dad on January 12, 1971. "Thank you for your cooperation in this matter."

Kidnapping charges were filed against Carl by the FBI because I was a minor. But Dad never did find out where I was.

He didn't have to. It took me about six months out in Berkeley to realize Carl was not the man of my dreams after all. He was a real nut job. Not violent like some of the men I would wind up with later, but he sure as hell wasn't grounded in anything resembling reality. He was undependable and unstable, an immature, greasy drug dealer nine years my senior. Other than that, he was fine.

I was smart enough to know it probably wouldn't be a good idea to simply tell Carl I was done with him. He would lose it, I felt certain. Going back to my father's house also didn't seem like a good idea. So, my addled brain concocted another master plan. This time the goal was to get away from Carl and find my way back to Minneapolis.

I told Carl I wanted to visit the Twin Cities to see some old girlfriends. I would talk my dad into buying me an airline ticket and then, after about a month, Carl could come get me. Off we'd go again, and no one would be the wiser. Cool, Carl said.

I called my father from a phone booth on Telegraph Avenue in Berkeley, asking him to buy me the ticket. I knew he would be happy to learn where I was, that I would be returning to friends and family back in Minnesota. I was no longer a child, I told him. He understood he could not force me to stay with him in St. Louis. I told him if he tried to get me to come back, I would just run away. He would never see or hear from me again. He was relieved to know I was safe. Reluctantly, he agreed to fly me back to Minnesota.

He arranged to have me stay a while with Jackie, a woman whom he described as one of his friends. I figured I had nothing to lose by going along. She was a sweet-natured divorcee, with a couple of teenage kids of her own. I realized pretty quickly that Jackie had been seeing Dad while he was married to Mom, but that didn't matter to me now. Jackie was kind and compassionate; I liked her.

I had been at Jackie's about a month when Carl figured out where I was and started calling. It was time to follow through on our plan and come pick me up. That's when I told him, change of plans. Sorry, but that's not happening. We were done, I told him. I never wanted to see him again. He yelled into the phone, crying like I suspected he would. He said he would jump off one of the tallest buildings in San Francisco if I didn't come back.

"Go ahead and jump," I dared him. "I don't care." He was fooling with the wrong customer when it came to the subject of suicide. I coldly called his bluff. I knew he didn't have the nerve to take his own life. All I could think about was getting away from him permanently.

I hung up on him, but he called a few days later to inform me that he was going to turn himself in to the FBI if I dumped him for good. He would happily go to prison. Be my guest, I said. The crazy son of a bitch did just that, and after he was in custody, two FBI agents came to question me at Jackie's house about him kidnapping me. I told them the truth, that it had been my plan to leave St. Louis in the first place. That took most of the wind from their sails and by the time they left, they realized they had no case against Carl.

The final straw came after I went to a party with Jackie's two kids. We had been to the record store earlier in the day and bought the new Sly and the Family Stone album, There's a Riot Going On, a funk masterpiece with a title that seemed to sum up my life at the time. We took it to the party but never had a chance to play it. A fight broke out when a white girl showed up with a black kid on her arm and words were exchanged.

One of the kids was stabbed in the temple with the stem of a wine glass. The boy went down hard, convulsing and bleeding like he was going to die, right onto my lap. I was covered in his blood. Wrapping his head in my favorite lambskin embroidered coat, I tried applying pressure to stop the bleeding until an ambulance came. The cops showed up and we were all questioned. I came home smeared in blood. Seeing me like that — on top of the visit from the FBI — was more than Jackie could handle. A few days later, Jackie asked me to leave. She had become increasingly and understandably unhappy with the drama surrounding me. She was worried about her own kids being subjected to Bill Magness' youngest daughter.

Apologizing sweetly as she did it, Jackie told me she couldn't have me in her home anymore. I heard her call my dad and say she was sorry, but she had her own kids to worry about. Who could blame her? I was bad news. I kept getting into crazy trouble, whether it was my fault or not. Drama followed me like a lost dog. I called an old classmate from the neighborhood, Tina Fynbo, the girl I had been on the phone with when Artese drowned. I filled her in on the latest craziness. She offered to talk her parents into letting me stay with them. I told her they might be able to get some money out of it if they applied for a Foster Care license, an angle I was aware of from my time on the street in Berkeley.

It seemed like a perfect solution. Tina's parents liked me when we met and agreed to give the new arrangement a try. They applied to be Foster parents soon afterward and were accepted. So began my travels through the Foster Care system.

Unfortunately, the welcome wore thin with Tina's family, too. I was only there a few months when they decided I needed to move on. I was a bad kid, they said, and would have to leave. That was a verdict I heard a lot. Her parents were scared I would be a negative influence on Tina and their other kids. It hurt to hear that shit again, and I was pissed off, but I had no cause to blame them. They were reacting to what they heard with their own ears and witnessed with their own eyes. They also knew that I had run away once, gone to California and been involved with a guy much older than me. They knew I used drugs and that I was not a virgin. To Tina's Catholic parents, this was scary stuff. I was damaged goods, still beating myself up over Mom and Artese, but I knew I was not a mean or malicious person. I was still down in the dumps and drinking, getting loaded as often as I could. I knew how to hide it pretty well. You could say I was a young functioning alcoholic, just as my parents had been for so long. But not long after Tina's parents kicked me out, someone else would offer an opinion on my mental status, an assessment that would bring a whole new set of dire consequences.

Nine - Otis Rush

Once Tina's mom and dad had been approved as Foster parents and taken me in, I was officially and legally a ward of the state. Fourteen and I belonged to the state of Minnesota. After Tina's folks said I needed to leave, it was now up to my court-assigned social worker to find another placement for me. It didn't take her long. She located a nice couple in Stillwater who took me in. They were kind and loving, too loving as it turned out for my tastes. The mom helped me get work down the block from their house at a Dairy Queen, the first job I ever had. I was terribly shy and reluctant to talk to people, and the job was good for me because when you're serving up dip cones and ice cream sundaes, you are required to interact with other human beings. But as much as I craved love and attention when I was living in my house, I cringed when other people noticed me. From my head to my toes, there was not one ounce of self-confidence. I was so lacking in social skills it was frightening when someone actually did pay attention, even if it was only to say they wanted chocolate on that vanilla cone. I ran away from that place after a few months, living on the streets or "couch surfing" with people I knew for a night or two here and there.

Moving around every few nights was awful. Not knowing where I would crash from one day to the next was more randomness than I could handle. When the social worker asked me if I would go back to the couple's house if they were willing to take me in again, I knew they were "too normal" for me but I said yes. To my dismay, it was the foster parents who said "no" this time. They didn't want me back. That stung, but it hurt a little less when I found out later that the mom had been diagnosed with breast cancer and had other things she needed to deal with besides trying to get through to a stubborn and distant teenager who didn't seem to want help from anyone.

Thanks to the LSD episode, I was also on probation. That led to my eventually being required to undergo regular psychiatric exams. I took them so many times, I became an old hand at the exercise. I was never serious about any of them. One big test was called the Minnesota Multiphasic Personality Inventory. That's a mouthful and a half. Invented decades ago by two University of Minnesota professors and updated multiple times since, I believe it is still the most commonly used personality test in mental health. It has about six hundred true-or-false statements and questions asked over and over, worded a little differently each time to catch someone in a lie or a distortion. Statements like, "I work under a great deal of tension" - true or false. Or, "A person should try to understand his dreams and be guided by or take warning from them." Or, "My sleep is fitful and disturbed," "I have not lived the right kind of life." "I wish I could be as happy as others seem to be." "I am a good mixer." On and on and on. There is even one that says, "I am very seldom troubled by constipation."

I took the test so many times, I can practically recite parts of it by heart. It became a sort of joke amongst troubled kids. The diagnosis I got back was stern and ugly: "schizophrenic, maladjusted, manic depressive and highly suicidal." I still have the paperwork. I suppose it was more or less accurate. But we know so much more about diagnosing adolescents today than we did in the 1970s, especially budding alcoholics. If that same messed up young girl were somehow examined today, the results might be different. I know they had the suicidal and depressive parts right. Nonetheless, the test results had consequences. I soon found myself in a group home for "mentally retarded" girls in St. Paul, the first of two placements there. After that, there were three psychiatric hospitalizations at a psychiatric hospital in St. Paul, each for a longer period of time than the one before.

At the time, the person calling the shots in my life was one Charles T. McCafferty. He was the Juvenile Court psychiatrist in Ramsey County assigned to my case. He was a big believer in Freud and dry as a pile of toothpicks. Sometimes during our sessions, I would not say a word. He might say two. He just sat behind his gigantic desk with a note pad. Waiting for something to accidentally spill out of me or drop from the sky. I was sealed up tight. I wasn't about to let anything get out. I was just marking time with him. It was a power struggle. In my mind, I was sure I was winning. I decided he was square as a block and knew nothing. Then one day he surprised the hell out of me when he blurted out, "You know, until you relive parts of your childhood, you will never mature or move forward."

Whoa. Words from on high. I couldn't believe my ears. So I got angry. Who the hell did he think he was and HOW the fuck was I supposed to relive my fucking childhood? What an idiot, I told myself.

He didn't articulate it well. That was seemingly beyond his capabilities. I was a damaged teenager and we might as well have been talking different languages neither of us understood. But, of course he was spot on. Bastard!

It was his idea to have me spend time in a psychiatric hospital where he felt there were counselors who could help me do what he was convinced I needed. Plus I would be under observation. Ugh. The first time in there, I was so beaten down and lost that I reluctantly agreed to extended treatment; I wound up staying a month. I didn't get much from it, and after I was back on the streets a while and checking in with him for my court-scheduled visits, I came around and surrendered to the idea of trying again. This time I was there two months. Same result. My armor was impenetrable. I wasn't interested in reliving anything or cooperating with anyone. But after a while, lost again in the streets with no permanent or safe place to go, we reversed roles. I went to him and asked to be sent back to the psych ward. I was exhausted, worn down from fighting the world and life. I was tired of being me. It took so much energy to keep going and hold everything bottled up inside me. My depression was getting the upper hand, keeping me in a funk so deep and full of despair I wasn't able to do much of anything. I was desperate for a break. I went to see him and asked him to commit me for a third time, tears streaming down my face from the utter sense of helplessness I was feeling. I don't know what I was hoping for other than a place to go, but I could at least exhale and get some rest without having to think where I would sleep, how to feed myself or other essential human activities.

The place was structured to the nth degree. Every moment you were in your room, in a group, in an art class, at a meal. The only color in the place was beige. We had no free time, which was the idea. You were rarely alone, always being watched by someone somewhere. There was a mirrored window in the group therapy room so the other staff and doctors could watch the group, but we could not see them.

It was surreal. I didn't know a soul in the place. I did my best to size up people and hung around a little only with the ones who didn't seem completely wigged out. Not unlike high school or prison. Adolescents and adults were on the same floor, in two wings behind locked doors with bars and wire in the windows. Windows were secured shut. They couldn't be opened, but we sure tried. The story in the ward was that some kid had tied sheets together and climbed out the window to escape, putting an end to windows that could be opened.

We were not allowed to have a radio that connected us to the outside world or anything sharp in our room. We only had spoons to eat our meals. Knives and forks were too dangerous. They made sure we didn't have anything that could be turned into a rope. Those things were confiscated upon arrival. Shoelaces. Jewelry. As I said, it was like prison.

A nurses station and a so-called "community room" where a television, some ratty chairs, a sofa and tables were set up so we could socialize and play cards if we liked. The adult and adolescent wings were separated, but the whole place felt like One Flew Over the Cuckoo's Nest, without Jack Nicholson. Some of the adults were getting shock treatments. Just about everyone was on heavy meds. I don't remember much scintillating conversation or socializing going on in the common area. A lot of staring and a fair amount of drooling. The adolescent rooms were livelier. We had our own separate TV room, but you had to exhibit good behavior for extended periods of time to earn various privileges. The orderlies were young guys, and if you acted up they would put you in restraints or a straitjacket. That seemed really fucked up, but I was smart enough to mind my own business. They never got me.

Every once in a while, they'd haul off someone who was making a lot of noise or causing trouble, and away they'd go for shock treatments. I never saw the actual treatments administered, but we all knew what was happening. Someone would be taken away and get wheeled back to the ward a few hours later looking like a zombie. They got their brains fried. That's what we called it. Sometimes the orderlies would station them in the community room for all to see. They'd just sit and stare. Forever. There was one woman they gave the shock treatments to because she couldn't shake her depression. She cried all the time. All she did was lie around and weep. Loudly. Meds didn't help her. When she returned from the treatments, she was a freaking vegetable, barely moving as she stared blankly off into space. That lasted about five days. Then she started crying again non-stop. Only now she didn't seem to understand why because her memory had been zapped. Shit like that scared the living daylights out of me.

One time we somehow got hold of a bunch of cans of whipped cream and barricaded ourselves with a chair into our little TV room to have some fun. I don't remember how we got them; a visitor probably smuggled them in. We had an awesome whipped cream fight. It was a blast, the only fun we'd had in weeks. We paid for it with all kinds of oppressive restrictions for weeks after that. No field trips. No art classes. Nothing. Boring times a thousand. Enough to drive you, well, insane.

The art therapy classes were the only ray of light in the entire place. And yes, I swear we actually did weave baskets, make sculptures, and paint by numbers. I can laugh my ass off about it now, but it wasn't funny at the time. I made a beautiful clay sculpture of a woman, kneeling down, trapped in a shadow box. I am sure the shrinks had a field day trying to analyze what was going on in my brain when I came up with that.

At one point, they put me on Thorazine, but I was smart enough to take the pills and tongue them, then spit them out when the orderlies weren't looking. I never swallowed one. Stashed a pile and traded them with a visitor, a boyfriend who came to see me. He brought me some LSD; I gave him the Thorazine as a trade. Another kid and I wound up doing the acid. It wasn't as if the staff could tell if we were tripping. Psychedelics in the psych ward. Perfect. That was a fun day. I remember we spent a lot of time sitting in the hallway rolling a tennis ball around. Not very ambitious or demanding, but it killed time and provided a little bit of comic relief anyway.

I seldom had visitors. I think my sister came once to check in on me, but I'm not sure. Maybe Sam came once. There wasn't a lot to say. Seriously. Hi. How crazy are you? Do you feel better? Did you make anything in weirdo art class today? When do you get out? Not exactly the conversation anyone wanted to have with me. The feeling was mutual.

Most of the orderlies were jerks. Into power trips, not at all cool and not very smart. But there was one, I don't remember his name, who was super cool. He took us on a few field trips, which were a big deal. Orderlies always wore hospital whites, so it was obvious if they took us out of the hospital that we were mental patients. He took us to the park a few times. To a movie if he could get one approved. He managed that a few times, too, and it was always a welcome break from endless monotony.

Toward the end of my third stay, this cool orderly took us to a park and to a movie. He had convinced the higher ups in a staff meeting that it was a good idea to allow us to go to select, pre-approved movies. Somehow he got the film Harold and Maude on the list. It's the great 1970s dark comedy about a young guy fascinated with death and his close friendship and eventual romance with Maude, who was about eighty and played brilliantly by Ruth Gordon. Maude was so eccentric. So was he, of course. The turning point of the movie is when Maude eventually is able to break through to Harold and convince him that life is a precious gift, meant to be lived to the fullest.

The movie was an epiphany for me. Sitting in that dark theater and watching it made me realize there was nothing "wrong" with my acting out and being rebellious. My behavior made perfect sense, given some of the things that happened to me. That movie drove home the idea that I was merely reacting to my environment. Not always in the most productive or intelligent way, mind you, but there were reasons for my behavior that started to make some sense to me. It sounds like a simple and obvious concept, but when you're depressed and suicidal, you are depressed and suicidal. That's all you feel. At least that's all I felt. I wasn't thinking about how or why until I saw that damn movie. I was 14 pushing 40, and for the first time in my short life, it started to dawn on me, hell, maybe I'm not a bad seed. Maybe I am just different. And maybe like Harold and Maude, different is fine. It's not terrible or shameful. It felt like a breakthrough. It's hard to believe the hospital approved us going to a movie about suicide. The Harold character kept coming up with macabre ways to stage his violent and untimely death. It was nuts, but maybe the "experts" back in the psych ward knew something. I doubt it. They probably had zero clues about the film. The orderly knew his shit, though, and I'm forever grateful he did.

Seeing that movie made me feel for the first time that I was not as off-the-wall as I thought I was. I felt empowered somehow. That wasn't a word anyone used back then, but it's how I felt. That movie opened up something in me, and some of my fellow adolescent psych-ward patients felt the same way. We talked about it among ourselves and with the orderly. He was quite pleased; he'd wanted to make us think, and he did. We came back from that outing — dare I say? — happy. I realized later he was a renegade trying to help us. He did, but it didn't last long. He eventually lost his job. No one ever said why. But not before he managed to take us back to see Harold and Maude a second time. I was just as transfixed.

We did not get out anymore. It must have made administrators nervous to see us happy. Pretty soon, we were acting out again. Raising hell, refusing our meds. Trying to take back some power. Needless to say, that didn't go over well. We got locked down and put on serious restriction once more. No outings or special privileges. But now I had a plan. I knew what I had to do. I knew I was not alone with my suicidal thoughts and depression. Suicide and depression were the theme of a major Hollywood movie. It made me feel a lot less weird and alone.

After seeing the movie, I told Dr. McCafferty about how it made me look at myself in a different light. I said I felt ready to be released. I wanted to go back to foster care and get out of that place, but he did not see it that way. This time, he refused to let me out. I needed more time in the unit, he said. Even though I had a new perception, it wasn't enough to make me dump the new plan.

I bided my time, working to get privileges back. I had no other choice. I was a ward of the state and a juvenile. One day, I managed to get out with an orderly and a few others who were taken to a park on a small outing after our restrictions had been lifted. I made my break when the orderly was distracted. Just walked the hell off. I learned later that he lost his job because I bolted on his watch, but I was desperate. I walked to a phone booth. I called McCafferty collect and told him I was out of there for good and that he may as well sign release papers for me or he would never see me again. He said I was right and promised to do it. He told me to come get my belongings, but I knew that was a trap. I told him to send them via my social worker. I was done with that place forever.

That's when I went back to the group home for mentally retarded girls in St. Paul. It sounds terrible, but it beat the psych unit at McCafferty's snake pit. The truth is, for different reasons, almost all my Foster Care placements were bad fits. Some were downright bizarre. One couple were alcoholics and wanted me around so I could babysit their twin sons. The dad was a mortician, if you could believe that, convinced his wife was having an affair. He hired a private detective to spy on her. He would come into my room late at night drunk, sit on my bed and cry on my shoulder about his suspicions and broken heart. That was creepy. I grabbed my stuff, threw it in a bag and split as fast as I could after two of his tearful episodes.

I can't remember where I was living when a friend wanting to cheer me up said there was a blues singer coming to a bar on the other side of town who I had to see. Frantic to do anything out of the ordinary, I followed the tip and hoped for the best.

The Union Bar was a dive in Northeast Minneapolis, across the Mississippi River from downtown, not too far from the University of Minnesota. It was in a nondescript brick building, nothing fancy or upscale about it. The bar was dark and smoky. If you got too close to the bathrooms, your senses were assaulted with an acrid smell that would make you want to run outside for a breath of fresh air. It was a skanky bar filled with skanky people. What The Union had going for it was that it managed to book a lot of great touring acts that came through the area.

I didn't know who Otis Rush was when my friend said his show was something I should not miss. At the time, I was like a wounded animal. I felt like Katie Pickles, one of my rescue cats, who was with me for about ten years until she died in 2012. There was sweetness inside her, but she had been through so much trauma, it took years to get her to let me pet or soothe her. Katie didn't trust anyone. I was like her: isolated, completely disheartened, unable and unwilling to let anyone in. I poured as much booze as possible over that state of mind. I consumed as many drugs as I could get my hands on. Anything to erase the negative chatter in my head. And my head was relentless. It kept playing the same tapes about how fucked things were. How I only had myself to blame. Whatever insight I gained from Harold and Maude did not last long. Or should I say that it was not enough to drown out the internal radio I constantly had going… KFUK. So I figured I would go see this guy Otis Rush if for no other reason than to get lost for a few hours in something other than my own brain.

On the night he played, the Twin Cities were hammered by a fierce Minnesota blizzard. Traffic barely moved. The entire metropolitan area was all but shut down. You could barely see in front of your face. But it would take more than a whiteout to stop me. Magness resolve said "fuck you" to the storm. I needed something new. I stuck out my thumb and hitched a ride. After a slow, tedious journey through the blizzard, I walked into the bar, flashed my fake I.D. that said I was eighteen, and for a three-dollar cover charge, bought a ticket to the beginning of the rest of my life.

I found the darkest spot in the back of the place and set up camp, standing quietly against a wall where no one would notice me. I could sip my gin and tonic without being bothered. I must have sent out a powerful "fuck off" vibe, because everyone did.

When Otis and his band came on stage, I couldn't believe how menacing they appeared. They were a bunch of hard-edged Chicago musicians who looked like they'd kill you just as soon as glance your way. Naturally, I loved them immediately. There was an obvious edge and excitement that came on stage with them. Otis was tall and thin, handsome with a high, well-kept hairdo and a slim Xavier Cougat mustache. Cool cat that he was, his eyes were covered by dark shades. I didn't understand the fine points of his talent at the time, but Otis was a rarity among blues guitarists. Being left-handed, he chose to play his guitar backwards and upside down. This gave him a distinct sound, where the notes seemed to burn and bend as his fingers picked the strings. Modern guitar legends like Eric Clapton, Carlos Santana, Jeff Beck have all said they were influenced by his unique way of playing the blues.

Some of the details of the night are a haze after so many years. I don't remember what Otis played. He already had an album out and a bunch of singles like, I Can't Quit You Baby and Reap What You Sow. He surely did his big hit, Double Trouble. I lay awake at night, can't sleep just so troubled . . . Bad luck and trouble have taken me. I have got no money to show . . . He and the band could have played nursery rhymes and I would have been transfixed. A wave of emotion poured through me. It thrilled and scared me shitless at the same time.

Every note, every word out of his mouth dripped with pain and honesty. The blues coming out of Chicago at the time, where Otis and legends like Howlin' Wolf, Muddy Waters, Buddy Guy and Koko Taylor made their mark, was ferocious. That's what Otis and his band were. Fucking ferocious. Intense. Ruthless. Otis sweated bullets. He packed every ounce of his passion and energy into each song. The emotion he sent out into that dirty little club hit me in the chest and pinned me to the wall. There's no other way to describe it.

I stood at the back of the bar, shaking. Not long into his set, I began to cry uncontrollably from all the strange and unfamiliar emotions that were unleashed in me by his performance. I didn't understand or know where it came from, but my guts were churning. His music sliced through all my protective armor and laid me bare. I was glad it was dark inside that club and glad I was alone because I was melting down in public and wasn't sure I could put myself back together again.

For a brief window in time, I started to feel like maybe I belonged somewhere. That was another new and strange sensation for me. When you rage through life like I had, no place feels right. There is no comfort zone. My idea of existence at the time was to kill time and plan a way to end my life. Like my mother had done. I believed she was finally at peace somewhere in the cosmos. I told myself often, if I were dead, my pain would die, too.

As I stood at the back of that smelly bar watching Otis and his band, a wave of unfamiliar feelings coursed through me. Pain I had pushed down for as long as I could remember. I wasn't sure what any of it meant, but I am not exaggerating when I say the sensation scared the hell out of me. It was so unfamiliar. And with the fear came a foreign and intoxicating feeling that I wasn't alone in the world. Maybe it was part two of the Harold and Maude epiphany. The first part was that glimmer of light in the movie theatre that got me to start thinking maybe I wasn't such a bad person after all. And now Otis and his gut-searing music that seemed to suggest maybe there's something in this world that I actually can connect to.

Years later, I read that Bruce Springsteen once said that when he discovered rock and roll as a young man, it quickly became a matter of life and death for him. That until he realized that the music was his connection to the rest of the human race, he felt as if he had been isolated from humanity and slowly but surely dying. He couldn't say why, but that's where his head and life were at. Man, do I get that. It was exactly how it's been with me and the blues since that snowy night in Minneapolis. Otis Rush sang and played his upside down guitar while I wept in the dark. In that instant, I began the gradual process of starting to believe there might be something in the world to rival the idea of checking out from life once and for all.

After the show, I immediately began to immerse myself in live music, especially the blues. Of course, I was obsessive about it. No half measures for Magness. I saw the late, great B.B. King a few months later at the old Met Sports Center. I went to shows by Bonnie Raitt, John Mayall, Sonny Terry & Brownie McGhee, Lazy Lester, Roland Kirk, lots and lots of local bands—whatever and whoever I could see. I was spending a lot of time with Sam in those days. She always seemed to be "with the band" or had a guitar player boyfriend who allowed us to hang around backstage at one of the local clubs.

Seeing Otis was as if I had been flailing around in the middle of the ocean and drowning when suddenly a life raft appeared and magically rescued me. I scrambled aboard, but there would be plenty more treacherous waters to navigate before I could ever find dry land.

Ten - My Dark, Terrible Dream

Seeing Otis Rush wound up becoming a touchstone of the life I lead today. It awakened something I didn't know was inside me and connected me to the human race, even if the feeling was fleeting. Seeing him pour so much of his heart and all of his soul into that performance at a seedy nightclub in the middle of America on some random night on the calendar, showed me something that still resonates strongly with me today. I can't count the number of interviews I've done where the meaning of that one night comes up again and again. Otis showed me the power of being able to connect with other people through music that is sent into the world with skill, passion and above all else, honesty.

Witnessing that when I did was like attending a master class session on life. I felt like I aced the course. Loud and clear, I got the message he delivered. But my life has never been a straight, uninterrupted line toward anything. I've always been someone who has taken a step back even while pushing forward. I have been split in two by conflicting emotions, which I think is true with a lot of people. But in my case, with chronic depression and loneliness thrown in, the only energy I could summon much of the time was the energy I used to plan and carry out my demise. Yet, at different times, I'd be on fire, powered by something so strong and deep inside me that made me shout, 'Fuck this, I will never be defeated.' That, after all, is what the blues is all about. Besides the fact that it sounds so good and makes my feet want to move, it is the reason I love the music so much. We suffer. We feel pain. But we persevere. We find a way to overcome. Human beings can be extraordinarily resilient, and the idea of overcoming pain and heartache seems universal to me. If it wasn't, the blues would not have been around as long as they've been or beloved as much as they are.

Because of the psychiatric diagnosis I received after taking that Minnesota Multiphasic Personality Inventory test for the first time, I spent two years and change after the Otis Rush epiphany sliding backwards. During that time, I was shuffled through 12 total foster placements, two of them being a group home for mentally retarded girls, and was committed to a psychiatric hospital three separate times. All this between ages 14 and 16. I was sent to the group home by a judge after I ran away from my last Foster placement. Even though I was not "mentally retarded," which was the vocabulary of the day. Nor was I developmentally disabled, to use a more current term. But during the last month I was in the group home, I was definitely out of sorts. In part that was because I began to be haunted by a repeated, very specific and frightening nightmare I found impossible to shake.

In my dark, terrible dream, somebody yelled my name for a phone call, but it was never clear where I was when the call came. I walked down a long spiral staircase. Someone handed me a phone at the bottom of the stairs. Jimmie's wife, Sam, was always on the line.

"Your father is dead," she would say, before hanging up. The dream haunted me like one of those scary movies I could never stand to watch. And it ended the same way time after time, playing in my head repeatedly.

The best thing about my new placement in the group home was that I met another Foster girl, Charlene, who became my best friend and running buddy. She was smart and rebellious, came from a real crazy background and liked to get loaded, just like me.

This repetitive dream I had was driving me crazy. I had to get it out of my head so I told Charlene about it. Bad idea. I was nervous about how she would react, and my hesitation was warranted. Charlene was not sympathetic and she was not in the least bit interested in talking about it.

"That's the devil talking," she loudly declared. "You don't say that shit out loud. That's Satan talking. I don't want to hear that shit."

My story scared her. Hell, it scared me. I didn't bring it up to her again. Then a few weeks later, in the morning on March 20th, 1973, when we were getting ready for school and making sandwiches in the kitchen, I started a conversation with her by offering my default plan at the time for making things better.

"Charlene, wanna get fucked up?" I had stashed a few hits of acid in my wallet for months.

"Let's do it," I said.

"Sure. How much ya got?"

Four hits, I told her. Two for me, two for you.

We put two little squares of thin white paper into our mouths. It was windowpane acid. We waited for the ride to begin. I loved acid. I know other people liked it because it took them away from themselves, bringing hallucinations and other imaginings that made them feel as if they'd given up control. For me, it had the opposite effect. Taking LSD was one of the only times when I felt I could be in complete control of everything, myself and my surroundings. Must have been the way I was wired. Maybe it's similar to the chemistry at work when a hyperactive child is given Ritalin, which is speed, and it calms him down. It's counter-intuitive to be sure. I can't explain it, but I took a lot of acid.

We finished making our lunches and got on the city buses that took us to school. We both were enrolled in an accredited free school that was called "Community School." It was in the middle of the Selby Dale neighborhood, which was straight-up ghetto. The school was across from the Martin Luther King Jr. Center, where we would sometimes hang out. On this day, by late morning, we were totally fried. I will remember the scene forever. There we were, tripping in Ruth Ann Muller's English class in the third floor library of the beautiful old Victorian that housed the school. I faintly heard the phone ring in the first floor office. Someone yelled my name. I went down the back stairs. A three-story spiral staircase led down to the first floor. I walked through the kitchen, into the office and picked up the phone. It was Sam, just like in my dream.

"I've got bad news," she said. "Your father's dead."

The only sound out of my mouth was, okay. That's all I said before hanging up the phone. I was calm. I had seen my dad's death in my dreams for weeks. It happened exactly as I knew it would. I was stoned out of my mind when the call came, but not the least bit surprised.

When bad things are coming my way, I have always had this weird, almost psychic deep level of intuition. It was a gnawing feeling that I hated, and I would do anything to squelch it. "Anything" usually involved drugs, alcohol, sex or stealing.

Dad had taken his life much the way my mother had. He was in his 1970 black Cadillac Fleetwood in the closed garage, the engine running. When I first heard some of the details, I thought he might have accidentally overdosed on pills and alcohol, passing out unintentionally in the car before he could turn off the motor. He had just come through a second surgery on his troubled back and was having a tough time. He was in a lot of pain. Toxicology reports put his blood alcohol level at .14. For a man as large as my dad, that meant he would have consumed between six and seven drinks in an hour.

The idea of an accidental death didn't last, though. A little General Electric AM-FM radio and cassette recorder and microphone were found on the seat next to him. Turns out, Dad recorded his suicide. Toward the end of the tape, before it ran out, he started to have second thoughts as he grew more delirious from the carbon monoxide.

I listened to the recording shortly after he died. It still doesn't seem real to me when I think about it today. I heard my father's life slip away as he gave up and could carry on no more, then change his mind! It is heartbreakingly sad.

"I don't mind dying," he said in a calm, emotionless voice at the start of the recording. "It isn't that. When a man is as proud as I have been in my life and having to die a failure, it hurts worse than any words I can come up with right now. . ."

Then he seemed to speak directly to my mother, who had been dead for three years, about the kind of father he had been to me and my siblings. He was particularly remorseful over his relationship to Carson, the youngest of his five kids. In her suicide letters, my mom had asked him to pay special attention to Carson. Dad was convinced he'd failed.

"I am sorry I couldn't live up to their expectations," he said. "I am sorry I couldn't be a better daddy to Carson. . . ."

On the tape, dogs were heard barking, which was duly noted in the police transcript, which I still have and which is why I can quote directly from the tape all these years later. You could also hear several blasts of the car horn, which the police report also points out. The horn is heard near the end of the 20-minute tape, when my dad was having second thoughts about wanting to die.

Dad had remarried about a year after my mom's death. His new wife, Betty, was an evil, deceitful woman hated by me and my siblings. She didn't like my dad very much either, we came to find out. Betty happened to have two poodles that yapped at the slightest provocation. I have always been suspicious about why she didn't go out to the garage and intervene once the dogs started barking.

At the time of my dad's death, he and Betty were living in Des Peres, Mo., another suburb of St. Louis, in a small house with an attached garage. They were fighting a lot at the time. I feel certain she looked into the garage to see what was going on, but left him there to die. She told police she last opened the kitchen garage door around 2:45 a.m.; the garage was empty, she locked the door and went back to bed. Carson was 8 at the time and was living with my dad and Betty. He told Sara and me that he heard commotion and noise apparently caused by my dad fumbling around in the garage, trying to get into the house and honking the horn. Betty told Carson it was nothing, ordering him off to bed. The next morning, in a cruel act that was also noted in the police report, Betty told Carson to go into the garage and get his overshoes. Carson opened the door and saw his daddy seated behind the wheel of his car. He tried to wake him, but Dad would not budge. "Daddy's asleep in the car and I can't wake him," Carson told Betty, according to the police report. Both my dad's eyes were open. His body was still "somewhat warm," police noted, when the officers showed up following a call from Betty.

Betty told the police that my dad fell asleep in the car on a number of occasions when he had been out drinking. So why did she send Carson out to the garage before checking things out herself? As it turned out, our worst suspicions about Betty and more would be confirmed by some solid detective work my siblings and I would pull off after a number of years beating our heads against a brick wall, but I will get back to that sordid little tale in a bit.

The night before he died, Dad called Sara and Joe, whose birthday is March 18. Sara said he sounded great. Upbeat, positive, much better than when she'd spoken to him three weeks earlier when he was in the hospital recovering from his back surgery. Then, she could hardly make sense of his rambling. But on the night before his death, he told her he was feeling better. He'd even mowed the lawn that day, something he hadn't done in months because his back hurt too much. He also said he and Betty were not getting along, and he'd been sleeping on the couch. It had become clear to him, he told Sara, that he and Carson were second-class citizens in the family, not mattering to Betty nearly as much as her other kids.

"Not mattering" seems to be putting it lightly. Toward the end of the suicide tape recording, my dad was sobbing uncontrollably. He was a proud man broken into a thousand pieces. One last ember of Magness will to live flared up before the very end. He seemed to be trying to reach out to Betty, hoping she would rescue him.

"I'm going to ask you for some help now," Dad pleaded. "If I can find the horn. God, I hope you hear it because I don't want to go like this, baby, and I'm not blaming you. . . . I'm getting pretty sleepy. The way my luck has gone, I (will) probably run out of gas. I am asking for help, Betty." The horn blared a final time. Betty's dogs barked non-stop as the tape ran out. The police report and transcript exist because the death seemed suspicious and a full investigation was launched, but it never went anywhere conclusive.

Miraculously, something tenderhearted happened between my dad and me a few months before his death. Even though I was in foster care and not living with him, I thought about him a lot. Mostly, the thoughts were about how much I hated him for everything that had happened. Truth is, nobody on the planet could piss me off faster, probably because we were so much alike. As a young woman, I prided myself on having a cool temperament when I was interacting with other people. No one was going to get to me. I was impervious, the master of detachment. No psychiatrist who tried to figure me out would penetrate my armor. No psyche hospital, no foster homes, no social worker. . . I rarely let anyone see that anything they did or said could affect me. I rarely broke down. I was despondent yes, but you could not cause me to flip out. I was too cool for that. But my dad . . . shit, my dad could get to me in ten seconds. I would be screaming and yelling, he'd be screaming and yelling. It happened just about every time we had any contact. But before he died, something came over me. I woke up one day and thought, I don't want to do this anymore. I don't know where or why the idea came from, but I distinctly remember saying to myself out loud, "I can't keep hating my dad. This is stupid. All this hatred, all this anger and bitterness—it's such a waste." I was visiting out at Sam's house in White Bear Lake at the time. My dad was living in St. Louis. I called him, blurting out what I had been thinking.

Dad, this is stupid, I told him. I don't want to do this anymore. I don't want to hate you. I don't want you to hate me. I'm sorry for all of it. Everything.

I didn't expect him to even hear what I said. I didn't think my words would sink in, but I said them anyway. I expected he would be his usual stubborn, bossy self and tune me out. Or tell me something I needed to get straight on and then we'd have another angry blowout.

"You know what?" he said with obvious fatigue in his voice. "You're right. Let's not do this anymore. It's no good. It's no good, kid. I love you." I melted. It was in that moment that we began to be friends again, father and daughter, instead of mortal enemies. I was shocked by his reaction because this was not his M.O.

We both fell apart and bawled like babies. I said I was sorry for all of it. I know this was right before I turned sixteen because very soon after he sent me a Sweet Sixteen birthday card and in it—this was his sense of humor—he wrote, "Sweet 16 and never been missed."

He was 52 when he died in that garage, alone and frightened, wanting to give up but also struggling desperately to fight and try one more time. Did I say we were a lot alike? The deep sadness I felt over losing him was much different than the sorrow I felt when my mom died. Thank God Dad and I had made a sort of peace before his death. We penetrated each other's armor and touched our common humanity in a way that my mother and I never could. It changed everything between us to have that short conversation. We finally cut through all the bullshit and leveled with each other. I was able to tell him I loved him. He said he loved me. Those were not words we used much before with each other. I know today that he was letting me off the hook in a profound way.

I'm pretty sure he knew he was going to kill himself when we talked. That he had been having what experts call suicidal ideations. If he had died and disappeared from my life while we were still at war, if the last words between us had been anything like what I said to my mom before she took her life, I would have blamed myself forever for his death. I would have been consumed with grief and shame as I had been with my mom. Despite all the rage we threw at each other, regardless of his violent and strict demeanor, I always felt enormous love for my dad. More than anything else, I wanted his approval and for him to be proud of me. What kid doesn't feel that way? Blaming myself for his death would have been another backbreaking load of guilt to drag through life even for me, and I had a pretty strong constitution when it came to lugging that kind of crap around. I don't know if I could have ever gotten free of it without that phone conversation from my heart to his.

There was a strange footnote to my dad's suicide, just as there had been with my mom and that caftan she had been knitting before she died.

In the tape recording found in his car, Dad kept muttering about seeing crows flying around his head, which seemed to frighten him. It sounded like delirium, but when his body was discovered, four dead crows were sprawled across the hood of his car. Somehow they had become trapped in the garage with him. They were desperate to escape as carbon monoxide rose to the ceiling.

Years later, without ever hearing that story, my then-husband, Jeff, would write a beautiful song about suicide that featured crow imagery that could have been taken directly from my dad's death. Bury Him at the Crossroads is a haunting song, one I could not resist recording on my 2004 CD by the same name. Jeff somehow channeled the imagery that haunted my dad in his final moments from a book about suicide he had picked up when we first got married because he was trying to understand my family history. Before he wrote the song, Jeff had never heard the details about crows being found in the garage.

"Bury him at the crossroads, where the dirt is sinking down. Where there ain't no sign a telling which way is back to town . . .I see four crows on the highway, one up in the air. I can't help but wonder what he's looking at down there. Bury him at the crossroads, where the dirt is beaten down. Where the crows will keep him company and the wheels can keep him down".

Accompanied by mournful banjo picking, the words in the song reflect old folklore that believed people who committed suicide should be buried at night at a town's unmarked crossroads. Out there, the story goes, the remote location would keep down the corpses, preventing their spirits from rising and finding their way home. Crows and ravens, of course, have often been used in mythology and folklore as symbols of death for a long time, but the connection between this song and my father's suicide spooks me still. I knew I had to record the song. I knew I could sing it with authority. And it was too brilliant and beautiful to pass up.

At the time of my father's death, I was a lost, sad and messed-up teenager with constant thoughts of suicide. Both parents were now gone. Their abandonment was final and permanent. I was filled with rage and hatred toward my own life and the train wreck it had been. I turned most of that anger and loathing inward. I was the target of my fury. I hated the word "orphan," refusing to embrace the idea that it fit or described me in any way. I didn't want to own any of it. Instead, I was laser-focused in my mode of absolute determination to do what had to be done. Like Mom and Dad, I resolved once and for all that it would not be long before I would fulfill my True North mission and be gone from this earth.

Eleven - Mr. Bad

When you are as much of a mess as I was, bad choices are as natural as breathing. They occurred all the time. That's how things were for me, especially with men. For more years than I like to acknowledge, I was the kind of girl who, if blindfolded and placed in a room with a hundred guys, and if just one of the guys was a total asshole and the other ninety-nine were wonderful, would steer straight to the single solitary asshole. The guy who could make me even more miserable than I was already. What can I say? I had an affinity for shitheads. They were familiar to me.

I met my first Knight in Shining Armor when I was just 11, but it would be a few more years before I'd let this asshole sweep me off my feet. I am keeping his real name out of this story for reasons that will appear obvious, so I will refer to him by his true identity: Mr. Bad. He was an ass hat of major proportions. I still feel grossed-out that I was ever involved with him. I shudder to think there was some need inside me that this jerk filled.

Mr. Bad was in the same high school class with my brother, but I didn't start the ever-so-rewarding experience of getting to know him until I was 14 and he was 23. This time, we connected through Sam. She was finished with Jimmie by this time, living with her guitar player boyfriend and hanging out with a lot of different musicians they knew. Mr. Bad was the singer in a local band – a pretty good singer, I have to admit. But it was his younger brother I had a terrible crush on. The brother wanted nothing to do with me.

Mr. Bad he was smart, I will say that for him. Too smart. One of those 180 IQ types, but not terribly functional in the world.

If good looks counted for points in the "character and integrity" column, he might not have been such a jerk. But it doesn't. He was tall and lean, with long blonde hair, blue eyes, and a thick beard. He was quiet and aloof most of the time. But he was obsessed with music, so eventually we actually had something in common.

Other than my interest in music, though, I'm not sure what he saw in me, since I was pretty clearly damaged goods. From the time I was 13, when my mother and Artese died, until I was 19, I might have three months out of twelve when, for whatever reason, I would feel kind of okay. Or not terrible. Most days, I existed in a state of deep depression. Because I was in so many foster homes during those years, I kept changing schools. My isolation and depression followed me to each new placement and school. The alcohol and drugs would make things tolerable for a while, but it was like trying to stop a hemorrhage with a Band-Aid. I'd only perk up when I'd decide I needed to die and would begin to plot my exit. I know that is sick. But it at least gave me a sense of purpose I never felt otherwise.

Mr. Bad and me, depressed and suicidal. A match made in heaven, right? Not really. I really was hanging around because I was "in love" (14-year-old girl love, that is) with his younger brother. One night at the gig it was break time. Mr. Bad left the bandstand and made a beeline for me – said he wanted me to follow him to his buddy's apartment – right across the street. He said he wanted to show me some artwork he had been working on. No, I'm not kidding — he actually said that. I was pretty drunk and wobbly by then, and I was naïve and ignorant in certain ways. Though I didn't really want to go, I was also very lonely and he acted very kindly towards me right then, so I went. We got up to the apartment, and I realized it was a mistake for me to be there alone with him. I was a terrified, drunk 14-year-old and did not have the capacity to stand up for myself or run away. He was 23. That seems to sum up the kind of asshole he was, and I am deeply ashamed to admit our first sexual encounter was not consensual. He forced himself on me. I didn't know how to fight him off. He pushed me into the dirty bathroom and locked the door, then told me to take off my clothes and lie on the floor. When I said I didn't want to, he demanded and then took what he wanted. He left me on the bathroom floor of this shitty bachelor apartment and went back to the gig he was working, telling me to straighten myself and the bathroom up, wait a few minutes so we weren't seen together and lock the door behind me. When I left, I was numb, without a clue about what to do. I came to find out many years later this encounter was based on a bet with his younger brother, who I had slept with one time. They bet that Mr.

Bad could get me, too. It's ugly when you think something could not get any more rotten than it was.

This was the early 1970s. To say everyone was fucking everyone would be very close to the truth. No one I knew viewed this as wrong or promiscuous. It was just what was happening. At the time, it seemed like an okay thing to do, as long as the sex was consensual. No one thought about the damage or fallout that might result from such reckless behavior.

After a while, Mr. Bad—for lack of a better term—said he fell in love with me. I was sickened by the sight of him and wanted nothing to do with him. He became like a forlorn puppy around me, as if some romance had occurred, when nothing like romance had happened at all. Eventually I made myself forget what happened that night. Enough alcohol and drugs can do that — at least for me they did. I decided to like him.

I am embarrassed even now to say that. But I understand today that my being with him had mostly to do with the fact that he paid attention to me. He would allow his focus to fall on me from time to time. That was more attention than I was used to having from a man. He would speak to me like a person and he fit the bill of what I was attracted to. An older, mentally questionable guy who said he liked me and drank a lot. Great profile, huh? Not the kind of guy you'd go looking for these days on dating apps. Plus, he was creative. He was a singer. He loved music. Eventually it became a bonding point for us, love of the music. The absolute satisfaction found in sitting and listening obsessively for hours to the Youngbloods, Grateful Dead, Jesse Colin Young, Otis Redding, Aretha Franklin, Van Morrison and Muddy Waters. Devouring liner notes as if they held the secret to life and until we both knew them as well as our own names. That was true happiness, or so I thought.

Unfortunately, I still can't rationalize or dismiss what happened with this creep and several other men I got myself tangled up with. The unvarnished truth is that these were ugly, sick episodes. When I think about them today, they seem like sordid stories from someone else's life. At the time the relationships were going on, I didn't really think they were anything but normal. I didn't really know what that word meant, but normal for me was kind of twisted, so I didn't think much about what I was doing. That makes me sad, but I will not deny this or any other part of my life.

As I write these words today at the age of 62, the good news is that I can look back at the girl I was and actually feel empathy toward her. Toward myself. I feel true compassion. I don't hate myself for any of it. This is truly the first time I can think about the men who abused me, and instead of beating myself up about the choices I made that allowed me to be demeaned and mistreated by them, I can feel sympathy and love for that young girl. Today I can look back and thank God I found a way to come through it and learn from my mistakes and bad choices.

Mr. Bad was part of the scene of people and players I was living with, by default as much as anything. They were around White Bear Lake, Minnesota, also known as Bear Town, at the same time I was. We fell in together quite naturally. Drugs and music were the glue. Some mental instability was surely part of it. We were all fucked up and broken to one degree or another.

Sam was another reason I was there. This seemed like a cool scene of artists and musicians that I was exposed to through her. They were Sam's friends. Her people. Her scene. She was doing what she thought made sense. And it's not as if I was some totally naive virginal young girl. I had been on the streets in Berkeley with a 23 year-old drug dealer, for Christ's sake. Sam knew I had already been around the block a time or ten. I'm convinced she believed I was better off with her, hanging out in her scene, than I would have been on my own searching for connections with God knows who, what and where. At least she could keep her eye on me. Besides, I adored the music.

There were some great local bands and musicians around at the time. Acts like Chicken Lips, Lamont Cranston, Doug Maynard, Willie Murphy and the Bumble Bees and the Rharettes. We called them Willie Murphy and the Bees or just the Bees. They were the first band to record with Bonnie Raitt. They made a great LP that stands up today as still a great record. I listened to that record so much. I should have taken Bonnie's words to heart when she sang the song Danger, Heartbreak Ahead. When you give more than you get, you're in danger. You may find that you're in love with a stranger. But who knows what evil lurks within the hearts of men? It's vanity, insanity. You play what you can't win. If you find that you are losing, Girl, it's time to get on moving. 'Cause there's danger, heartbreak dead ahead.

You see why I loved the music so much and still do? It sounds beautiful and it reveals the truth to us, whether we choose to admit it or not.

Everyone in Sam's crowd wore vintage 1930s to 1950s style clothing, so there was a fashion scene aspect to our crowd as well. Sam taught me how to shop Goodwill and thrift stores to find colorful second-hand stuff and cool old furniture. I already knew how to sew quite well, so I could alter the clothes to improve the fit or just make my own, which I did a fair amount of the time. I sometimes created my own patterns and designs, too. Each one of us had our own personal look. It felt cool. We felt cool. We were cool.

Minneapolis back then was a main stopping point for touring regional and national artists. That's how I was exposed at such a young age to giants like Otis Rush, B.B. King, Little Richard, Delaney & Bonnie & Friends (which included Eric Clapton), and many more.

There was fun, parties and a lot of laid-back, stoned hanging-out time. But underneath all the partying, fashion and fun, these were mostly dark days for me. My clinical depression was constant. If any one thing kept me alive, the music was it. It soothed me in a way I could not adequately describe or articulate. You know how fussy babies will sometimes calm down when they hear white noise from a vacuum or a radio stuck between channels? Music soothed me the same way. Good music, that is.

Since we were loaded most of the time we were together, Mr. Bad and I were never careful when we had sex. Pretty soon, I was pregnant. When I told him, Mr. Bad, chivalrous as always, made it clear he wanted nothing to do with me or a baby. It was not his child, he insisted. By that time, I didn't want to have any more to do with him, either.

I cried for days after I told him I was expecting a baby. My moods fluctuated wildly. One minute I was convinced life was impossible, that there was no way out but death. The next day I would feel certain that having a baby might be the reason I needed to keep living. I went back and forth for weeks. I thought my head would explode. It was an endless internal debate. Eventually, I settled on the idea that always made the most sense when things were too much to bear, and the idea of bringing a new life into the world was not enough to dissuade me.

I began planning my escape with the precision of a master thief, patiently waiting until I could stockpile enough sleeping pills and tranquilizers to get the job done. I did enough sleuthing so I knew whose house I could go to and steal a few pills without anyone noticing. I would wait a couple weeks, go back for a few more, and continue to plan and wait. I had time. It might take a whole year to collect my arsenal. I didn't mind. Stubborn, plodding and determined: Magness traits tried and true. It wasn't a question of if, only when. Plotting my suicide and beginning to put my plan in motion always gave my spirits a boost. I know how sick that sounds. I was a depressed ball of skin and hair masquerading as a human being until I was actively engaged in planning my suicide. Then I felt pretty fucking good. The end was in sight. I could see my goal and work toward it. My pain would soon be over. Actively working on my death took the edge off. There was finally a clarity and purpose to my life when I got out of bed each morning. I was relieved to be able to stop the debate in my head. I had plans for the future, I knew what they were. That was a good feeling. That made me comfortable in my own skin. Man, if that's not fucked up, I don't know what is.

After a while, I had socked away enough pills from various places; it was time to act. I saw no other way. How the hell could I take care of a baby? I was in no shape to be anyone's mother. I looked at myself and saw only despair. Mom had been right to end her misery. Dad, too. They were tired of feeling terrible. I understood. After all, they were my role models. I wanted what I assumed they had: rest, peace, and no more suffering.

I was crashing at my sister Sara's place at the time, a farmhouse in Anoka, a suburb north of Minneapolis. My brother Joe was staying there, too. I went upstairs to my room and swallowed all the sleeping pills I had saved; there were at least fifteen or twenty. Sara woke up in the middle of the night when she heard a crash. She found me passed out upstairs in the bed, lifeless, a suicide note beside me. Sara woke Joe and a friend of his, who were loaded and out cold in the living room. The three of them somehow picked me up and got me to the hospital.

The doctors told me later that my heart had stopped beating. I should have died, but they managed to revive me. When I woke up in the ICU, a minister from the Church of Christ sat next to my bed. Sara had called him to come talk to me. He was from one of the several different churches my folks took us to when we were kids. Sara was scared and didn't know where else to turn.

I let the poor guy have it, cursing a blue streak, yelling at him to get the fuck out. I was furious he was there, even angrier I was still alive. I wound up staying in intensive care for a week, muttering to myself over and over about how fucked up it was that I was not dead. Once again, I had failed.

After I got released from the hospital, Sara said she was done with me. I needed to leave her house, she informed me. It was too risky for her to have me around her young children. I understood, but her words stung. She drove me to the highway to thumb a ride into town. It was twenty-eight miles from my sister's place to Sam's front door. When I finally showed up there, I asked Sam to put me up again for a little while, but she was on the same page as Sara. I was too messed up, she said. She was tired of my act. How could I blame either of them? They didn't want to get dragged into whatever came next. And we all knew with certainty there'd be something bad that would come next. That was my life at the time. I crashed from one drama to another. It seemed to me that everyone I touched seemed to get caught up in my crap.

When Sam turned me down, I broke into tears. All I could do was cry. It was late in the day on a Sunday. She wanted to help, but short of letting me stay with her, she didn't know how. She offered to take me to the local youth center in White Bear Lake to see if they could find me someplace to stay. My heart was breaking, but I agreed. I didn't put up a fight. There was no fight left in me. Sixteen, terrified, pregnant, no prospects for anything good. What was there to fight about? I felt as desperate as a person could be. But what I couldn't possibly know in that low, frightening moment was that someone new was about to enter my life. And that because of her, everything would begin to change in ways I could never imagine or believe.

Twelve - Carrie's Garden

The White Bear Lake Youth Center was in a nondescript, single-story building tucked into an anonymous part of old uptown White Bear Lake. As Sam and I walked nervously up the stairs, there was certainly no reason to feel hopeful about anything other than maybe a warm bed for a few nights. The full-time staff was gone because it was Sunday, and the building was about to close. A young male volunteer talked with me a few minutes, asked a couple questions and ushered us into his office. He seemed younger than me, utterly unequipped to help a damaged soul. But this fresh-faced, earnest young man was all I had. He reached across his desk, pulled out his list of people known to take in underage girls from the street, and scanned the names. I could see it was a short list. If he was able to find someone, he told me, I would be able to stay with them for only three days — seventy-two hours and girls had to move on and find something else. As I sat in a hardwood chair fighting off panic and tears, Sam and I held our breath. The volunteer called the first six names on his list. He dialed number after number, letting the phone ring as my heart beat faster and faster. Each time, he hung up without registering much of a reaction. Or he would get someone on the line, ask if they had space and then put the phone back down on the receiver after being told there was no spot for me. My stomach twisted tighter with every call. The center was now officially closed. I was out of options, starting to think of doorways or alleys I could sleep in safely. Finally, on what I'm pretty sure was the seventh call, a woman answered. Her name was Carrie.

The volunteer told her I was 16, pregnant and fresh out of a week in the intensive care unit as a post-suicide attempt. I needed a place to stay. Carrie didn't hesitate. The volunteer listened for a few moments, jotting down directions to her place.

Sam drove me out to 843 East County Road F, White Bear Lake, Mn.,55110. The address, her zip code, the phone number . . . They are all such markers in my life between "Before Carrie" and "After Carrie" that I will forever remember them.

Carrie lived out in the country, her house surrounded by thick woods at the end of a long dirt driveway off the road. Sam dropped me off and gave me a tight hug. We both had tears running down our cheeks. It was a miracle she could even look me in the eye after the tragedy I caused in her life. She said she would call to check on me in a few days and was off. All I had as I watched her drive away was a backpack stuffed with some clean pants and shirts, the only belongings to my name.

Once inside Carrie's, I clammed up. She showed me my room and said we'd talk later. Once I was there, I did my best to help around the house with cooking and cleaning. No one had to tell me to do anything. I was raised to be respectful. You help out. No one should ever have to clean up after you. Especially if you were a guest in their house.

I was as polite and well-mannered as I could be. Never chewed with my mouth open, no elbows on the table. I sat up straight, said please and thank you very much. Inside, I was trembling. Three days would be over in a flash. It was warm and comfortable at Carrie's. Where would I go when my time here was up?

Carrie told me a little about herself. She was a divorced mother in her thirties. She had five kids of her own and clear boundaries. Her ex-husband was a deadbeat, providing no support. She had to rely on welfare Aid For Dependent Children and work she did on the side cleaning houses. She was also trying to go to school to become a chemical dependency counselor. She was stern but sweet, with a gleam in her eye that let you know she had a big heart.

One of the things I remember most warmly about Carrie is her beautiful gardens. She loved caring for her creations as attentively as she cared for the stray kids and critters who came to live with her. She planted wildflowers and vegetables, nurturing them all with loving attention. She had rock gardens. She used to tell me they represented gardens of the soul that would flourish through recovery and self-awareness. Her children, she liked to say, were like a garden of wildflowers. All they needed was love and nurturing. I never heard anyone talk like that before. She was so kind and caring, much of it was so foreign to me. But I could tell from the way she spoke that there was something real behind her words. It was not just idle talk.

After letting me be for the first two days at her house, Carrie asked me to sit down with her in the living room for a talk. I can still see the blue-green '70s-era shag carpeting, the big picture windows. Outside, on three sides of the room, were woods and one of the wildflower gardens Carrie had planted. There wasn't much furniture, other than two recliner rockers with a table lamp between them. A black and white television sat in the corner, a couple of bean bag chairs and an old antique tea cart were in front of a window. She also had a stereo in the room. I would learn later that she loved to play music, usually accompanied by loud laughter and spontaneous dancing. Despite her tough circumstances, Carrie was a joyous person, clearly happy and feeling blessed to be alive. For now, it was just the living room of a woman old enough to be an older sibling, whose house I had been living in for two days. Carrie sat herself down in one of the rockers, motioning for me to take the other.

So tell me, dear, she began, what happened to you? Carrie looked intently at me with her steely blue eyes. She had beautiful, milky white skin and short curly blonde hair. She was tiny, but pleasantly round. Kindness radiated from her.

She wanted to know how I wound up at the Youth Center and the hospital, recovering from a suicide attempt.

Where is your family, dear? Do you have any family?

She might as well have asked if I had any plutonium or rare diamonds.

Not really, I mumbled.

I tried to answer her questions with as little information as possible, as was my wont. But as the minutes passed, I found myself disclosing some things I had not spoken of in a long, long time. Maybe never. The words came slowly. She began to prod, gently culling information out of me. I'd only shared my story up to then with a few people, in bits and pieces. It was a new experience to be spoken to like this, by someone who seemed to truly care why I was such a sad and hopeless mess.

Carrie wanted to know how I had become so broken that I wanted to take my life. What's happened in your life that you think you would be better off dead? she asked me. I did the best I could to give her the bare facts. Short, straight answers, unadorned. I told her I was low as low could feel. I was pregnant. I saw no hope or prospects for my life. Both my parents were gone. I felt like a loser with zero going for me. Tears welled up in her eyes as I spoke, but I felt detached from the information I was letting slip out. It was as if I were talking about someone else. I was in PTSD mode, coolly reporting data, doing my best to keep down the feelings and any trace of emotion.

She thanked me for talking with her and answering her questions. Imagine that, her thanking me. That threw me for a curve. It was late; we were both exhausted. It was time to go to bed.

I fell asleep thinking how the next morning would be the beginning of my last day at her house. It was a Tuesday. I would have to leave for who knows where one day after that. I awoke in a state of terror. I felt truly fucked, and spent much of the day puttering around her house, straightening up here and there and watching the clock hands move like a condemned prisoner waiting for her execution in one of those bad B movies. Early that third evening, when I was feeling so anxious I knew I would never be able to sleep, Carrie sat me down once more in her living room with the blue-green shag carpeting. It was time for another talk.

She wanted to know my plans. Where was I going next? What did I intend to do? I broke down and sobbed as I sat there in front of her. There were no plans. There was nothing. I had nowhere to go. There was no next. I was lost.

Carrie lowered her head for what seemed like a long moment before lifting her face and gazing directly into my eyes, as if she was about to make a point. Her face was a few inches from mine. It felt as if she were looking through me.

Well, dear, she said, I've been thinking. Here it comes, I thought to myself. I'm about to get the boot. But she continued, "What has happened to you is awful, I have to tell you. Just awful. No one should have to endure what you have had to endure."

I braced for the part where she would tell me she hoped I would get back on track somehow and wished me the best. That she would drop me off tomorrow wherever I wanted to go. I had heard that one so many times before. I steeled myself as best as I could.

Instead, Carrie said she had been talking things over with her kids. Bobby, Ronnie, Marie, Kenny and Helen. They all agreed. "If you don't mind," she said, "you're not leaving."

I stared at her, utterly confused. "Excuse me?"

She repeated herself, telling me again that everything that had happened to me was awful. But it can stop here, she tried to reassure me. Right now. If I wanted to stay with them and be part of their family. I could not believe what was coming from her lips. I had given her and the kids no reason to care about me. I didn't open up or connect in a way that could explain why she was willing to ignore the three-day limit on my stay and offer me refuge from being alone and on the streets.

"We would love to have you," Carrie said. "We will figure out a way. You can stay here with us. The kids all love you and so do I."

To say I was stunned doesn't begin to capture it. All the emotion I had been fighting to tamp down came pouring out of me. Tears streamed down my cheeks. I could not stop sobbing. I felt mortified and relieved all at once. I wasn't used to hearing someone try to talk me into staying with them. With words like "love" and "family," no less. I was too exhausted and worn down to fully absorb what she had said. What she was offering me. I just felt an enormous sense of relief wash over me because her gracious invitation meant my brain could stop obsessing over the question, Now what?

You'll have chores like the rest of the kids, she said. Doing dishes, taking out the trash, keeping the house neat and clean. They would expect me to pull my own weight. But she and the kids would welcome me into their family. My unborn baby, too. I could not believe what I was hearing. 843 E. County Road F, White Bear Lake, Mn., would be the beginning of many miracles to come in my life.

Carrie would turn out to be all I ever needed and wanted in a parent. She was kind, loving, strong, and funny and had a great sense of theatre. She encouraged all her kids to be artists, singers, actors, painters—anything having to do with creativity and the arts. She and several of her own children worked in the local community theatre. When I was extremely pregnant and my belly was the first thing you saw when you glanced my way, she enlisted me to help out in the costume department for the production of a fantastic musical called The Merry Adventures of Falstaff.

One night when we were talking, I had told Carrie that I sometimes daydreamed about Glinda the Good Witch of the North from The Wizard of Oz. I loved Glinda from the moment I saw the movie as a little girl. I imagined her coming to me and changing everything that had happened in my sad, shitty life with a single wave of her wand.

Within a week of sharing that story with Carrie — on the morning after a night when I was feeling lousy and down — I sat in her kitchen as she came floating down the stairs in a white, floor-length Glinda-style gown made from yards of netted tulle fabric, just like the dress Glinda wore in the movie. Carrie even wore a crown and had a magic wand in her hand. You could have knocked me over with a ball of cotton. She was the picture of goodness, looking as if she were there to protect all the creatures of the world with her special powers. Carrie appeared to be walking on air as she approached me. She touched my head with her wand and said she had been sent to wash away the pain.

"You have had the power all along my dear," she said in her best Glinda voice. "You have had the power all along." It was, and still is, one of the sweetest and most loving gestures I've ever experienced. I felt so much love and affection for her at that moment and felt her love and affection for me. She was a princess, not a witch. I will adore Carrie forever.

It would take a long time to trust what she said, but eventually I came to see she was right. It was just one of the many reasons I will always love her.

Carrie was the first person ever to offer me encouragement about my singing. One afternoon, when I thought I was home alone, I put on a Roberta Flack record of Carrie's. Singing along to the soulful music, I was startled when Carrie came into the room.

"You sing so beautifully, dear. You really should consider doing something professionally with that voice of yours." I flushed with embarrassment.

Change has always come slowly for me, like the time it takes one season to gradually flow into another. With her gentle heart—with her kindness and encouragement—Carrie planted the seed of an idea that I could doing something with music besides listening to it in my heart and in my head. It was Carrie who watered and nurtured it the way she did her beautiful wildflowers. After that, with constant encouragement and conversation, she did everything in her power to help make sure that seed of a dream to do something with my singing didn't die from lack of attention and light. I wouldn't do much with it for quite a while, but she saw something in me and helped me catch a glimpse of it, too, even if it was fleeting and impossible to hold onto. After all, I was pregnant, soon to give birth at the ripe old age of 17.

Thirteen - Pearl

My brain raced back and forth, imagining the various scenarios. One minute I was convinced I needed to terminate my pregnancy. Who was I kidding? I was in no shape to be a mother. Then I'd land on the equally firm conviction that having a baby would be awesome. A game changer to lift me out of my depression. It was an opportunity for two new lives—hers and mine. She would provide the focus I needed to feel alive. Thinking about a new start was not my usual M.O. It represented hope, a foreign concept. In the end, I came down on the side of keeping the baby, convincing my heart it was the right thing to do. My head was another story. So I was only seventeen. Big deal. The Magness in me said I could conquer anything, even things I knew absolutely nothing about, like how to care for a tiny baby, alone. How I could bounce from the firmest conviction to the most profound and troubling doubt is something I never questioned, but bounce back and forth I did.

Once I made the decision to have my baby, it dawned on me that maybe I should cut out drugs and alcohol. It wasn't hard to pull off. I wish I could say I thought of the need to get clean on my own, but the inspiration came from an unlikely source. A drug dealer I knew lectured me outside the Sunset Bar one night when he saw me with drink and cigarette in my hand despite my big belly, telling me I should quit smoking and drinking so my baby would be born with a clean slate.

"That's the least you could do," he admonished. Somehow I heard him. Funny where you can find good advice if you're open to it.

Life was even more chaotic than usual in the months before the baby was born. I worked with Carrie cleaning houses and as a hotel maid. I also had a job for a while as a bus girl at an IHOP restaurant. The manager didn't want to hire me because I was young and pregnant, but I guess he felt sorry for me and gave me the job.

This was 1973. People were far more judgmental about these things than they are today. Everywhere I went, I felt people staring at me in disgust and disapproval. The pregnancy also brought physical complications. I had to quit the maid and IHOP jobs because I was spotting blood. I didn't have the jobs for very long, but the work made a lasting impression on me. To this day I am unable to leave a hotel room without cleaning up after myself. I always leave generous tips for my bus person and table server. They do some of the hardest work around; I have to show my appreciation. I remember.

I did not want to move out of Carrie's house, but I had no choice. I needed to demonstrate my independence to qualify for welfare, which I had to have so I could take care of myself and the baby. For a little while, I lived in a big house in northeast Minneapolis with a roommate named Theresa. She was employed and stable. The rent was reasonable.

Things were not too bad until I made a mistake about three months before the baby was born. My brother Joe got in touched and said he needed a place to stay. At the time, I had no conscious memory of his abuse. The episodes were buried somewhere in my subconscious. What I did know very well, however, was that Joe had a long history of drug abuse and dishonesty. He swore to me that he was clean and staying out of trouble. Theresa was cool with it so—against my better instincts—I let my brother move in with us.

Not smart. Joe was at the house a matter of weeks before it became obvious he was using dope again. I would find him nodded out all over the house at strange hours. One night when a friend came over to go to dinner with me, a bunch of unmarked police cars suddenly pulled up to the house and in the alley behind it. I parked my pregnant self in front of the door until they showed me their search warrant with the name Joe Magness and my address on it. Shit.

The police tore up the place. Literally tore open furniture, beds, walls, even the damn ceiling. They eventually found what they were looking for: a cache of drugs Joe had stuffed into the ceiling of his closet. They arrested him and Theresa, who had one joint on her. I stood there in shock as the two of them were cuffed and carted away. That same week, the house got broken into three times, apparently by junkies looking for what they thought was left of Joe's stash.

I soon got out of there, moving into a studio apartment in Loring Park, back then another Minneapolis ghetto just off downtown. I didn't have much money, but I was able to get food stamps, which helped. Good thing I loved creamed corn on Texas toast. It became a staple.

I finally got a job in the customer service department at Dayton's department store, which was on a bus route and close to my new place. For some reason, I wanted to work the front counter because I thought it would make the time go faster, but they didn't like the idea of an unwed pregnant teenager interacting with customers. They kept me hidden away in a back office. It was demoralizing, but I worked my full eight-and-a-half hour shift until the day before I was supposed to have my labor induced. Waddling and exhausted, I climbed up onto the bus and soon walked into the hospital alone.

On May 6, 1974, against all odds, I gave birth to a healthy baby girl at St. Paul-Ramsey Hospital. Believe it or not, Sam met me at the hospital and was my birth coach. I still can't believe the grace and kindness of that woman. I named my daughter Pearl Corrina, for my maternal grandmother and a beautiful song by Taj Mahal, "Corinna, Corinna," which I've always loved. The little angel weighed in at eight pounds and one ounce.

We stayed at the hospital for three days. I decided to go to Sam's place for a week or so after being released, which was a blessing. I was scared to be alone with a new baby and could use the help and companionship. Sam was a saint to invite me to stay with her. When we got there, Mr. Bad, the baby's father, was waiting for us. I hadn't seen his sorry ass in months. Not since he had been telling everyone he knew, including me, that the baby was not his. Now he insisted he wanted to see "my" daughter. Maternal instincts I didn't know I had came roaring out of me. In that moment, I could have killed him as easily as taking a sip of water.

He moved close to reach for Pearl, and I tore into him. "How dare you," I said with contempt. "Who do you think you are? You wanted nothing to do with us for nine months. Now you want to hold her? Fuck you."

He refused to leave. Rather than cause a knock-down confrontation, I told him he could have fifteen minutes alone with her before I kicked his pathetic, good-for-nothing ass out. Sam told me she had no idea he would be there, but the ugly encounter left me feeling unsafe. After the week at Sam's, I went back to my apartment. By that time, post-partum depression and my fears about raising a baby had kicked in. In Darkness Visible, his masterpiece about his own depression, author William Styron brilliantly describes what it feels like to be laid that low.

"The pain is unrelenting," he wrote, "and what makes the condition intolerable is the foreknowledge that no remedy will come—not in a day, an hour, a month, or a minute. If there is mild relief, one knows that it is only temporary; more pain will follow. It is hopelessness even more than pain that crushes the soul. So the decision-making of daily life involves not, as in normal affairs, shifting from one annoying situation to another less annoying—or from discomfort to relative comfort, or from boredom to activity—but moving from pain to pain. One does not abandon, even briefly, one's bed of nails, but is attached to it wherever one goes." I'd say that pretty much summed things up. In another section of the book, he continued painting his dark picture: "Mysteriously, and in ways that are totally remote from natural experience, the gray drizzle of horror induced by depression takes on the quality of physical pain."

I could never come close to expressing it so eloquently or precisely. But this was pretty much the state of mind I was in a few weeks after my baby was born.

My depression felt like quicksand I was sinking into. When it came time to take Pearl to the county hospital for her first check-up, I could barely put one foot in front of the other, but I knew she needed to be checked out so I forced myself to go. The poor little thing was yellow with jaundice, like a lot of babies can be, and I was told she needed to be in an incubator, under blue light, until she improved. Being a mother was hard enough when everything went right. Now I was thoroughly challenged. I knew I did not want her at the county hospital, where I understood from life on the streets that the care was less than stellar. I raised a stink and they agreed I could take her to the children's hospital in St. Paul, which was known for its excellent neo-natal care, and have her treated there. The little thing was in four-point restraints so she wouldn't pull the intravenous fluid line out of her scalp. It tore me up to see her like that. The nurses would not let me hold her because they assumed it was my milk had made her jaundiced.

I was a young welfare mother. Even at the children's hospital, the picture was clear. They never tested my milk to see if that was the cause. They simply figured it had to be something wrong with me. Finally, after a few days of driving myself crazy with worry, I marched into the neo-natal ward, removed tiny Pearl's restraints, lifted her ever so gently from the incubator and put her to my breast to feed her. A nurse rushed in, yelling that I was violating policy and had no right to be there.

"I want my milk tested," I yelled back at her. "You've never tested it. This is bullshit." The hospital finally relented and did the test. Of course, it was clean. I went there on the bus every day to be with Pearl and spent hours with her, holding her, singing her little lullabies and feeding her until her coloring improved and her blood tests came back normal. After about a week, she was released to me.

When I told Carrie what had happened, she suggested I move closer to where she lived so it would be easier for her to help me out. In a few days, I found myself in a ratty apartment in St. Paul. I soon came to learn that tenants referred to the place as "Cockroach Towers." That says all there is to say about the place. I was on the third floor. There was no elevator. I liked the apartment OK at first because at least I had a porch off the bedroom that allowed me to get some fresh air. But after standing out there for a while, I realized the porch was unstable. It creaked and groaned beneath me. The entire building was infested with monster cockroaches. These motherfuckers could fly, for God sakes. And they were fearless. I, on the other hand, was not. Not when it came to flying cockroaches and porches that could topple at any moment. I spent a lot of time on the bus going to Carrie's because hanging around in that shithole was more than I could bear.

Carrie was always trying to help me. She came to me one day and said she decided to give me her old car, a 1963 Ford Fairlane, so it would be easier for me to get around. It was a police special, black with a baby-blue hood and a "three on the tree" transmission. The steering was loosey-goosey. The car also had no muffler and was loud as hell. I didn't care. This was my first car. I loved floating down the road in that big, noisy beast. Having wheels was a great help getting back and forth to Carrie's with Pearl. I eventually moved out of Cockroach Towers, renting a back bedroom in a basement apartment in White Bear Lake with a friend of Carrie's.

My introduction to motherhood was fairly brutal, causing me to wonder more than a few times how my mom even attempted to raise five kids. Pearl was colicky. No matter how I tried to soothe her, she cried incessantly. Neither of us slept. Thoughts of suicide invaded my brain once more. I could not get them out of my head. I soon convinced myself I was wrong to think I could handle my new responsibilities. I resolved yet again that the only way to find relief was to end my life. There was no other way. It was just a matter of time before I would have what I needed to pull it off.

As Styron wrote, "The pain of severe depression is quite unimaginable to those who have not suffered it, and it kills in many instances because its anguish can no longer be borne."

True enough. I was engulfed in sadness so heavy my limbs hurt. It's so hard to describe what it feels like to exist in that state. When I was in it, nothing could cheer me up. Not my baby's smile, not a friend, not thoughts of something good that might come along to drive away my blues. I desperately wanted what I was feeling to go away. As quickly and as completely as possible. Forever. I knew only one way to make that happen.

By the time I got to that basement apartment in White Bear Lake, I realized I was not mentally equipped to raise a child. After so much hand-wringing and worry about what would happen next, I came to the conclusion that I had to give away my baby. That's the only way she would have a shot at a decent life. And then I would be free to do what I had to. I was haunted by the idea that I would do to her what my mother had done to me. That was what made my decision for me.

I kept my new suicide plans to myself, but told Carrie about my decision about Pearl. She didn't judge. I asked her to help me figure out how someone goes about giving away a child. We both found it terribly sad, but I think Carrie knew it was the best course of action for me and my little girl. I found a lawyer, a friend of my old neighbor at Cockroach Towers. He took care of all the paperwork so everything was straight-up and legal. The process took about a month or more. Pearl wound up going to the friend of a friend's family. I wasn't told much about her new parents. Just that the father was a farmer and that the mother had been a school teacher. They were good, hard-working people who were unable to have children of their own. They had adopted another girl, so Pearl would have a big sister. She would be raised in the country. That's all I knew, but it sounded good, far more promising than anything I could hope to provide for her.

I gave my baby away confident she was going to parents who could see to it that she had the love and stability she would need to make a good life for herself. Doing it filled my heart with a pain deeper than I had ever felt before, pain worse than I'd felt when my parents took their own lives. This little girl was mine. I gave birth to her. She came from inside me and I had to give her up because I was fucked up so bad I couldn't take care of her or myself. I sat in a daze for hours after Pearl was driven away from Carrie's house. Finally, I stood up, put on my coat and walked down the street to the nearest bar. I flashed my fake ID and got stink-assed drunk until I was cross-eyed. I didn't know what else to do.

After the alcohol fog cleared, the gears in my teenaged brain started to turn. Once again, I became obsessed with hatching the details of my next suicide plan. It would take me a full two years to make this next attempt, but making the decision lifted a heavy burden off my shoulders. I knew that once I finally hit on the right strategy, I would carefully plan it, slowly and methodically coming up with a recipe for success. This time, it had to work. I would make sure of that. No more failures. No more close calls.

Over the next few months, despite being in a frame of mind that can only be described as giving a shit about nothing, I somehow managed to muster up the energy to move several more times. I sleepwalked through the hours of the day. I went back to Cockroach Towers, started dealing weed to help pay my bills and eat, and then connected back up with my former roommate Theresa, who told me she was planning to move to California. I could come live with her, she said, and off we went. We got as far as Denver before our car broke down. I wound up staying there six months and started living with a guy named Michael, a handsome cabdriver friend of hers who was kind enough to let us stay with him while we waited to get the car fixed. I started to feel a small shift in my emotions, like maybe I could figure out a way to make my life work after all. I was around people. That probably made it harder to sink into my own despondent and isolated depression. I even called the lawyer who handled the adoption and told him I needed to get my baby back. I was adamant about it. I didn't care what it took. That was impossible, he told me. I should have known, but over the next few weeks, I sobbed pretty much non-stop as the finality of my decision to give up Pearl hit home.

I eventually took a Greyhound bus to the Twin Cities, moving in again with Carrie for a while, then to another ghetto apartment in St. Paul. My life was a swirl of change, none of it good. I couldn't stay anywhere for long. I was not connected to anything. It felt like I had been dropped out of an airplane, no parachute, but with the ground moving farther and farther away so I was perpetually tumbling through space.

Back in the Twin Cities, I started volunteering at the Chrysalis Center for Women, which offered mental health, recovery, assertiveness training and other programs. Some of the staff went through the assertiveness training and we were asked to do an exercise called "Name in a Jar." What we call ourselves and everything we associate with our name can have a powerful effect on our lives and self-image, we were told, so the goal of the exercise was to discover our "true name."

My given name was Lisa Maria. I never liked it. Every Lisa I ever knew struck me as meek, passive and sad. It seemed like whenever I read or heard a story about a girl named Lisa, she was in trouble or pain. I'd listened to so many stupid songs about girls named Lisa and they all annoyed me. Like Sad Lisa, for instance by Cat Stevens.

She hangs her head and cries on my shirt, she must be hurt very badly. Tell me what's making you sad . . . Lisa, Lisa, sad, Lisa, Lisa.

Fuck that. I needed something different, something strong. If I was alive, I felt desperate to be anyone other than me. I was still obsessing about ending my life, but I lived in two worlds, which is not uncommon for someone deeply depressed. I would fight for my survival and a new beginning even as I methodically planned my death. The name exercise opened me up to the notion of a new identity. I latched on to it. A different name would transform me, I felt certain.

During the exercise, one name kept running through my head: Janeva. That was the name of a cool woman I'd met when I was living in Denver. She was smart, kind, strong and funny. We'd hung out together a few times. I'd been immediately drawn to her, the rare bird I somehow felt I could trust.

I rolled the name around in my brain for a long time, trying it out on people for about six months. In my mind, I changed the spelling to Janiva to make it my own. I told members of my family that's what they should call me from then on, explaining why a new name and identity were so important to me. They cut me no slack, ridiculing the whole idea as stupid, pointless and disrespectful to Mom and Dad. I told them use my new name or I will not respond to any of you. They let me know in no uncertain terms that they would not go along. It didn't matter. I was accustomed to them not understanding the first thing about me. When I told Carrie about it, she was gentle and supportive; she got it from the gate.

Here's the thing: I did feel different, as if it was just me now and none of the ghosts I carried around from my past. Finally, when I was eighteen and could do it legally, I went down to the local courthouse, filled out a few forms and was now Janiva Marie Magness.

The name change worked wonders for a while. I felt freer, liberated. But the thing I wanted to change most was my history and the sadness that came along with it. Sorry to say, those were set in stone. I was no longer Lisa, but I still dreamed and obsessed about taking my life. My parents were still gone. Artese had still drowned because of my reckless behavior. Giving away my baby still left me feeling cut and dead inside. These were terrible losses. I grieved none of them properly. I didn't have the first clue how. The only times I felt right were when I was loaded or listening to music full blast, preferably both. But it became harder to be loaded because I knew it was nothing I could sustain. At the same time, it became impossible not to get loaded because when I was sober, I felt like I was losing my mind. I could not get the dark thoughts to rest. They would not leave my head without something to wash them away. It really was time to fix things once and for all.

Fourteen - Nineteen

The movie that won the Oscar for best film at the Academy Awards in 1976 was One Flew Over the Cuckoo's Nest, with Jack Nicholson starring as a rebellious patient in a mental health ward. He was so hard to control; they gave him a lobotomy to bring him under submission. His performance won him the Oscar for Best Actor. The Grammy that year for best album went to Paul Simon for Still Crazy After All These Years. Must have been something in how the planets were aligned that year. Madness was a popular topic. It certainly was with me. I turned nineteen in January, 1976, and the year was a watershed for me for another reason: It marked the last time I tried to take my own life. And when I say I tried, I mean I tried. I planned that son of a bitch down to the letter. It's obvious, since you're reading this, that once again, I failed. I couldn't pull it off, despite my best efforts.

I was living with two girlfriends at the time. They had been renting a beautiful old three-bedroom Craftsman-style house on Lyndale Avenue, a big, broad street in Minneapolis that cut through the city north to south. It was a hip neighborhood everyone knew as "The Wedge". Lots of older homes and brownstone apartment buildings. Our place had tons of charm and personality, with wood floors, leaded windows, a sitting room, dining room, basement, front and back porches. One of my roommates was a woman by the name of Randy, who I had befriended when she lived in a commune next to the group home I was in. Later on, she got hired to teach the English at the Community School I was attending. That was the same year my father died. There weren't the customary boundaries at that school between teachers and students, and she and I had become close friends. We stayed in touch after I graduated and she eventually asked me to come live with her and another girl from the commune when they needed a third roommate. I liked Randy. I needed a place to live, so I jumped in.

We partied heavily at that house. There was a ton of drinking and drug use while I was there. Everyone I knew lived that way, so it seemed like no big deal. It was the '70s, after all. I made some cash selling drugs and working down the street at a seedy bar and pool hall named Occies. That dive was a perfect place for me to hang out. I could wait on tables and shoot pool, which I got pretty good at, and I loved being with all the small-time criminals in the area. They were my kind of people. Occies was known as a gathering spot for that style of customer. Plus, I could walk to work, get drunk and stumble home. What more could a fucked-up nineteen-year-old girl want? It was perfect.

Randy, I learned soon after moving in, was diabetic. What a great fringe benefit that turned out to be. She took insulin shots every day. Once I made that discovery, and when the time was right, I gradually and methodically began to quiz her about her routine. She told me she was supposed to inject thirty units of insulin a day. If she took too much, it could kill her. To me, that was a nugget of gold. I grabbed it and patiently panned for more details.

You go into diabetic shock first, which is incredibly painful, she told me. I paid rapt attention to every word, as if my life — or more importantly, my death — depended on it. Then you lose consciousness. Your body shuts down from a diabetic coma. Most diabetic comas are fatal. People don't come out of those. They inflict too much damage to your body and brain to survive. You're toast.

She was adamant about that part in particular. Once you are in a diabetic coma, there's no coming back.

Bingo, I remember thinking. Randy just mapped out my escape route.

I would take sleeping pills and drink enough alcohol to be sure I passed out and slept through the painful part of the diabetic shock. But not before shooting a shitload of insulin. That part didn't intimidate me. With two older brothers who were junkies, I knew what to do. I was nine when I first saw Jimmie put a needle in his arm. It disgusted me, but the lesson proved to come in handy.

I'd be unconscious from the pills and alcohol when the insulin started shutting down my organs. It felt like a foolproof plan, filling me with a sense of relief that was palpable. I knew it would take months to steal enough of my roommate's insulin and find the pills I needed to pull this off, but that didn't bother me. I had a plan. I was on it. I had a purpose. I could stop worrying and start doing.

A single vial at a time, I started pirating Randy's medicine. Her insulin came in time-release and regular doses. I slipped into the kitchen fridge when she was not around and took a little of each so it was less likely for her to notice anything was missing. I stole a syringe. Randy was like me. She got stoned and drunk a lot. She never noticed anything was amiss.

When I had squirreled away about a thousand units, it was time to act. No matter what else was happening, nothing would deter me. This was show time. Late one afternoon, I went upstairs to my bedroom and locked the door. I imagined I could be up there for days without anyone thinking something was wrong. They'd just assume I was sleeping off another binge.

I swallowed a fistful of sleeping pills and drank a bunch of wine. It didn't take long to get a buzz on. I was loopy from all the crap in my system when I filled the syringe and shot three hundred units of insulin into each thigh. It makes me cringe as I write these words and flash back to that terrible, desperate moment. I can see myself lying in bed, filled with wine and pills and insulin, knowing my pain would soon be done.

It could not have been long before I passed out. But sometime later, I think it was a couple of days, instead of being dead, I came to. I dripped with sweat, hairline conscious but aware enough to be furious that I was still alive. This time, I planned for such a contingency. I was alone in my room. No one had missed me; we partied so hard, that wasn't unusual. I reached over to the side of the bed where I had laid the syringe and the rest of the insulin. Through the fog that had engulfed my brain and body, I managed to draw out two hundred more units. I hit my thigh again and fell back on the bed thinking that I had finally pulled it off.

I don't know what happened after that. My next conscious memory was of me somehow lying on the antique blue velvet sofa in the downstairs living room being yelled at. Now it's daylight. I have no idea how much time passed. The light cut through my eyes like a sharp knife. I had no idea which day it was or how I got from my bed, down the stairs to the couch. Randy was not a big girl, but she hovered over me. She was shaking me, shouting at the top of her lungs.

What did you do? What did you take? Tell me right this minute or I am calling an ambulance and they can deal with you. She kept screaming, What did you take? What did you take? Tell me, God dammit. I need to know. Tell me. Tell me.

She wouldn't stop. She slapped me, screaming and screaming. Her lips were two inches from my face. Go away, I pleaded in words that must have been barely audible. Let me sleep. My mouth was so dry, it was nearly impossible to speak. The pain in my eyes was stabbing my eyes; I could not focus. I spit out a few syllables. An ambulance can't take me against my will, I mumbled. It's illegal. I won't go. I made it up, but Randy seemed to buy it.

Still, she didn't stop. She kept at it. She put her hands on my back and forced me to sit up. I was soaked with sweat. She kept slapping my face so I would not pass out. I could have killed her, if I had any idea how or the strength to do it. Finally, I mumbled something about insulin and she shrieked. But she was no longer hysterical. She became calm. This was useful information. She knew what had to be done.

Within seconds, she had me sitting up, force feeding me orange juice with honey in it to counteract the insulin. She helped me into the kitchen. I was so weak and disoriented that I had to crawl along the wall for support. I was pissed off, but there was no fight in me. There was no way I could sit in a chair. She refused to let me lie down. To get her off my back, I finally told her to take me to the emergency room. Bless that girl for being so persistent. I owe her my life.

When we got to Hennepin County General Hospital, the ER doctor didn't believe my story. I muttered the bare details to him, my speech slurred, my head feeling like it weighed a hundred pounds. He insisted I couldn't have taken that much insulin and still be alive, let alone conscious. Another doctor told me later that if I had taken as much insulin as I claimed, some of it must have been so old it had gone bad. Otherwise, I would not be talking to them. I'd be laid out on a slab. But there I was. Alive. Barely. Not dead again, despite my best intentions.

For weeks after, I was a physical and emotional wreck. Broken from top to bottom, inside and out. I still couldn't see straight or focus my eyes. I slept for days. My body was desperate for recovery. Everything was a blur. After a few days, I found myself sitting face to face with the one person I could not bear to see me this way.

Carrie and I had stayed in touch when I moved out of her home. Once I was out of the hospital, Randy called Carrie to let her know what had happened. She asked her to come talk to me and of course, Carrie did. Having Carrie see me in such bad shape broke my heart. I felt so ashamed. I knew she loved me, and I had let her down. As soon as she laid eyes on me, all washed out and battered, Carrie broke down crying. I didn't think I could feel any worse, but now I did. Her tears hurt more than any pain I felt through the whole ordeal.

After composing herself, Carrie got serious. She insisted there had to be a reason all that insulin and everything else I took didn't end my life. There must have been some kind of plan I couldn't see and didn't understand that kept me alive yet again. Carrie was certain God wanted me around for something other than all this self-destructive shit. To her, there was no question; she believed it to her core. She had all the proof she needed. She was gentle and soft, but she told me I needed to find out why I survived. Something big was going on, she said, and I needed to figure out what it was. Your survival is a gift, Carrie told me; I owed it to God and myself to accept it. Life was too precious to squander. I had to do whatever it took to figure out what I was meant to do with my life because—clearly—there was a reason I was alive, and it was bigger than anything I was able to comprehend. To Carrie, this was an incontrovertible truth. I had taken enough pills, booze and insulin to kill three people. And here I was, still breathing, for God's sake. Carrie, who I had never known to force her views on me or anyone else, demanded that I put in the effort to find out why. This is bigger than you, she told me, and nothing anyone could say would make her feel differently.

Do something with your singing talent, she told me again. Do something. Get out of your head. Stop being so selfish. Live. All this misery is a profound waste of your precious life. You are alive. Act like it! I don't know if I have ever felt more confused, conflicted or ashamed.

I always believed in God, but until I was in my 30s, I was pretty sure the son of a bitch had it in for me. Why else would He have put me in that fucked-up family of mine if he wasn't out to get me? If He really gave a shit about my life, why wasn't I born into a normal, loving household? One with parents equipped to deal with life's ups and downs. Parents who could be there for their children and help them figure out and navigate life. It was black and white in my mind. I was born into a sick, screwed-up family who didn't seem to give a shit about me; it had to be because God didn't care whether I lived or died. What other explanation could there be? Kind of self-centered, I know. Today, I realize life does not work that way, but it was the way I saw things then. At least until I survived that insulin overdose. Until alternative possibilities started seeping into my brain. I respected and loved Carrie too much to dismiss what she said. Didn't I owe it to her to at least consider that she might be right?

As the insulin fog lifted, my brain began working overtime. Now it was preoccupied with something other than planning to die. What would happen if I tried suicide again? There had always been a next time. After each failed suicide attempt, I would eventually plot another try. Would I have to get a gun next time and stick it in my mouth? With my luck, I'd blow off half my face and live because there was some stupid plan God had that I wasn't privy to or was too blind to see. That scared the hell out of me. But so did the idea of having to give up the notion of suicide as a safe escape. If that was off the table, it meant I would now have to find a way to live and function in the world. That seemed impossible. Carrie was in my corner, but there were no parents or other family members to help me figure this shit out. It was on me.

The idea of suicide had always been my ally. An old friend. A reliable trap door I knew I could open and escape through when life became too much. Just as important, it was something I could do by myself. I didn't need anyone's help to end my life the way I needed help to live it. The idea made me feel in control – something I never otherwise felt. Once again, the writer William Styron articulated this all-encompassing mindset better than I ever could.

"As I went about stolidly preparing for extinction," he wrote, "I couldn't shake off a sense of melodrama— a melodrama in which I, the victim-to-be of self-murder, was both the solitary actor and lone member of the audience." Yeah, what William said.

Now things were upside down. Everything was changed. I had to do something different because, above everything else, one fact was perfectly clear: My old ways were getting me nowhere. They were not allowing me to live, and they would not allow me to die. Something else was called for. Could Carrie be right? Was there some reason other than dumb luck that I was still in this world? Could there possibly be a plan for me? Fuck. Fuck. Fuck. How could there be a plan for a miserable little druggie from Detroit who no one save for Carrie seemed to give a damn about? It made no sense whatsoever. As hard as I tried, I could not shake her idea from my brain. I tried talking myself out of it, but Carrie's words rang in me like a bell. You are alive for a reason. God made sure you didn't die. He wanted you around for something important. Go figure out what that is and get on with your life.

Fifteen - Alive For A Reason

Just a few months after the insulin debacle, with Carrie's encouragement, I somehow managed to summon the courage to audition for a singing gig. A friend told me about a group in Minneapolis called the John Stafford Band that was looking for female singers. The idea of trying out for the band scared the living hell out of me, but I decided to go for it anyway. I'm not sure what compelled me to put myself out there and risk getting humiliated and rejected, but it's not as if I had anything else to do. Or anything much to lose. Carrie's talk probably had something to do with it, but I'm not sure I really bought the idea that there was any real purpose in my being alive. That was a concept I was probably not ready for, but I had reached a point where I was more frightened by the idea of not trying. Living with the idea that I had no guts and would never know if I was any good scared me more than putting myself out there to see what might happen. If I was alive, if none of my suicide plans worked, something inside was compelling me to put some effort into the idea of starting to live. Novel concept, I know. It was a giant step away from the past. It was time to see how I did with a clean start. Magness, I told myself, you are going to try out for that band. Fuck what your head is telling you. Fuck the idea that you're no good. You don't know unless you put yourself out there and try. I had to work myself over to summon the guts to take the leap, but I did it.

Carrie and a few others along the way told me they liked my voice when they heard me sing around the house, but I never believed I had any real talent. It didn't fit with my view of who I was or what my life had been about. If that were true, if I really did have a voice that made people stand up and take notice, if I could sing, well, that meant I had something to offer the world. It meant I had value as a person. I'm not being dramatic when I say this was an alien concept. Yet, something was agitating me to try and the feeling would not let me rest. No matter what steps I took, I felt certain I was destined to die young. Even when I decided to give life a try, that's how I saw things. Only now I was determined not to leave this earth without at least seeing if my singing was worth a damn.

I had taken to heart the crap I got fed from the other destructive man I am including in this book, someone I have chosen to call Mr. Worse. We met in Minneapolis when I was about 20, after the insulin overdose. That I would get involved with a cruel man like him, and stay involved for 2 years after everything else I experienced makes me shudder; it's such a loud proclamation that I was more messed up than I could even admit. But there is no denying that it happened.

I actually had met Mr. Worse a few years earlier, when I was living in south Minneapolis and had gone to a recovery meeting one night because I was worn out from getting loaded all the time. I wanted to see if I could find something that might help or make me feel a little better. I think I went as much to see if there were any cute guys there, but what I found made my life even worse than it had been before.

Mr. Worse had one thing going for him: he was gorgeous. I will give him that. He was very rock and roll, and at the time charming and very kind. Shoulder-length honey blond tresses, olive-colored skin and big brown eyes, and Oh Lord, he played a guitar. All of which spelled trouble for me out of the gate.

I was infatuated from the moment we met. To say I was not good at relationships would be like saying I didn't have a head for physics. It would be the understatement of the century. I kept coming around the rehab place and going to recovery meetings. It was like trolling a vaguely defined mental institution for a relationship candidate. Brilliant, I know.

I chased him hard, even though he wasn't really interested in me. Hmm . . . see a pattern here? I chased a cruel guy who wasn't into me, and I would have been better off without him. Like the father of my child, Mr. Worse was hot for another girl. Her name was Susan. She was in recovery treatment, too. Cozy deal all the way around. But I dug him. Or I thought I did, so I wasn't about to be persuaded otherwise.

I wound up becoming his mental and emotional hostage. Sadly, this was a position I would volunteer for in my life again and again.

As I remember it, some weeks after we met, he left rehab on a relapse, then moved in to the house I shared with Randy on Lyndale Avenue. Except he brought

Susan, the girl he was hot for, with him. Again, not exactly brilliant on my part. They didn't stay there long. They got another place not far away, but Susan soon went off the deep end and had a bit of a mental breakdown. Truth is, just about everyone in my crowd was half-crazed or worse. One day, she just started crying and could not stop. Susan eventually left him; Mr. Worse was alone and on the prowl when we finally got together. We wound up getting a place together in Minneapolis, the start of another very ugly stretch for me.

Later on, I realized that he probably saw me as a good bet because I was a free ride. I was far more stable than he was. I had a job and worked hard. I am sure he never actually cared for me. I was a convenience for him. It's the old joke: What do you call a guitar player without a girlfriend? Homeless. That was this guy, only worse.

I got us an apartment at Aldrich and 26th Street in South Minneapolis. It was a studio that had a Murphy bed and stained glass bay windows. It was sweet, except we shared a bath down the hall. Eventually we dealt and shot coke together in that little apartment.

I thought I was in love with Mr. Worse, but I realize today that what I felt wasn't anything remotely close to love. It was a familiar obsession and addiction. All I knew at that time was negativity and self-loathing. He was just what the devil ordered.

As it turned out, Mr. Rock and Roll was an angry, violent, and most likely a sociopath. I know what you're thinking: No one is perfect, right? But this guy was bad fucking news. There was choking, screaming, furniture-breaking, and yelling in the street. We had the whole sick package.

To this day, I avoid the sun for two reasons. The first is that it ages skin prematurely, and who wants to look old before their time? The second equally important reason for me is that when I spend any time in the sun, it brings out the permanent marks he left on my body. They turn a darker brown, as a scar can do, and remind me of that asshole and a deeply painful period of my life.

Mr. Worse was involved with some old friends of his from Milwaukee who were into serious drug trafficking. Mostly cocaine, and I'm talking volumes. There was a lot of money changing hands. This was the first time in my life that I actually began to recognize sociopathic behavior. This guy got away with an incredible amount of wrong doing. He was coated in Teflon. He'd get arrested for drunken behavior, and for burglary, then for fencing stolen property and his friends would pay his bail in a flash. Or he'd give the cops some false names and details on someone he knew and that guy would appear in court as my guy. In one case, the dude and Mr. Worse were old friends. The other guy did the time for him. I am not kidding. I don't know what kind of hold he had on the fall guy, but it was some of the most surreal shit I'd ever seen.

At the time, I was driving a 1961 VW Bug, the second car I owned. It was beige. It was the first of three Bugs I would end up owning over time. I loved that little car. By the time we reached the end of that relationship, if I dare call it that, the Bug was littered with rusted one-edged razor blades, syringe points and roaches. They filled the ashtrays, glove box, and inside door pockets . Just everywhere.

During the worst of it all with this guy, I actually had a legit job: working with kids as an intern in the probation office for Hennepin County in Minneapolis. Don't laugh. It's one more example of the conflicting and opposite forces in my life. I was working with kids in a law enforcement agency. I was also living with a criminal, selling dope, shooting cocaine. Lovely. I was a walking contradiction, and a felonious one at that.

I was in my early 20s, anxious to find gainful employment, but the truth was I didn't have too many marketable skills. I did some brainstorming about what I thought I might be good at. I can't recall exactly how this idea popped into my head. Carrie might have helped me come up with it, suggesting that I might be able to help kids who faced troubles like mine, but I'm glad it happened. I was able to talk myself into sitting down in the county office of someone in authority and did a Bill Magness sales job on them.

I was good with troubled kids, I told them. I knew from my time in foster care and from my own experiences how it felt to be young, messed up and lost. Whoever I spoke with put me in touch with a gentleman, who ran a juvenile probation office in Northeast Minneapolis. I gave him the same spiel and he hired me. Pretty amazing, especially given what was going on under my own roof. But I was good with those kids. They related to me. They could see I was one of them. I loved working with them, trying to boost their spirits, listening to their worries and concerns. It made me feel useful. I only stayed there about six months, but it made me feel like I had something to contribute to the world and the lives of these kids who needed help. Too bad I couldn't apply any of what I offered those kids to my own fucked up life. Even as I was helping them, I was sinking deeper by the day.

It was during the time I worked in the probation office that Mr. Worse tried to kill me for the first time. Yes, kill. We had an argument. It got physical. The fight began because I'd spilled the beans on his brother, who had been cheating on his wife, a good friend of mine. He was cheating with someone I knew and I couldn't hold that secret anymore. When my girlfriend asked me if I knew anything, I gave her the truth. That ended their marriage, and of course I was blamed for it.

Mr. Worse and I got into it. At one point, he picked me up by the neck and began choking me, slamming my head against the cupboard in the kitchen of our apartment. When I finally got away, I resolved to leave him, taking advantage of an opportunity to get out of town for a while to help my girlfriend move back to Milwaukee. She drove her car and I commandeered the U-Haul. I figured I would just get away for a while, maybe start a new life. I asked for two weeks off from work and they said yes. I went to Milwaukee with my girlfriend; we stayed drunk nearly the entire time. Milwaukee is a great place to do that. Who knew? Drink, drink, drink! That's about all we did. Alcohol dulled pain. We were helping each other the best way we knew how.

After two weeks, I was feeling homesick. I drove back and, of course, immediately found a reason to go see Mr. Worse. Since he was afraid of losing his good thing, he was now sweet and kind, so happy to see me. I understand today this is a typical pattern for an abuser, but back then I just wanted something I didn't have, and I thought it was him. I went back with him to the apartment and was blown away at how nice it looked. It was completely furnished; he seemed to be doing quite well. I couldn't figure it out. I know he didn't have a legit job. And I had taken everything with me when I left with my girlfriend. All the belongings from the apartment that were mine had been put in storage; here he was with the apartment totally refurnished. When I asked him about it, he said someone gave him a bunch of stuff because they had owed him money for drugs and paid him in "furnishings." Didn't ring true to me, but I wanted to believe him. I found out later he had been burglarizing places with a couple of his friends.

The only job he ever had when I knew him was working for a commercial cleaning company. How he got that I will never know, but it was convenient for him. He and his pals were going into businesses, cleaning offices at night and stealing anything they could. Man of my dreams, right?

I wound up moving back in with him in spite of every warning sign that doing so was a terrible idea. It pains me to write these words: I went back with him. What on earth was I looking for? What was wrong with me? If he was the answer, what was the fucking question? You could have called us Sick and Sicker. You would have been right.

During this reconciliation, he shot me up with coke for the first time. Here's how messed up it was: I put a needle into my arm and shot cocaine into my veins so I could be closer to him. I thought it would bring us together. That's what I believed at the time anyway. Today, almost three decades later, clean and sober, I have to say this still makes me sick to my stomach. More than anything, it makes me sad, even after so much time has passed. Some memories you just can't forget or reconcile.

If that wasn't bad enough, there was a point near the end of the year we lived together that the drug use got even more depraved. With no explanation or warning, one day he disappeared. He took all the coke and cash and split without a word. After about ten days, friends of his started calling me at the house and at work saying I needed to get him under control, that he was going to get arrested. He was running around town with way too much blow and cash in his pockets. He was reckless, even by the standards of the dealers and thieves he hung around with. I finally tracked him down in a hotel penthouse suite with another woman. Textbook, right?

He came to the door in a towel, indignant that I was there, and began strong-arming me into the laundry room and pushing me around. Demanding I stay out of his business. I went home and put all his crap out on the lawn. It didn't amount to much. Maybe three boxes of shitty odds and ends. Somehow he showed up pretty fast. He must have figured I meant business this time. He worked hard and talked fast, trying to charm his way back in, and guess what? I didn't say, "Go fuck yourself. I never want to see your face again." I took the lying sleazebag back.

Shortly after that, he had a severe episode of cocaine psychosis. He got so high for so long that he freaked out. He was convinced someone was trying to break into our apartment and kill him. Unfortunately, it wasn't true. He did call the police, though, and then hid in the attic when they showed up. That happened twice. The second time, he threw empty wine bottles through the bay window in the kitchen and tried to escape as the police broke down the door. He went to jail that time, but miraculously he found a way to get off scot-free. I never understood it.

I finally got away from him after the next big fight, the one that almost resulted in my demise. He had asked me to pawn a camera that he'd brought home. He swore up and down it wasn't stolen; I knew better, but I wanted to believe him. We needed the money. We had been stealing food from the neighborhood market, mostly lobster tails. We were broke and figured why not? Gonna' steal some food anyway, might as well be lobster!

So off to Hy's Pawn shop in downtown Minneapolis I went, camera in tow. The pawnshop guy happily gave me a quick hundred-dollar bill for that nice equipment. Just as quickly, I am certain, he must have called the police when that camera showed up on a stolen property list. A few days later, I got a call from the Minneapolis P.D. burglary division. They called at my job, for God's sake. They wanted to talk with me about the stolen property I pawned. Jesus. I knew enough to realize I was cornered. I arranged the next day for a lawyer to meet me at the police department, but I made the mistake of stopping home first to confront Mr. Worse about the camera and his lies. Again, not exactly sound thinking on my part. We started to argue. Next thing I knew, he was punching me and slamming my head on the hard wood floor. It must have occurred to him that I'd probably try to get away again, so he ran outside to my car and frantically ripped whatever he could off of the engine, including the distributor cap.

I was barely conscious when he reached for the phone to bash me in the head with it, I'm sure. In that exact moment, miraculously it rang. Even more miraculously, he actually answered it. It was his probation officer. He had to take the call and act as if everything was cool. I ran into the street, jumped on the bus and headed downtown to meet my lawyer. When my attorney saw me tattered and beat up, he couldn't believe his eyes. We spoke to the detective from the Burglary Division who had called, and for the first and only time in my life, I turned evidence against another person. Every cell in my body was screaming at me. There was no way to pretty up any of this. I was in hell. Something had to be done and it had to be done by me.

After that, I managed to get my own apartment in what I thought was a safe building, cutting all ties with the maniac and his friends. I left everything I owned at the place we lived in at 26th and Aldrich, moving into a studio apartment and not even putting my name on the mailbox. I was really scared. I had two kitchen chairs and a dark red area rug that I had gotten at a garage sale. A pillow and a couple of blankets. I slept on that rug on the floor. I was insanely broke. Days and nights were a blur. I was frightened all the time, waiting for the other shoe to drop. Did it ever.

About two weeks later, the maniac found out where I was living. I woke up in the middle of the night to see him standing over me. He was snickering, telling me I couldn't get away from him. That I would never get away from him. It was one of the scariest moments of my life. Then he left. Just like that. Gone. He must have been really high.

That happened three separate times before I figured out how he got into my apartment. Through the old ironing board wall cabinet in the kitchen. It had never been properly secured from the outside hallway – so bingo! He was always loaded when he appeared. Once, he stood over me holding a big kitchen knife. My survival instincts took over. I acted unafraid and ordered him to get the hell out. I think I was in shock. I know I felt real terror when I saw him.

I finally split that place, too, and went back to Carrie's. Mercifully, she let me move back in. I knew I would be safe there. At least I could breathe and not worry that he would find me again.

I was finally free from this madman. Then years later, in 2011, social media allowed him to locate me. He turned up at a festival show in Northern California. I had a premonition and alerted my booking agency. Security guards who had been warned in advance by the promoter, removed him. But true to form, as he was being taken off site, he got away!

I see it all pretty clearly now and understand the pathology that was my life during those sick, fucked-up years. I didn't need proof or reminders that I was a self-destructive mess for so long, but this episode brought it all back home. In a lifetime of lows, my time with him might be the lowest. Much as I would like to, it's impossible to pretend it didn't happen.

But deeper than the scars this man left upon me, is the knowledge that I not only volunteered to be with this guy, but I worked hard to get him and I kept going back again and again. I was unquestionably damaged. I hurt for me when I see that. I hurt for that young woman I was, with zero self-worth and in so much pain.

I have hope that by telling this particular story, it could help someone else who is in an abusive relationship. It's not anything they should put up with, not for a minute. Get out no matter how lost you feel. Find help. It's out there if you want it. But get away from whoever is hurting you and protect yourself. I know it's not easy. It never is. I have nothing but empathy for anyone in a similar situation. But it tears my heart apart to think of anyone feeling so terrible about their own self-worth that they would put up with physical or emotional abuse the way I did. The way so many women, sad to say, do.

The physical wounds Mr. Worse inflicted on me have all but disappeared. As long as I stay out of the sun, no one sees them. Including me. But the emotional scars, those were much tougher to mend. For years, it was impossible for me to move past the insults he hurled my way when I sang even the tiniest bit around our apartment or followed a song on the radio.

You can't fucking sing, he'd snarl at me. Who do you think you are? You sound like a cat in heat. Stop that shit. He was someone who could detect my worst weakness and go right for it. When other people told me I had a wonderful voice, it was his insults that stayed with me. They carried far more weight. I believed them more than any compliments I ever heard.

Yet, despite my deep apprehension about whether I had talent, there was no denying that something incredible happened when I finally did sing in front of people. I felt alive. I had a power that was never there when I did anything else. Singing took me to another place. Just as it did when I was a little girl, back in my bedroom, hiding out, putting on shows for the cat and dog, pretending I was someone else. For those brief moments, things were right. People liked my music. And seeing them react positively touched something inside me. I could feel their reaction. It was a tangible, physical sensation that started in my gut and made me all warm and tingly. It was good. But it also filled me with anxiety and discomfort. If you see me on stage now, beaming from the love I get back from the audience, you wouldn't believe I had so little confidence earlier in life. I know what can happen on stage. If I go out there confident I can win people over with the music and my honesty. Being truly myself and putting my heart and passion into a song I believe in. Back then, when Carrie was prodding me to do something with my talent, my negative Magness brain would go into overdrive. It told me: don't believe it. So I squelched my desire to sing. Whenever the feeling came up, I found a way to ignore it and move to something else.

When I forced myself to try out for the John Stafford Band in spite of all the resistance to the idea I'd built up in my head, the reaction from band members was amazing. Everyone in the group loved my singing. I wanted to believe that would happen, but how could I? I went through a few songs with the band and began to feel comfortable. I was singing, for God sakes, and it felt good. John said I had the gig if I wanted it.

As things turned out, we spent about six months rehearsing a couple nights a week. I loved having that regular time to get in line with the music and use my voice on a regular basis. Don't get me wrong. This was no slick act. We were not destined to sell out anything. The band included three female singers and an Elvis impersonator. We played what was popular at the time—soul music, Miami disco, K.C. and the Sunshine Band, Elvis. We did a handful of gigs at the Burnsville Bowl outside Minneapolis. It felt good to be part of something. But it didn't last. After a few months, somehow Stafford was unable to pay the band. All the players quit. That was the end of that. My brain was hardwired to believe bad things would always happen, so it was no shock when things fell apart. My first real gig as a singer and it was gone before it really got going.

After the gig tanked, I felt too low to look for other work. The familiar feeling of isolation was back. No one wanted anything to do with me or the black cloud lodged above my head. I was unreliable and flaky. I had alienated everyone who cared about me. Carrie, my family, Sam. They were all tired of my shit. How could I blame them? I was twenty-one, now drinking nonstop, taking whatever dope I could get my hands on. Mostly cheap speed and some hallucinogens. I was still numb from that abusive relationship I'd been in. I was always in a shitty mood, hardly a joy to be around. My unemployment payments had run out. I was broke, for a change. Nothing I did turned out right. I couldn't even kill myself, for God sakes. I was beating myself up pretty bad once the safety net of singing with the Stafford Band disappeared. I needed something to shake me from my latest doldrums.

Magness Family Home Coalgate, OK

HEAR
Brother
C. A. Magness
Of Coalgate, Oklahoma
AT THE
CHURCH of CHRIST
106 Van Buren Street, Taft
COME, LET US REASON TOGETHER
October 6th - 20th
EVERY ONE WELCOME
SONG SERVICE 7:30 P. M.
BRO. PAT MOORE OF BAKERSFIELD, SONG LEADER

C.A. Magness

C.A. Magness family Coalgate, OK 1931

Grandma Pearl and Charlie Kirby Mt. Clemens, MI

Mom and Grandma

Mom and Grandma Michigan

Mom's Glamour

Gettin' Hitched Arkansas

Olan Mills Mt. Clemens 1957

Happy Baby 1958

First Precinct Downtown Detroit

Officer Magness

Daddy's Girl

Daddy's Girl

Early Blues

Happy Mom

The Farm

Dad with a cold one

Company Christmas 1961

Elementary Awkward

Sara, Kits, Carson, & Me 1964

Mom & Carson December 1966

More Elementary Awkward

Eggheads

Choo-choo

Jimmie 1969 That Was Then

Heading to Jimmie's Wedding
St. Peter Hospital for the Criminally Insane

A Boy and His Bike

The St. Louis Gang

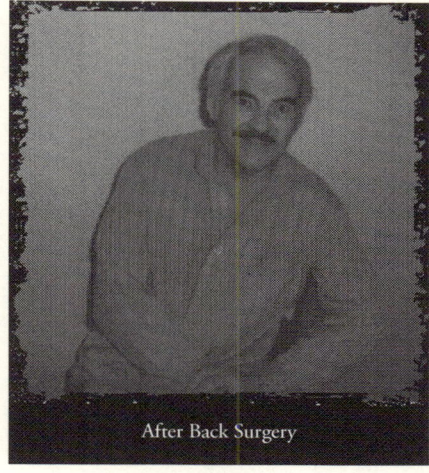

After Back Surgery

Me and John Paul

9th Grade…Right?

High High High

High Again

Me and Pearl 1974

Halloween Visitation, Stillwater State Prison Carrie, the girls, & David

Soft Landing 1978

Struck Sober 1978

Waking up clean 1978 Minneapolis

Classic Carrie

Carries Family Michelle, Me, Marie, Elaine,
Kenny, Ronnie, Helen, Bobby

Dance Party

Jimmie Sober 1979

First Cover Story Minneapolis Jazz Magazine

In Way Over My Head First recording session 1979
Steve McCloone & Co

Me &Nanc heading to the Black Hills

Me & Nanc Saloon girls

Phoenix Headshot

Yours Truly and Scotty Spenner

The Blues Connection Matt Roe, Emerson Carruthers, Bob Tate, Elmer Scott, Me, Bob Corritore, Jed Allen, The Chief
Photo by Paul Cantrell

Janiva Magness & The MoJomatics
Presents
All Star Blues Jam
Every Tuesday 9:00 P.M. — 1:00 A.M.

At Club Macayo Lounge
7005 E. Camelback Rd.

"The Best of the Valleys Blues Performers"

Mojomatics Phoenix

Best of Phoenix 1986

That Was a Great Band Andy Kaulkin, Me,
Tyler Pedersen, Steve Mugalian, Rick Holmstrom
Photo by Stan Weinstock

LA Baby 1991

Sunday night Nyala photo by Jan Jensen

One Night in Orange, NJ Bettye, Me, and friends

Kid, Leach, Me, Horwitz, and Boogers

Mississippi Valley BF
Dave, Scruff, Horwitz, Me, Alan, Paulie, Debbie, George

Gone Tits up! San Diego BF Me, Little Ed, Zach Zunis

JR House Party Tonight. Gonzalo Bergara,
Dave Kida, Me, Gary Davenport

Sangin' in Orange, NJ
Me and Bettye LaVette

Me and Steve Samuels at the King King

Hamming it up backstage at Buffett 1991

Kay's Salon. Sara Fleetwood, Miss Kay, and Me

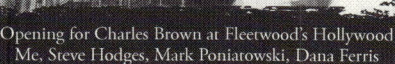

Opening for Charles Brown at Fleetwood's Hollywood
Me, Steve Hodges, Mark Poniatowski, Dana Ferris

Steve Samuels, Yours Truly, & Floyd Dixon Topanga BF

$100 Love Shack Sara & Me

Juan Carlos Queso. Ron Thompson, Yours Truly, Lenise
Bent, Carla Fredericks, Sara & Mick Fleetwood

Early Jeff & Me

Me and Junior Watson

Lila and Me

Me & Some Boys. John Baz, Gene Taylor,
myself, Jimi Bott, Jeff Turmes

Messin' With Kid Yours Truly, Jeff Turmes,
Kid Ramos recording date

Joking with Queens. Backstage House of Blues Chicago
Denise LaSalle, Koko Taylor

Kirkie Fletcher and Me

Yours Truly & Robin Rogers BMAs

Randy Chortkoff and Yours Truly

No Green Zone! Bluezapalooza in Iraq

Memphis in May baby! Me, Jimmie & Scruff

Blues in Hell Me, Scruff & Zach
Photo by Patrick Frontéri

Helena, AR Anson Funderburgh & Me

Texas Nights Me, Scruff & Zach

Train to Hell, Norway

B.B., Bonnie & Me
Photo by Merete Eide

B.B. King Called My Name
Photo by Merete Eide

The Asking
Photo by Dick Waterman

Snot Rag

Motown Hometown

Song of the Year 'N Stuff
Me and Dave Darling

The Future is Female Thornetta Davis,
Candye Kane, Gina Sicilia, Yours Truly, Laura Chavez

Gimme' Back My Wig   LRBC   Me, Gina, Priscilla, Alice, Teresa

Catch a Red Coat
Portland Waterfront BF

He's Out of Control!   Matt Tecu & Me

Persistence

Woman Bites Dog

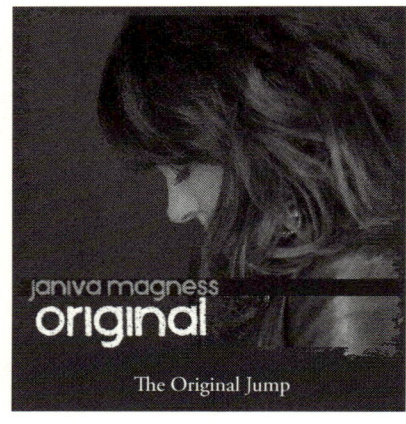

The Original Jump

Original The Musical   Jeff Richards,
Dave Darling, Rachel Nee Hall

A Scene from Original The Musical

Women Who Cook: Robin Rogers, Thornetta Davis & Me
Photo by Aigars Lapsa

Happy Carson

Carson Happy 2

Brothers in Arms Joe & Jimmie

Me & Ronnie Magness   The Borderline London

A Good Day Sara & Jimmie

Cake! Mr. & Mrs. Norton

Memphis Happy Me & Tim
Photo by Deb Lubin

2016 Leslie.Joseph@Blues411.com

Doin' It Me & Zach Zunis
Photographed by Leslie Joseph

A Moment With Ike Turner

Kid Ramos Fights Back
Photo by Kim Culbertson Juniper

Me & Fruteland Jackson

Best Publicist Ever Me & Cary Baker

The Earl of Ronnie & Me

Me & Some Fellas Hubert Sumlin,
Yours Truly, & Pinetop Perkins

Love Is An Army Arlan Scheierbaum, Dave Darling,
Yours Truly, Davey Faragher, Stephen Hodges

Oh No! Me & Jim Lauderdale

Judith Owen, Lee Sklar & Me

Ian McLagan & Me Woodsongs

Life Is About Friends
Bnois King & Smokin' Joe Kubek

Friends Nick Nixon & Me

2016 Grammy Nomination

Winning Live at The Troubadour Hollywood, CA
Photo by Earl Gibson for Blue Elan'

Sixteen - Bleak City

With nowhere to live, my friend, Inez, let me crash for a while in her unfinished basement. With no more than a bare cot and a couple of cardboard boxes filled with my stuff, this was Bleak City. I wasn't hanging around with an abusive psychopath any longer, but I felt like shit. Then Inez confronted me.

Are you an alcoholic? Do you have a drinking problem? Do you need help? You seem like the walking dead. You need to get into rehab before it's too late.

I just stared at her blankly and cried. Inez was undeterred, God bless her. She picked up the phone and made some calls, finding an alcohol treatment center that would take me in forty-eight hours. Minnesota is known as the Land of 10,000 Lakes, but I've heard people say it's the Land of 10,000 Rehab Clinics. Inez knew where to find one she thought could help me. Thanks to experiences with her own family, she was well versed in drug and alcohol recovery programs. I had no other options, good or bad. I'll give it a try, I told her through the tears. I promise.

I meant it, but this was not something I was about to rush into. First there would be one more night of getting loaded. My money was gone, so I told people at the crummy bar I went to that it was my birthday. It worked. They bought me drinks. I got loaded for free. This would be the last hurrah, I told myself. I would catch a buzz and march off to rehab. Typical addicts' thinking. Reminds me of the line in that wonderful Gillian Welch song, Look at Miss Ohio, where she sings, I wanna do right, but not right now. That was me in spades.

I followed through on my commitment to Inez, though, and got myself admitted to the rehab program she found, throbbing hangover and all. I don't remember the name of the place, but I wound up staying thirty days. Then I moved to a halfway house for seven and a half months of what they called, "extended treatment."

It was torture of sorts, but I needed it. After the insulin episode and all the abuse and insanity from my time with Mr. Worse, I could not deny that my life was out of control and that I needed something or someone to help me manage. At the halfway house, we had group therapy every day. Ten counselors and forty women called me on my shit.

I liked taking advice about as much as I enjoyed being sober, which was not at all. When someone asked me a question, I was quick-witted enough to blurt out what they wanted to hear, but I rarely meant it. I knew what to say to get some space and have them back off. When it came time for a meeting at the halfway house, I was chronically late, like I didn't give a shit. I was late for lunch. Late for breakfast and dinner. My heart was clearly not in it. We got to go out at night if we told the staff what our plans were and made it back by curfew, which was 10 p.m. I was late for that, too, so those privileges were taken from me. I needed help and could admit to myself that was the case, but there was no way I would let my guard down enough to allow someone else to get close or tell me what to do. My lies and aloofness probably came across as arrogance or bravado, but I eventually came to learn they were protective armor I wore so nobody could get close to me. Like when I stood in the back of that seedy bar drinking and watching Otis Rush back when I was fourteen. I sent out a powerful "stay-the-hell-away-from-me" vibe because, God forbid, if I let down my guard someone might see the real me. I was an orphan. Stoned or drunk whenever I had the chance. A scared-to-death young girl with terrible taste in men and no purpose or meaning to my life. I caused the death of a child, for God's sake, because I was such a mess. Who'd want to let anyone in on all that? I was willing to check out rehab and go for the extended treatment, but in my mind it was little more than something to kill time and keep me off the streets. There was no way I would commit to any of it. I could B.S. the counselors and everyone else in the group. I was a master at it.

So I liked to drink and get loaded. BFD. My life was a mess, but I told myself I wasn't a drunk or an addict like the other women in there. I was a Magness. My father's daughter; C.A. Magness' granddaughter. I had my own way of doing things. If you don't like it, fuck off and leave me alone. It's your problem, not mine. I didn't believe anything the counselors told me. I barely heard what they said, because I knew I was smarter than them.

The counselors and the other women had pretty strong bullshit detectors, unfortunately for me, and they lost patience with my crap pretty quickly. I nearly got my ass booted out of the place because I refused to open up to the group or to the counselors trying to help me. They kept a list of infractions, scoring us for house rules we violated. My count was off the charts. If I was a baseball player, I'd be in the Hall of Fame. You had to really fuck up to get tossed from one of those programs. I was a star fuck-up. I went into the place for help, on my own accord, but I was putting on a false face with everyone I came into contact with. And guess what? They were a lot smarter than I thought. They had seen through bigger bullshit artists than me. Worst of all? I was being dishonest with myself. But the sad truth for me at the time was that without drugs or alcohol, I had no clue how to live or act. I was wandering around the wilderness with blinders on and no map to lead me out.

It dawned on me years later that I was little more than a younger version of my brothers, Joe and Jimmie. They were hustlers. Inveterate liars and con-men. They would bullshit about everything because they thought they had to in order to get by. Even when a lie served no purpose. Deceit was second nature to them. Why tell the truth when you can lie and mislead people? I suppose it provides some semblance of power or control when you don't have either. Or so you think. I couldn't understand why the counselors in the program made such a big fucking deal about any of it. It seemed pretty normal to me.

Finally, one day, I hit the wall. Or, I should say, I was slammed into it. The counselors called a house meeting and I got "grouped" on by them and all the other women in the program. I sat in the middle of a circle as they pummeled me with questions and accusations about my attitude and behavior. I shut down completely. I couldn't say a word. It was impossible for me to defend myself. I will never forget the counselor I was working with—her name was Ginny—throwing up her arms and abruptly calling a halt to it. She saw I was broken. She put her arm around my shoulder to comfort me, taking me out of the group and sitting me down so we could talk with no one else around.

You are going to have to get real, she told me. She was compassionate, but stern. You are going to have to get real right now. Not tomorrow, not in a week. Today. You have to get honest with yourself or you are not going to survive. Plain and simple.

Of course, she was right. I raised the flag and felt myself surrendering. What the fuck, I thought. Nothing was working. I had no defense, nothing to say but "I know."

"Magness, you got nothing else," I told myself. "This is it." Maybe they could teach me something new. It was a huge leap I did not want to make. I had just been screamed at by more than forty people for two hours. In recovery groups, they sometimes say life can beat you up so bad you wind up in a state of reasonableness. If you don't die first. I suppose that's what was happening to me. I was exhausted from being out on the streets or sleeping on a cot in a cold basement. I was worn out from running into loaded friends, dealers I owed money to, people I had lied to about one thing or another. I was exhausted from being me.

The practical implications of getting clean and trying to stay that way was that it made the idea of singing at nightclubs even more terrifying. Recovery wiped that idea right off the table. I knew I was not strong enough to avoid the temptation to get high if I was surrounded by people with drinks in their hand. The only thing that gave me some feeling of being alive, my singing, now had to be put on ice for the foreseeable future. In my mind at least, there was no way I could get clean and sober and sing.

I began to convince myself it made sense to give up the idea of singing altogether. I was despondent over this, but it took me off the hook. It's hard to be rejected and told you're not any good if you don't put yourself out there. I had a higher calling now. I needed to get off drugs and alcohol. That was something to feel righteous and serious about. I had to give it my all. The dream of singing, the dream of a life in music, would have to be squelched.

I cried for days after making that decision. It felt like another big defeat. But I really did want to get off this road to nowhere with drugs and alcohol. It wasn't long before I had a classic Magness brainstorm, a way to shake off my funk.

I decided to do the next best thing to singing. I would become a sound engineer. I'd be surrounded by music, musicians and artists. Music would be part of my life. Maybe this was something I could live with. I'm not sure where I got the idea, but it made sense to me. I told myself I would be the best damn sound engineer who ever lived.

No big deal that I knew nothing about being a sound engineer. Who cares if there were no women doing that kind of work at the time? I was channeling my dad and his determination to get something done no matter what. No women in the field? BFD. I didn't care. There will be now. I'd need to go to school to learn my way around a recording studio, but that was no problem. No money to pay for the schooling? So what. I'll find a way. Thanks to the DNA that came from my father, I could sell skin to a snake. I can do this, I told myself, and it was another example of the dichotomy that was my character. A marriage between total despair and fierce determination. They took turns getting their way.

I soon found myself sitting in a chair at the Minnesota Vocational Rehabilitation Services Department, talking one of their employees into giving me a scholarship to attend electronics school. I had heard from someone I knew that the state had programs for people in my situation. I wanted something that would pay well, keep me focused and, above all else, allow me to stay clean and sober. The state gave me enough money to enroll in a few classes. Pretty soon I was cold-calling recording studios to ask if anyone needed an intern. I found out the state would match any money I made in an internship, so I pitched the idea of matched pay to one of the studios I called, and they bit.

I got a valuable lesson in how the universe seems to respond if you're out there showing up and going after things. Before long, I was employed at Sullivan Sound Recording in St. Paul, hired as an assistant engineer. Truth was, that meant answering phones, wrapping cables, go get this, go get that, grab me a cup of coffee, make some cassettes, scrub the toilets.

If I was lucky, I would be able to cut some tape. That's how editing was done back in the days of pre-digital recording. We recorded on tape, using a razor to splice and fit together the pieces. It was a delicate operation. For some reason, it was something I did well. You had to listen closely and cut the tape in the exact right spot, splicing it to the other piece with precision so the sound was seamless when the tape played back. This felt like a big honor and thrill for me. It certainly beat the hell out of cleaning the toilets. I took pride in being able to do it well.

One night when I was at the studio, Herman Jones, a local rhythm and blues singer, had come in and was cutting demos with his band, Herman Jones and the Exciters. It was late at night. I was wiped out after being there all day and doing whatever my boss needed. I was napping with my head down on my desk when Pete Martinson, the engineer at Sullivan, called out to the front of the studio.

"Hey, Janiva, get in here," Pete shouted over the intercom. "We need some background vocals. You've sung before. Come on. Get in here. We need you."

I tried to beg off. Are you fucking kidding me, I thought to myself? The mere mention of singing in the studio in front of these guys scared the shit out of me. I didn't want to be under that kind of microscope. Pete was adamant. If I wanted to keep my job, I better get the hell in there and fast.

I was so tired, I couldn't think of a way to escape. I felt trapped and began tearing up, but I quickly realized the worst possible thing I could do was fall apart. I pulled myself together with another one of my little pep talks and trudged back into the studio.

Herman Jones and the Exciters were just starting out, but they developed into a popular St. Paul band that mixed Motown, funk and R&B. With Herman on drums and vocals, the band wound up opening for some big acts when they came through town. Ike & Tina Turner. The Temptations. Curtis Mayfield and the Impressions. They also backed up stars like Jimmie Reed and Al Green once in a while. Herman was passionate about his music. He still is. When he heard me sing, he was ecstatic.

He told me he loved my voice. A few days later, he came back into the studio with some other songs he hoped I would help him demo. I said no, man, you need to get a real singer. And he said no, no, no right back. You're good. I want you to do this. You have a lead voice. You're no background singer. Again, I said no, no. Again, he said yes, yes, yes. This was strong validation of my talent. Although I didn't see it that way at the time, I will always appreciate Herman Jones for his strong show of faith.

I wound up doing other background vocal work for the studio and sessions with some talented local musicians. People like Tommy Wiggins, Steve McCloone and a popular band called Judd. Once I started getting into it, the switch inside me was back on full throttle. The switch that made me feel alive and human. But it cut both ways. It felt like torture, too, because I was still afraid that singing and being sober didn't go together. Not for me, at least. I didn't think I was strong enough emotionally to make that work. And no matter how many compliments I got from Herman and other artists who came to the studio, I could not allow myself to fully believe them.

Whenever I sang, my legs literally would shake. My heart pounded. This is embarrassing to admit, but I got locked into this awful pattern of coming down with diarrhea right before it was time to perform. My nerves were killing me. The notion of being an artist talented enough to make a living? Who the hell did I think I was to believe that fairytale?

Somehow, I kept moving forward. I was in my early 20s now and was soon landing other singing gigs. Rock and roll, background vocals, ensemble stuff. Something was pushing me. I had no choice but to go after it. Fuck the fear, I kept telling myself. I was going to act as if everything was fine. Whistling in the dark. It's what I do. The world could be ready to end and I'll be out there whistling a tune as if everything was fine. It was a ruse I needed to employ so fear would not paralyze me. Keep moving, I told myself. It's something I do even now. Down time with nothing happening has never been my friend. I don't want my brain to start telling my heart all the reasons I can't succeed. So I have to always stay busy. I need to keep moving and pushing.

After a few years of working in the studio, flirting with some positive reaction to my singing, I actually started to play around with the idea that maybe I could make a go of this after all. I don't think I bought the idea a hundred percent, but I was anxious to see where I'd wind up if I gave music a real shot. A good test presented itself when the opportunity came to leave Minnesota and move to Los Angeles. I felt compelled to jump. It was time to see what I had. Filled with my usual dread and conflicting emotions, I figured, why not? I'll try this and see where I land. What else was there to do? Get out there, Magness, I told myself. You're alive. Give it a shot. What's the most terrible thing that could happen? Whatever it is, you've been through far worse. Whistle in the dark and go for it.

Seventeen - City of Angels

I wound up hitting the road and driving to Los Angeles with Gary Starr, an engineer friend I had gotten to know in Minneapolis. We met on a session at the Sound 80 recording studio made famous by Prince and artists like Bob Dylan, who recorded some of Blood on the Tracks there. I had done some work with an all-black production company; why they had hired me I had no idea, but I was pleased and proud to be working with such talented players. We had been brought on to work for various artists. Gary had engineered those tracks and we became friends. It turned out he wanted to return to L.A., where he had lived before. He kept telling me I was too talented to be playing around like I was. Over and over, he told me I needed to go to L.A. and commit to pursuing a fulltime music career. It sounded enticing, but I wasn't convinced. One day he said it at just the right time, when I was feeling particularly restless. Okay, I said, let's go. I'll drive! I wasn't sure he was serious, but once I gave in there was no turning back.

It took four days to make it out to Southern California in my little Dodge Colt. When we got there, we were ecstatic, driving straight to Hollywood to see a good friend of Gary's named Nancy Boykiss. She worked at Alan Zent Mastering Labs, a renowned studio where a ton of great records were mastered. I loved her last name—Boykiss. Too perfect. I was drawn to her instantly. This woman was dripping with energy to spare. When we walked in, she was on top of her desk dancing to loud, rock music, hair and arms flying. She jumped down in a move that was perfectly in sync with the song, wrapping her arms around Gary in a warm and loving hug. Shit, I thought, this place is awesome. Nancy and I became fast friends.

But I was soon back to my anxious, impatient self. Los Angeles was so big and fast. The freeways and traffic were overwhelming. I was twenty-four and insecure. I didn't think I could ever get comfortable there. L.A. was more than I bargained for. I knew there was a lot I needed to learn about being a professional singer and started to think I would have a better chance somewhere a little less intimidating. I gave Los Angeles a try, but within six months I was ready to pack it in.

So I upped and split again. This time, for Phoenix. I didn't know anything about the place, but since Phoenix was relatively close to L.A., I figured there must be a music scene. Makes sense, right? That was the extent of my research. Remember, there was no Internet back then. No Google. I was traveling blind.

I also had a boyfriend who lived there. His name was Scott. I had lived with him in Minneapolis for a while. He wanted to marry me. I told him yes and we never broke it off when I left town. I thought I would get back together with him and check things out. Scott would be my safety net in Arizona. Felt like a solid plan to me.

Once I got there, it was apparent that Scott and I were no longer a good fit. He had become an investment banker. My dream was to become a professional singer. We were not in the same book, let alone on the same page. The relationship crashed and burned in no time. But unlike in the past, I didn't cut and run when things didn't work out. I hung in and in time, Phoenix became the place for me where things finally started to solidify musically. Not before a few more tough and painful lessons, of course.

First I had to decide how much of my toe to stick in the water. I was torn as usual by wanting to jump all the way and still holding back so the pain wouldn't be too bad if I dove into the pool and the pool was empty. The debate raged in my head like it did when I was trying to decide whether to keep my baby. The stakes were higher back then, of course, because another life was involved, but it was the same endless back and forth in my brain that made me tired. "Come on, Magness," I kept chiding myself my first few months in Phoenix. "You in or out? Don't be such a loser."

For about a year, I treaded lightly. I allowed myself to get distracted. That's how it went with music for a long time. One step forward, two steps back. It's like a romantic relationship when your heart says it's the one but your head keeps saying be careful. You pull back when things start to feel right because you don't trust it as much as you should.

As I navigated through town and around the local music scene, there was another consideration that couldn't be avoided: rent. I needed a place to live and money to afford it, so I found a job driving a commercial limousine. The work was pretty stress-free, the money excellent. I wore a suit and a tie, a cute little chauffeur's cap. I didn't have to talk much. I just drove. The rich guys I took around town seemed to enjoy that. After a while, I landed another part-time gig working the front desk at a health club. Once the owner heard I had experience as a driver, he asked if I wanted to be his personal chauffeur and assistant. He enjoyed the idea of being squired around town by a pretty young woman.

I found him a Cadillac Seville stretch limo. Man, this baby was cool. Two-tone, maroon and black. I had the inside redone so it was fresh. I was now his personal assistant and driver. I worked six days a week. He owned the house I lived in, the car I drove. Everything belonged to him. I had one day off a week. I was on call all the time. I felt like he owned me. Suddenly I was so busy, there was no time for music or anything else. I was wiped out all the time.

Despite what I said to myself about wanting to really give music a chance, I seemed to keep falling into this type of arrangement. It was automatic, an obvious self-defense move. If I didn't have time to fully commit to chasing my dream, there was no need to worry about obstacles that got in the way. Life was the obstacle. You can't fail if you're too busy to go for gigs. But the same thing happened every time I squelched the urge to sing by making myself busy with other things. After a year of running myself ragged for this guy, I heard music in my head all the time. I was ready to blow my brains out if I didn't get back to the music.

For the first time in ages, I had money in the bank. My bills were minimal. But I didn't even have time to shop or do anything else that would make me feel better. (That's when you know something is fucked up, right? You finally got bread and you're too busy to spend it.)

I was terribly lonely; I had no friends or social life. Depression took ahold of me again and it wasn't long before I was off the deep end and in despair. The idea of suicide was front and center again; it seemed preferable to the constant back and forth in my head. It had been a while since I drifted into those dark thoughts, but I had not forgotten how. I spent lots of time crying. My friend Gary had stayed in Los Angeles when I split for Phoenix. I was alone, with no friends or support. The familiar and debilitating depression had me again in spades.

Then something bizarre happened. Driving home from work late one night, a fierce, violent desert thunderstorm struck. The kind that barrels across the Sonoran Desert, rolling in so quickly it looks almost fake. Angry, dark clouds swirled in and swallowed the brown, dusty landscape. Flash floods typically follow such storms because the ground is too barren to absorb all the water that drops from the sky.

The windows in my little Dodge Colt were shut tight, but I could still hear a grotesque, screeching sound that I was unable to make out. Rain poured down in sheets, bombarding my car with a steady noisy thud as I tried to drive. It was all I could do to keep the car on the road; it was impossible to see even a few feet in front of my headlights. The sky was soupy and black. Desert on both sides of the road filled with water. Through the din of the storm, there was an awful, anguished sound.

It came from swarms of jack rabbits desperately gathering themselves on the highest patch of sand they could find to keep from drowning. Through the rain and bolts of lightning lighting the sky, I saw hundreds and hundreds of them, piling on top of each other, scrambling to stay afloat, frantically fighting to stay alive, screeching. I have never heard anything as haunting. Those rabbits were literally scared to death. No one could save them.

The sky was dark, but this was an instant burst of clarity. I remember asking myself, what the fuck am I doing? In my day to day life, I was drowning. But unlike those trapped rabbits, there was someone who could save me. Me. Yet I was running from the very thing that could keep me afloat. The life preserver was in front of me. I had refused to grab it. I felt a sense of panic as I sat in my car, rain noisily pouring down, the rabbits squealing for a miracle that never came. I distinctly remember telling myself, okay, Magness, you are either blowing your brains out or quitting that fucking limo job and finding something more manageable. You have to sing. End of story. Forget all the bullshit excuses and distractions. They're killing you. The rabbits are drowning and so are you. Wake up or give up. One or the other, it's up to you.

That storm shook me out of my depression. Within a few weeks, back on dry land, I had a new sense of determination. Then the universe plopped another game-changing experience in front of me that reinforced my new sense of urgency. I scored a ticket to see Etta James and James Brown at the Celebrity Theatre in Phoenix. Martha Reeves and the Vandellas were also on the bill, but this was Etta's show. She snatched it away from her co-stars and made it Etta James Night.

I loved Etta and knew a little about her story. She'd had a hard life, an up-and-down career battling drugs and alcohol for decades. I identified with her troubles and marveled at her singing. This show took place right before she had the first of several career resurgences. She had dropped off the face of the earth musically before I saw her, working as a cashier in Riverside, if you could believe that. The great Etta James handing out change. But on this unforgettable night, she opened the show and could have been charged with felony theft for stealing it from two other legendary acts. She didn't have her own band to back her up, but she still blew them away. I loved her even more for that. She was audacious and had the talent to back it up.

She borrowed Martha Reeves' bass player and drummer. On guitar, she had Leo Nocentelli, a pioneering New Orleans musician who was a founding member of the great funk band, The Meters. Etta ambled out on stage in black stretch pants and a black, stretchy Big Girl top. She wore no jewelry, no bling at all. She flipped her black flats off those swollen feet and started to wail. Barefoot and honest as anyone could be.

The instant she appeared, I sat transfixed. I had been listening to her music for years. Like millions of her fans, I loved her songs and the power and emotion she put into them. Before her first number was over, I bolted from my seat in the nosebleed section and went straight toward the stage. I had to get closer, so I made nice with a security guard to let me sit in one of the empty seats in the front row.

Etta could sing as ornery as she looked. The show had barely started and like the words to one of her signature hits, All I Could Do Was Cry. My cheeks were wet with tears. Like B.B. King and Otis Rush, Etta sang as if this was the last night she would spend on earth. I was consumed. The entire crowd and I were in her hands.

Mesmerized by every expression on her face, her contortions and grimaces as she reached for a note, the deep breaths for air needed to belt out her songs, I knew I was witnessing what a real blues singer put into a performance to make it the truth. To make it her own and sell it to the audience. Every ounce of pain and misery in those songs, every shred of joy and longing, you felt it with her. She transported you to another place. She had the power to pick you up and take you along for the ride. Seeing her made me profoundly aware of how much I would need to give to do this the right way. The way brilliant Etta James did it a few feet in front of me. There were no half measures with her, no half measures with the blues.

Etta's animal, lusty intensity and commitment to craft were a huge gift to me that night. Seeing her enabled me to feel the heartbreak and triumph in her life. The show was more than thirty years ago, but I've been reaching for that mark of hers ever since.

I was on fire to sing again. The spark came during that storm in the desert. Now it was fully ignited after watching one of the greatest singers to ever pick up a microphone. It was on me to find the oxygen to make that spark survive. There had to be a way.

Within days, I gave my notice and quit working for the health club owner, finding a much less-demanding job in a construction company office. My income was cut in half. I lost the car and the house my boss let me live in. I didn't give a shit. It had to be done. For my sanity and for my life. Gradually, I started to feel okay again. Rather than plotting how to end my life, I started going to shows to meet local players. The new job was low-key. The best thing about it was it allowed me time to chase the music again.

Pretty soon, I was getting gigs with small bands here and there, sitting in for lots of jobs. I was learning how to sing because I was doing it, honing my chops and starting to have a good time doing it. Some confidence even crept in. But just as things started going well, I was about to get a lesson about what life was like for a woman singer in a blues universe dominated by men. Lucky for me, the blessing side of being a Magness kicked in while the curse side of the coin took a rest.

Eighteen - Tate

Early during my six years in Phoenix, I had become friendly with a gal who called herself Rollo. She sang in a local blues band and asked me to go to rehearsal with her one day just for fun. She knew I sang a little and the band wound up asking me to sit in on a couple of numbers. It was only later that I realized what a set-up this had been. Rollo wanted out of the group, but she didn't feel right leaving it without a singer. She told the band then and there she was out and suggested I take the gig. The guys thought it was a great idea and just like that, I was a member of Cattanooshoes.

Say that ten times fast and see how it sounds. Cattanooshoes. I didn't dig the name, but it felt good to be part of something again. One of the biggest benefits of being asked to join the band was that I was suddenly getting introduced to a lot of other top-drawer musicians. I began going around town to see who was playing in the local Phoenix blues scene, which was lively and diverse.

Through Cattanooshoes, for instance, I got to know Big Pete Pearson and the Detroit Blues Band. Pete was a local legend who had been singing the blues since he was nine and his grandma let him belt it out in the church choir she ran back in Austin, Texas. Over the years, Big Pete was on bills with legends like John Lee Hooker, Muddy Waters, Ray Charles and B.B. King, to name just a few. But Big Pete was also mercurial. One night, he fired the whole band. Must have been the umpteenth time he did it. His harmonica player at the time was Bob Corritore, who taught himself to play after first hearing Muddy Waters when he was a twelve-year-old kid growing up in Chicago. So Bob and the rest of the guys formed their own group. They called it The Blues Connection. I came to their rehearsals and a few shows. Pretty soon, some of the band members were lobbying Bob to bring me in. He was reluctant. He said I didn't have enough blues material. That pissed me off. It also motivated me. Two weeks later, I showed up at one of their sessions with a two-page list of blues tunes I could sing with as much authority as if I had written them myself. I got the gig.

I was one of two singers in the band. We were a pretty good ensemble. Two of Sam Cooke's former band members, Bob Tate and Emerson Carruthers, played horns. But the work was not steady. It was a big ensemble, which meant a lot of mouths to feed. The band drifted apart when a couple guys returned to their day gigs. So that band gave way to the Mojomatics, a smaller group. Corritore handled most of the bookings; I was the lead singer.

It was a good gig; we started doing well right off the bat because Corritore seemed to know all the club owners in town. We were busy, working a lot. Then I learned that Bob had booked the band to play with my hero, the great Otis Rush. We would open for Otis and play behind him. But the deal Bob cut was for our band to back Otis without me. Bob rallied the other players for the gig first and then told me it was a done deal. For a hundred reasons, I was furious, mostly because it was done behind my back. Corritore had no idea at the time how much Otis meant to me. If Bob had been straight-forward about it, I would have understood. The club had a limited budget. Otis didn't need a singer. He was the singer. Even so, getting sliced out of the picture like that was not cool. I felt betrayed.

I fumed quietly for a while before a good friend of mine, Val, helped me realize I had actually been handed an opportunity. The best way to respond to Corritore, she said, was hit him in the pocketbook. I should start booking all the work, but on my terms. Put him on notice, she said. If he wanted to come to the party, fine. If not, that was cool, too. If that was the case, I'd move on. But that status quo had to change.

Over a period of two weeks, I started doing my own secret work, calling bars and clubs in the area and nailing down more than two months of bookings. With a bunch of commitments locked in, I told Corritore what was up. I spelled it out to him in black and white: the band I got hired to play all over town was now called Janiva Magness and the Mojomatics. I knew the Mojomatics were not as marketable an act without a lead singer and I was the lead singer. Take it or leave it, Bob. It was a brash move on my part, but it worked. Bob was the one pissed off now. I didn't back down or get into a conversation with him. It was the first time in my life as an adult woman that I felt the presence of my father when I conducted my business. I handled it just how my dad would have: balls out, as if I had all the leverage, take it or leave it. Fuck you very much.

I took back the power in my relationship with Corritore and the band. I showed him I would not be taken for granted just because I was a woman. After it happened, I remember thinking, shit, I can't believe I did that. It felt powerful and a little scary at the same time. I don't know where I got the courage to take him on like that. Val's encouragement certainly helped. So did a fierce survival instinct I didn't know I had. But I was channeling my father and after I did that, everything was different.

These were my bookings. The act was locked in. The other players were cool with it. They wanted to work. From here on, Corritore and the band could do whatever they wanted without me and call themselves anything they liked. But if I was on the gig, my name would be out front. That way there could be no mistaking or misrepresenting who was playing. Bob gave up trying to book the band. I was landing all the gigs and doing a good job at it, too. We were kicking ass. So much so that we were named Phoenix Blues Band of the Year in 1986, no small feat given the depth and quality of the local competition at that time.

As satisfying as that was, the absolute best part of hanging around with Big Pete Pearson's Band and being in the Blues Connection was that forged a connection between me and the dear man who probably had more influence on my development as a professional blues artist than anyone I have ever known.

Bob Tate was a kind and generous soul who played tenor, alto and soprano saxophone. He had been musical director for the legendary soul singer Sam Cooke until Sam was murdered in a Los Angeles motel shooting in 1964 when he was just thirty-three. The good-natured Tate and I became tight from the start. He took me under his wing because he liked me. He was a natural mentor to a lot of up and coming musicians. He was charitable in sharing his legendary knowledge of music, composing, arranging, band politics and life. We talked on the phone for hours at a time. He walked me through what to do and not do in a band. What to do and not do as a woman in a band, which was a different trip altogether. The Blues Connection disbanded and Tate did not join the Mojomatics, but his wise counsel was invaluable to me.

Tate told me it didn't matter what I did or how I acted. All the guys in the band were going to want to fuck me as a show of power, testosterone or who knew what. He was emphatic: I should never sleep with any of the band members. Solid advice.

No matter what, he said, they're gonna mess with you because you're a woman. He'd use Aretha Franklin and Sarah Vaughan as examples. If the band wasn't playing what she needed, Aretha would show them the part on the piano so there would be no question. The same with Sarah Vaughan. Those ladies knew what they wanted and how to get it. They sure as hell didn't take any shit. Musicians they worked with had no choice but to treat them with respect because those women had full command of their instrument. They knew how to lead a band so it fit what they wanted to accomplish.

You've got to have full command of your instrument and your bandstand, Tate told me. Be hard as nails. If they don't give you what you want, get rid of them; find someone who will.

Don't let them determine the keys you sing in because they're only going to make it comfortable for them, not you. And for God sakes, don't let them count the songs off for you! That's your job. You're running the band; they need to know it loud and clear.

They ain't gonna make it comfortable for you and you got the only instrument that ain't going to the shop, he'd say. If you ruin your voice, that's it. Game over. There's no band without you.

Tate helped me understand all these things when I was auditioning new cats for the band, which I now felt empowered enough to do. Tate always called them cats. I should look for cats who would help me rise up, not the kind of cat who would pull me down and step on my throat while he crawled over me. That's a common occurrence in the music business. Fuck that cat, Tate said. It doesn't matter how good he plays; you don't need him.

He mentored me like this from around 1981 to 1986. It was manna from heaven. God, what a gift. I needed it, too. I wasn't even 30 yet, and he was like a father looking out for his daughter. It was a graduate degree in how to survive in a band and run it as a business.

People thought there must be something romantic between us, but that was never the case. This was a sacred relationship to me, much more powerful than sex between an old man and a young woman. I loved Tate. So many people did. He mentored a lot of young artists right up to his death in 1993 at the way too young age of 61. He had been sick a lot at the end, suffering from diabetes and a host of related ailments. I owe that sweet, wise man more than I can even say.

Tate was a great judge of talent, too. His father owned a nightclub in South Phoenix. When Tate was growing up, Duke Ellington and all those cats stayed at his house. He got to know every one of them. Tate later hired the legendary Texas blues star Guitar Shorty right off the farm. Sam Cooke and Tate pulled up in their bus to where Shorty lived. He came out and hopped on, wearing no shoes, a pair of coveralls and holding his guitar with no case for it! Shorty played like someone twice his age. When Tate was Sam Cooke's musical director, he hired Lou Rawls to sing background. That's how Rawls got his start. Tate was one cat who knew his shit. He knew talent.

When Tate talked, I paid attention. If he thought I was good—and he told me all the time that I was—maybe I could start to believe it myself. He did so much to build up my confidence as an artist. After six years in Phoenix, I felt it was time to branch out again and push myself. I was still insecure about a lot, but my time in Phoenix and Tate's mentoring helped me start to get comfortable with the idea that I really was a legitimate singer. I could do this. Shit, I was doing this. It was time to give it another try in Los Angeles, where my career and my life would soon be turned upside down.

Nineteen - God's Time

The universe always seems to have its own plans and timetable. Over my years in recovery and therapy, I have learned that life happens on God's time, not mine. No matter how hard I push things, I don't always get what I want when I want it. Things tend to work out okay, but on their own schedule. God doesn't check with me so we can synchronize our watches. I have my own timeline and She does, too. Yes, I said She because that is what works for me now. Funny how that works. It can be extremely frustrating, but there is no use denying or fighting it. Once I made my mind up to leave Phoenix and head back to Los Angeles, God and the universe said "Not so fast, young lady. Slow down."

Less than two weeks before I was to move to the Coast, my drummer and I were in my Dodge Colt, at a Tucson traffic light. It was pouring rain again when some guy and his car hydroplaned and plowed into us. It was the last time I was ever in a moving vehicle without a seatbelt on. I didn't think or care about things like that at the time. Both my drummer and I crashed into the windshield and lost consciousness. We were hurt pretty bad. Over the next six months or so, as I was recovering, I suddenly had a lot of time to think about where I wanted my career to go. I couldn't do much more than lie in bed and heal. And think.

I had been making a living with my singing before the accident, but the crash was a big setback that helped put me back in my customary state of depression. Sometimes I was clean and sober, sometimes I wasn't. Even then, I found it hard to face everything that had happened to me. I needed a way to escape and when the darkness came over me. I turned to my old, trusted friends for relief; I got loaded on drugs and alcohol.

When I finally felt up to it, I got in the car and made the drive to Los Angeles. I was no longer a kid trying to break into the Southern California music scene, but I was compelled to try.

Now that I was back in L.A., not a whole lot was happening. I needed a day job, so I found one at a grocery store. I also did a few local gigs here and there. The pace was slow, but I was getting by. Then I read a front-page article in the Sunday newspaper that changed everything.

I rarely read newspapers, but on this Sunday morning, something made me get up early to go out and pick up the Los Angeles Times. The fat weekend edition of the newspaper was laid out in front of me as I rolled a joint for some early morning medication. My eye was drawn immediately to a big story on the front page. The date was Feb. 28, 1988. The article was about a mother who had given up her child for adoption. Later, she tried to find out how the little boy was faring and she learned that her son was beaten to death by his adoptive mother. It was a heartbreaking story, eventually turned into a book and television movie after the article led to the killer's prosecution. Incredibly, the woman who had adopted and killed the boy lived in my old neighborhood in Birchwood, MN. When I was a young girl, some of us neighborhood kids used to jump over the retaining wall outside the woman's house to steal her rhubarb. I could not believe what I was reading. I was stunned by the birth mother's heartache over what happened to her child after not knowing anything about his situation for so long. The story landed on me like a bomb. It could not have hit any closer to home.

By the time I finished reading, my heart was thumping out of my chest. My eyes were dripping with tears. Where was the baby girl I gave up? Was she alive? Was she healthy? Did her adoptive parents love her? Did the people in her life treat her well? Does she have friends? Is she happy? What does she look like? I had no idea about any of it, for God's sake. I was suddenly down on my knees weeping uncontrollably. I began to scream at God like a crazy woman. It's not as if I didn't think about what had happened to Pearl since giving her up for adoption. I never stopped thinking about her. Especially around holidays. Every Christmas, Easter and New Year's. Every Thanksgiving, every birthday, every Halloween. I cried my eyes out for her, wondering whether she was okay. But this article in the LA Times made my fears more visceral. I felt them in my gut. I had to find out how things turned out for her after I said goodbye.

I was on the floor, alone in my apartment, buzzed, screaming at God. All right, you Son of a Bitch, if you want me to get sober again, prove to me that she's OK. Show me, you fucker, and then I'll try. I'll give sobriety another shot, damn it, but I need proof my daughter is OK. I said this out loud, head in my hands, crying, snot and tears running down my face. I was seething with anger. At myself. At God. At the world. I was terrified about what had become of Pearl and the fact that I had no idea whether she was even alive.

It took a week for the name of the lawyer hired by the family who adopted Pearl to float up from my subconscious. When I say float up, that is exactly what I mean. I had buried the details from that chapter of my life in booze, alcohol and sorrow for nearly sixteen years. When I finally remembered the lawyer's name, I dialed directory assistance and asked for Don Beneke in Pocahontas, Iowa. I don't know what I expected. When the operator said, "Home or office, dear?" I could not believe it.

I took a deep breath and nervously dialed his office. I got an answering machine and left a message. Just my name and number. I didn't say why I was calling. My stomach was churning. What would I learn if he called back? The last time Beneke and I had communicated was a few years after I gave up Pearl for adoption, after he sent me a letter saying she was fine.

I didn't handle it well. He reached out to me from the kindness of his heart, but in my letter back, I bit off his head. The last thing on earth I wanted to be reminded of was that I was such a fuckup I could not raise my own child. That I had to give away my own flesh and blood. I resented him for taking me there. I acted like a monster to Beneke when all he ever did was what I asked him to do. He was just being kind with a follow-up note to reassure me that my daughter was fine. Now I had called him back to ask a huge favor. I kept repeating in my head all the awful things I said in my letter. But kind people are kind because that's who they are. The following Monday, he returned my call.

He was so courteous. Of course he remembered me, he said. I apologized for my angry letter, confessing how sorry I was to have lashed out at him. I was sick at the time, I started to tell him, but he cut me off. You don't have to explain, he reassured me. I understand. Better still, he eased my fears by telling me once again that Pearl was well. She lived in a small Iowa farm town. She was her high school valedictorian and would be graduating soon. He asked how I was doing. Was I OK? He wanted to know if I was holding up after everything that happened. I was trembling, trying to catch my breath. Somehow, I spit out the words to ask for another favor. If I wrote a letter to my daughter's adoptive parents and sent it to him, would he make sure they got it? After all these years, I felt an overpowering need to explain to Pearl why I was not able to keep her.

The last thing I wanted was to upset anything in her life or with her family, but I needed my daughter to understand that I had not callously abandoned her. I needed to tell her how it broke my heart to let her go, but that I did it to save her. I needed her to know I gave her away because I loved her and still did. I wanted her to be raised by someone who could provide her with the love, stability and sanity I could never hope to provide. I also wanted to let her parents know that if they required any kind of family tree or medical history about her, I would happily provide it. But the real reason was to tell Pearl I never stopped loving or thinking about her.

Write your letter, Beneke told me. He would deliver it when the time was right. It was a difficult letter to compose. I must have started it and torn it up ten times because the right words would not come. Finally, I got it done and sent it to him, not knowing if anything would come of it. A short time later, I received a letter from Pearl's mother. My hands trembled as I opened it.

"The world is a tough place," her mother wrote. "If there is someone out there with real love for our daughter, my husband and I don't want to deprive her of it." It was an incredibly loving, brave gesture. I am forever indebted to my daughter's adoptive parents.

Soon, with their permission, my daughter and I started exchanging phone calls and letters. I'll never forget the day I came home and found a message from her on my answering machine. It was right before Christmas. Her voice sounded like mine. It was like hearing a younger version of me on the tape. Her name wasn't Pearl Corrina anymore, but that didn't matter. Hearing her speak made my heart swell. I must have played that voicemail a hundred times just to soak in the sound of her voice.

She and I exchanged a lot of letters and phone calls, a feeling out process of getting to know one another gradually after all those years apart with no information or contact. It seemed like she had as many questions and doubts as I did. I desperately wanted to see her, but it took time for us both to get to the point where we felt ready. We finally met face-to-face in June of 1991, the day she graduated from high school. I was 33. She was 17. We had been apart for all but the first few months of her life. We bonded quickly and love each other very much. With a lot of help from people in recovery and an extraordinary therapist, I quit drinking and getting high the same year my daughter and I reconnected. You can say I kept my word to God. I honored the promise I made on that stoned Sunday morning to get clean and sober if I knew my daughter was safe. This time it stuck. I am still clean and sober today, more than twenty-five years later. My recovery is something that gives me a tremendous sense of gratitude. There is nothing in my life more important to me because I cannot have a life without being clean. It's not easy sometimes. I have to work at it. I go to meetings, write, try to take good care of myself, practice yoga for flexibility and peace of mind. I rely on friends and my therapist. Above all else, I try to stay brutally honest with myself and have an open heart as much as possible. I practice the art of forgiveness because that is the foundation of everything for me. I work to forgive other people, my parents and siblings, myself, the universe, God. It takes energy and effort, but it's worth it. It is more than worth it. Like air or water, I can't live without it.

My sobriety started for a reason I'm not sure I will ever understand. I went out one Sunday morning with the unusual idea of wanting to pick up a newspaper, and found that story about an adopted child. It led to my daughter and my sobriety promise to God. If those aren't miracles, I don't know the meaning of the word.

When all this was going on, I was playing with some L.A. bands and doing solo gigs here and there, but I still needed my job at the Santa Monica food co-op to pay the bills. When I began working there, they had me unloading trucks and stocking shelves. Eventually, I was moved to night manager.

My emotions were wildly up and down. So much was happening. I would play a gig, feel pretty good about it, then get overcome with despair because, well, because I worked in a grocery store and was convinced I was trapped. I finally volunteered to work in the walk-in freezer because I could be alone for much of my shift, with no need to interact with anyone. I spent a lot of my time inside that freezer, weeping to myself, oblivious to the cold and the rest of the world.

A couple months after finding Pearl, a girlfriend called me up with some information that turned out to be another gift from God. Debbie Davies, a dear friend who was playing with blues guitar god Albert Collins, told me Jimmy Buffett was looking to put together an all-female blues band. It would back up his harmonica player and open for Buffett's upcoming summer tour. Buffett was looking for a lead singer; Debbie said I should go for it. I didn't hesitate.

I soon heard via the gossip mill that Buffett wanted someone quite a bit younger than me. My chances didn't look promising. But Greg Taylor, aka "Fingers" and Buffett's harmonica player, was in my corner. He knew what I sounded like. He wanted me in the band. Debbie gave me a strong recommendation, too, which got Buffett's attention. Fingers, bless his heart, had a plan.

I was booked one night to play at My Place, an L.A. club on Wilshire Boulevard. Fingers came to town and got Buffett to attend the show. We're going to jam it down Buffett's throat and make it impossible for him to say no, Fingers told me. So that's what we did. Fingers and I played a couple of tunes. We killed it. Fingers was down on his knees, wailing on his harp. I was on my back singing like it was my last night on earth. The audience hollered its approval. The place went nuts. That night turned out to be a proving ground for me. I was so pissed off about Buffett's snub that I held nothing back. To sing the blues, you have to feel the emotion in whatever you're trying to get across. I don't think it was possible to have felt it any more than I did that night.

When the show was over, Fingers and I walked through the club to thank people for coming. I was drained. When we got to Buffett's table, I told him how much I appreciated him taking time from his busy schedule to be there. "Great show," he told me. "Whaddya got going week after next? You want to come to New Orleans and open for my band?"

I said yes so fast I'm not sure my lips moved. I was afraid he might change his mind.

Good. You got the gig, he told me. That might have been the best news I had ever heard. As things turned out, 1991, was a watershed year for me. I miraculously reunited with my daughter. Just as miraculously, I got sober again. So far, it's sticking. And I landed the Buffett gig as lead singer in his opening act. These were tremendous blessings. I was grateful for each one. I knew getting sober was the key to all of it. I never could have been focused enough to land that gig had I still been drinking. It always blows my mind how one decision or action—good or bad—can trigger profound changes in your life. Going out to get the newspaper that Sunday morning in Los Angeles, and getting down on my knees to make a bargain with God, led to so many wonderful places.

Buffett was a huge star with a deeply devoted following. We played all over the country, a three-month tour at big venues with thousands of people who loved Jimmy and the Parrothead culture surrounding his shows. Some of the stadium gigs drew 25,000 fans. Singing in front of that many people was heady stuff. I couldn't believe how big the crowds were. Turns out we were the third highest grossing tour that summer, behind only the Grateful Dead and Guns N' Roses. The whole adventure was a gas, without question one of the biggest and most validating breaks of my career. It was hard work, but I loved every minute of it. The band Buffett put together to open his shows was well received. My confidence as a singer was growing.

As the tour moved through the Midwest, there was some business I felt compelled to pursue during our stop in St. Louis. I had not been there in years. I got in the day before the show, checked into my hotel and couldn't stop reflecting on the dark old lake house we lived in when my mother took her life. It was driving me nuts. All I could think about was everything that went wrong there. I played the scenes in my head again and again. I'm not sure why, but I had to see that house of horrors again. The feeling would not go away, I finally took a taxi to the address, walked up and knocked on the door.

A young man answered, asking if he could help me. Yes, I said. I was in town on business and used to live there. I realize this is a little odd, I said, but would you mind if I took a look around for old time's sake? He let me in and we walked through the rooms while making idle conversation. He was very nice. I told him why I was in town, that I was a singer in a band opening for Jimmy Buffett. Turned out he was a big Buffett fan and a Parrothead, so we became fast friends. As we walked through the house, with my eyes darting everywhere and the memories flooding in, he began asking me questions. When did I live there? How many people were in my family? What did my parents do? Innocent questions, but not to me. He told me weird things happened in that house all the time, as if it were haunted or something. That's when I told him my mom died there, that she killed herself in the garage, and that my nephew drowned in the backyard pool.

"That was you?" he said in disbelief. From neighbors, he had heard stories about bad things occurring in that house. The stories were unsettling; now he had living proof they were true. Yes, I told him, that was me and my crazy family. When we got to the backyard, I looked at the pool. It was empty, down for repairs, which made me feel a little sense of relief. Seeing water in it would have been too much.

Our conversation was getting a little too weird for him, I could tell, so I said thanks and asked if he wanted tickets for the Buffet show. He was thrilled. I said I'd leave them at the door in his name. I was as anxious to leave as he was for me to go. I lived in that dark little house during what was probably the single most traumatic year of my life. It felt surreal to be back in it so many years later, in town to open for one of the biggest acts in the music business. It's like the classic song Truckin' by the Grateful Dead: Sometimes the light's all shinin' on me. Other times I can barely see. Lately it occurs to me, what a long, strange trip it's been. No shit!

After the tour, by the time I got home, it was the same old sorry story. I spent every cent of the $10,000 I got paid opening for Buffett. It was all gone in a heartbeat. But this time, it wasn't pissed away on booze or drugs. The money was poured into a battle that wound up uniting me with my siblings in a way that had not happened before or since.

Twenty - Insurance Scam

There was one more piece of business to attend to when I was in St. Louis for the Buffett show. Like the visit to my old house, it took me back to a darker and more frightening time in my life. This tale, which got its start in the days and weeks immediately following my father's suicide in 1973, brought my siblings and me together for a common purpose: We were united and going after the woman our dad married after Mom died , because the new wife had methodically stolen insurance money that was supposed to be ours. It was money our dad had intended us to receive if anything happened to him.

Proving we were right took years, but a judge eventually agreed with everything we claimed. During my stop in St. Louis for the Buffett tour, I was deposed for several hours and told our lawyer everything I knew about the case.

Even though I was so young when my father took his life, I'd been around the block enough times to realize there was something suspicious about his death. I had met Betty a few times before my dad died and never liked her. I'm sure some of this had to do with the fact that my mother was no longer alive and here was some other woman who moved in to marry my father and take Mom's place. I never could wrap my head around the idea of my dad being with her, but my dislike of Betty was about more than resenting her for obvious reasons. From the start, she struck me as a conniver and a schemer. She came across as cold, calculating and selfish. Later, we learned for sure that she was all that and much worse. She was patently dishonest and a thief.

My suspicions were first aroused because I was never able to understand how my dad could have died alone in his car inside the garage when he was leaning on the horn and Betty's dogs were barking while his life slipped away. My sister Sara and I listened to that tape recording he made when he took his life. We went down to the police department and they played it for us. You could hear the horn blaring. Betty's two poodles were yelping. There's no way she couldn't have heard all that racket. I don't think she killed him, but I am pretty sure she could have saved him had she wanted to. She had to have known he was out there. I will always believe she chose to look the other way and let him die. Then she had the gall and ice-cold heart to tell Carson, who was 8 at the time, to go out in the garage to get his shoes, knowing what this little boy would find once he went out there. You'd have to be a pretty rotten person to do that. You'd have to be Betty.

I know it didn't take my dad long to realize he'd made a mistake in marrying her; he had told us as much. My sister and brothers and I all knew he had a girlfriend while he was married to Betty. Betty found out too, if she hadn't known earlier, when the woman, whose name was Liz, showed up at our dad's funeral. My dad was in his early 50's when he died. Liz was in her late 20s and beautiful. Betty must have been furious when she realized my dad was with someone else. It wasn't long after that Betty started telling people that my dad had disowned us kids and left us nothing; we all knew that was not true.

We knew because Dad was a fanatic about life insurance. He spent more than twenty years working for the John Hancock Mutual Life Insurance Company and told us kids time and again that life insurance was essential for security and peace of mind for you and your family. It was something he harped on. He told me a number of times that he took out big policies on his life so if he died, the kids would be OK, they would be taken care of financially.

Rather than disowning his kids, as Betty had claimed, Dad had made peace with all of us before he died. He and I had that heartfelt phone conversation where we said we were tired of fighting and loved each other. He also went to visit Jimmie and Sara several times each before his death. Dad in fact visited Jimmie twice with Liz in the six months before he killed himself. Jimmie was living on a farm in North Dakota at the time with his second wife and a couple of kids. He and my dad had been estranged for years before those visits. I know it meant a lot to Jimmie and to my dad that they were finally talking again and behaving like family who cared about one another.

"My father and I became friends about six months before he died," Jimmie said in a letter he wrote in 1988 to our lawyers in the fraud case we filed against Betty. "Years of bitterness and intolerance and false pride fell away and we were able to talk to each other and be real people. We forgave each other for the harm we had done. I know I had harmed him far more than he had hurt me . . . I know that he loved us all, even me, and that he did not disinherit us. Betty used that to steal our insurance money because it was definitely easy for his peers to believe."

Dad also went to visit Sara, who was living in Minnesota with her husband and kids. She is still married to the same man and lives in the same town. When he saw Sara a few months before he died, Dad confided in her that he and Carson got the short end of the stick in his relationship with Betty. She had her own kids from an earlier marriage which ended when her husband died and left her a fair amount of money. Dad said he and Carson were after thoughts to Betty, but they at least had a place to live and some financial stability. He also let Sara know that he had taken out $500,000 in life insurance so the kids could split it five ways and get $100,000 each if he died. Sara let Dad know she wasn't interested in talking about his death or life insurance, but each time she tried to change the subject he insisted he wanted all the kids to know where things stood, just in case.

When we saw Betty at the funeral, we didn't say much to her. She seemed to keep her distance from us; we did the same with her. But a few weeks later, she called Sara and asked if she could send 8-year-old Carson to live with Sara. About two months later, she gave a truck driver she knew $100, put Caron's clothes in a garbage bag and asked the driver to drop him off at Sara's, which he did. Turns out, Carson started that trip to Sara's three days after Betty got the insurance money meant for us kids. We proved it in court and later again when an appellate judge court also ruled in our favor after Betty fought the original court order. But when it came to the next step, finding the money we would need to hire a forensic accountant who could prove what Betty actually did with the money she stole from us so we could recover at least some of it, we were broke. We finally had no choice but to let the case drop. I had put $10,000 of my own money from the Buffett tour into fighting that woman, but in the end, she got what she wanted. Our fucking money, money our dad paid premiums for so we would have something when he died. At least we got the satisfaction of exposing her for who and what she was. I'm not sure she cared as long as she didn't have to pay, but we felt like we accomplished something.

In the weeks following my dad's funeral, Sara began calling Betty to see if he had left anything for the kids that Sara could come and get. Among other things, Sara mentioned that she knew dad had several shotguns and other firearms he had promised to my brothers. Betty said there was nothing, insisting that my dad had disowned his kids and hadn't wanted to have anything to do with us. Sara called several times more because she knew that was a lie. Betty finally threatened Sara, telling her that if she came down and caused trouble, Betty would go to court and get a restraining order against any of us kids who were causing her problems.

None of us was in a position to take on Betty. We couldn't afford to hire a lawyer or investigator to find out what happened. We eventually called a colleague of our dad's from John Hancock, someone who was also his friend, and asked if he would look into whether my dad had any insurance coverage. The "friend" called back Sara a few days later. He said he was sorry, but Dad had nothing. No policies, no coverage, not a dime for any of us.

By 1978, Sara had found religion and moved on with her life. She decided to bury the whole mess along with her suspicions. She still had serious doubts about Betty and her role in my father's death. She had even gotten in touch with one of the cops who had come to Betty's house to investigate after my dad was found dead in his car. The officer told Sara he had a sneaking suspicion that something didn't add up, but he couldn't prove it. Nothing was done. As far as Sara and her new life were concerned, the whole sorry episode was best left in the past. Over the years, we would talk about it from time to time. I pretty much agreed with Sara, telling my other siblings we should just forget the whole thing and get on with our lives. Our suspicions were just that, suspicions, and if we couldn't prove them we might as well let them go. It hurt to give up the fight. But none of us kids saw any way to get anywhere with our cause.

That's how things remained until the fall of 1984, eleven years after my dad's death. All of the sudden, out of nowhere, someone from John Hancock's main office in Boston called Sara. The woman was looking for Carson. One of the checks the company had sent to him came back in the mail. One of the checks? Excuse me, my sister said into the phone.

Turns out, dad's surviving offspring were entitled to company survivor's benefits as part of his time working for John Hancock. My siblings and I had been entitled to monthly payments until we turned 23. Now we had our smoking gun. With concrete evidence, I thought it was a worthwhile use of my Buffett money to hire a lawyer and go after Betty.

According to the facts established in our lawsuit and agreed to by the Missouri Court of Appeals in a 1992 ruling, Betty forged our signatures, using the money that was rightfully ours however she saw fit. Under oath in court, Betty testified that she didn't realize what she was doing. She had been so traumatized over her husband's death; she was not in full control of her faculties. I thought the judge was going to smack her, he was so frustrated with her act. Everyone in the courtroom knew she was lying.

The company survivor's benefits were small potatoes compared to my dad's own personal life insurance policy. The company benefits paid to Betty came to about $34,000 during the years she was forging our signatures and stealing the money. Dad's personal life policy paid her a half million dollars; we never saw a penny of it. And we all knew suicide would void payment on a life insurance policy, but my dad's death was never officially ruled a suicide. The coroner said it was accidental death by carbon monoxide poisoning.

Betty is dead now. Needless to say, none of us kids shed a tear when we heard that news.

Once I was in Los Angeles again after the Buffett tour, I tried getting my job back at the food co-op, but they had given my spot to someone else. I couldn't blame them. I left to pursue the biggest, most exciting opportunity of my career; they had a business to run. Once again, as the litigation against Betty was playing out, I scrambled to find something to bring in some dough. I did a number of odd jobs, working as a movie extra for a while, playing gigs here and there. Then one night, I decided to go to a club not far from where I lived to hear some live music. It was a place I went to every now and then, and I had a lot of friends there. On this particular evening, I met the good man who would become my next musical partner and more.

Twenty-One - Billie's Blues

Getting married was never anything I wanted to do. Didn't believe in it. Never thought I would find anybody to trust enough or tolerate spending that much time with. My views changed after meeting Jeff Turmes at an infamous L.A. night spot called the King King. He is a wildly talented songwriter and musician.

We actually met for the first time shortly after I moved to Los Angeles. I was suffering my second relapse at the time, drinking and getting high, singing here and there locally, trying to keep at least one hand in the music. I was living with a musician named Steve Marsh, who spent more than twenty years playing saxophone in Lyle Lovett's Large Band. Steve and I had met in Phoenix; I hired him for my then band, the Mojomatics. We got pretty serious when he eventually followed me out to L.A and stayed together more than six years.

When I met Jeff, it was love at first sight. I knew it. And then there were those shoes: his oxblood wing tips alone got me thinking he must have been made for me. They were the same kind my dad wore, dark red with a lot of style. I felt hypnotized by Jeff's charm and good looks. I turned out to be right, but I wasn't about to step out on Steve. I've been a lot of things in my life, but a cheater was never one of them. So Jeff and I became musical pals. We would see each other around the L.A. scene, even getting together and doing some songwriting.

There was such an intensity between us that eventually some of our mutual friends began to tease us. I guess the attraction was difficult to hide, or maybe it was just a matter of us both eventually getting tired of pretending. Jeff was working with the James Harman Band, touring all the time. He'd write me friendly, slightly off-color notes and postcards from the road, and I saved every one of them.

Truth was, a distance had developed between Steve and me, in part, because I got sober again. That can draw two people together or make it glaringly clear that it's time to part ways. About eighteen months into my new-found sobriety, it became obvious to both of us that our relationship had run its course. On New Year's Eve, I told Steve we were done. It wasn't great timing when you are trying to celebrate the New Year, but having known sometime that we were done, I had to end it when we were face to face in the same city. To my mind, there isn't anything lonelier than being with someone after it's over and not having the nerve to face the truth.

In the middle of all this, I was scheduled to housesit for a musician friend and his two dogs in Van Nuys, Ca., while he was on tour with Eartha Kitt. Late one night, 4:31 a.m. to be precise, the Northridge Earthquake struck L.A. Magnitude of 6.7. The San Fernando Valley was the hardest hit.

One of the dogs I was babysitting for was a black lab mix named Lilly who was incredibly smart. She could open doors, undo latches and practically pick a lock. I woke out of a dead sleep, naked and face down on the bed, with Lilly spread eagle on my back and the whole house rattling. Glass broke; bricks, boards and everything else seemed to be flying. I knew this was a bad quake. It seemed to go on forever. I actually heard houses sliding off their foundations around me as I lay there pinned to the bed by the dog in the dark.

Things eventually stopped shaking and Lilly got off me. Dust and debris were everywhere. I scrambled for my glasses, shoes and clothing, but I quickly came to realize that I was trapped in the room because part of the roof and the fireplace had caved in. It took me the better part of an hour to dig my way out in the dark to see what remained of my friend's place. It was crumbled, broken glass and tipped furniture everywhere. The other dog, an older German Shepard boy who was deaf and nearly blind, hadn't moved a muscle during the whole ordeal. He was glued to the floor. I felt as if I was in shock from the violent turmoil of it all, figuring the dogs were as well. I crawled out of there with the dogs, eventually getting through to my friend in New York City so I could let him know what happened and tell him his dogs were okay. The house was trashed, so I had to get out of there, taking the pooches to my place for the time being, until my friend came back from tour.

It was stressful times, to say the least. Steve had not moved out of the place we shared; now I was hanging out there with two traumatized dogs and my cat, who I sequestered in the bedroom. It felt like living in a bad sitcom. Finally, my friend came home and gathered his dogs. Steve found his own place. I could finally start a new chapter.

Pretty soon, Jeff and I started dating. After meeting him at the King King on that Monday night a while back, I'd been unable to get him out of my mind. Steve Marsh used to tell me he was worried "some blues guy is gonna come along and steal you." Turns out, that's exactly how it looked. But we all know you can't be stolen if you don't want to be, right?

Shortly after we started seeing each other for real, Jeff quit the Harman band and I hired him to play with me. A little more than a year later, when I was 38, we got married on the Santa Monica pier. It was the cheapest place in town, with a gorgeously funky restored carousel from the 1920s that I loved.

We were very much in love, but our early years together were tough. I was still dealing pretty regularly with my PTSD. When we had a fight or I was on the brink of some kind of emotional meltdown, I would sometimes retreat to the back of our closet, unable to bring myself to come out. It was like I was a little girl again hiding from my dad and his belt. If I wanted more protection, I'd move our bed, wedging myself between it and the wall as tightly as possible. My back would be to the wall, so I could see someone coming but no one could get to me. I'm sure it was the emotional intensity of some of the conflicts I had with Jeff that set me off. I could usually see the trouble coming. PTSD sort of keeps you on high alert to meltdowns at all times. But I was still overwhelmed and immobilized when the panic hit. Jeff had to wonder what the hell he got when he married me, but as difficult as it may be to comprehend, I had no control over it. Not back then, at least.

About a year into the marriage, I realized I needed to raise the white flag and get a real job. There wasn't enough singing work around town for me to make ends meet. I found a position as a production manager for a composer who was pretty successful working in television and film. I didn't want it. Taking that kind of gig would mean I had given up again on my own music. I hated the idea. It felt like defeat, as if I was crawling inside a box never to get out to do what I loved. In the music business, you are either a player or you're not. You can't be a singer and an office worker. I needed work, though, so I took the job. Eventually, one more time, the music somehow broke through and found its way to me.

It took a while, though. I spent about five years in that gig working for Bill Bodine Music. Bill and I became close friends; during the time I spent with him, and a long time afterwards. There was such a shit ton of work, we were always busy and constantly under pressure. It finally became unmanageable, with Bill having two "episodes" with his heart that landed him in the hospital. The first was during a period of time when we were racing to fulfill our contractual obligations for a rash of Honda TV commercials, a weekly TV series and some repeat episodes of Judge Judy. We were under the gun, with a schedule that was busier than we could handle. Busy enough that Bill actually pulled together a small stable of composers helping him churn out the music because he couldn't get to it all.

When he was in the hospital, things were moving so quickly we could have suffered a setback and lost a lot of money and client base, but somehow I fired into another gear. I just stepped up to the plate and handled it. I'm not bragging. It's a reflection of the work ethic that was somehow instilled in me even in my toxic, dysfunctional household. When the work gets crazy, you don't run or consider failure as an option. You step up and manage things. Period. I know that may sound crazy, considering how my parents died when things got too much for them to handle. But I don't walk away from a challenge. I take pride in the fact that when the bombs start to fall, I am the person you want in the foxhole with you. I will figure out a way to get through that shit. I suppose it's just the way I'm put together; I'm not one to let things slide or fall apart.

In the end, even with Bill's health issues and all the disruptions they caused, the company never experienced more than a small bump in the day-to-day routine. I contacted all the clients, assuring them everything was on schedule, telling them Bill was fine. I controlled the flow of information and we met all our deadlines. We did it as a team: me, Bill, his amazing wife Beth, and the small group of composers working with is.

When Bill was well enough to come home, he was blown away at what got done in his absence. It moved our relationship to another, deeper level of trust. He knew I had his back. He was from a blue-collar background in Youngstown, OH, so he had his own brand of tough. That's one of the principal reasons we were such a strong team. Ohio solid, Detroit badass. Now he knew I wouldn't bail when the shit hit the fan. That meant everything to him; it was the same for me and how I felt about Bill.

When he turned fifty, Bill threw himself a huge birthday party. All his composer friends and heavy L.A. session players and singers came to celebrate with him. There were about two hundred people at a swank, catered affair at his home in Pacific

Palisades. A small jazz ensemble performed. It was perfect. The party was bulging with serious musical talent.

Different artists took turns sitting in with the trio, wowing the guests with their skills. After Bill had a few glasses of wine, he started in on me, bugging me to sing. That was the last thing in the world I wanted to do with so many great artists in the room. I didn't want to go to the party in the first place because I knew it would probably come down to him poking at me to sing. What if I sucked? But he would not let it go. I was so self-conscious. If I tanked, I'd be embarrassed in front of everyone. Those Magness demons got real busy inside my head. I was the production manager. That meant I ran the business, paid the bills, managed the schedule, handled the union contracts — whatever needed to be done. I was not the talent. I knew my place. Bill kept at it, though, and Bill was my boss. I finally said 'Fuck it.' I put my anxiety and other reservations aside, and told Jon, the piano player, what I wanted to do.

Jeff was at the party with me; he had my back, smiling and encouraging me because he knew I would own the room once I opened my mouth. I told the piano player to play "Billie's Blues," a medium-tempo 12-bar blues that is one of my favorite Billie Holiday numbers. I started counting off the tune and humming a little of it, just like I did when I led my own band.

"Well I love my man; tell the world I do, you know I love my man, tell the world I do, but when he mistreats me, it makes me feel so blue."

Like a scene in a movie, everyone at the party instantly stopped talking and chattering. A few bars into the song, the room fell silent, save for me and the tight ensemble. There was no microphone, but I didn't need one. I remember feeling like people were staring at me with who-the-fuck-is-that looks on their faces and their jaws dropping. A lot of them knew me from the office side of the house, but had no idea I could sing. Not like that, anyway.

When I finished, Bill was on his feet screaming, "Yeaaah! Do another!" Everyone joined in yelling for more. And they were shouting at Bill. Man, what the fuck, Bill? Where you been hiding this girl? I was kind of digging it by that time, so I did another song and people went wild with applause. The infamous Sid Page, a wickedly talented violin player who performed with Sly and the Family Stone's band and Dan Hicks and His Hot Licks and tons of sessions, jumped up with his violin and said, "I wanna jam with you." People were worked up and knocked out. Their applause and appreciation knocked me out, too.

To me, it was exhilarating and excruciating at once. My hands were shaking and my insides felt like I swallowed a stick of dynamite. I looked Jeff's way and said with a stern tone, "Fifteen minutes and we're out of here. He knew we both needed outta there."

Jeff and I had been playing together for a while by that time. In the end, we wound up working together for about six years. We made a living, had fun and got plenty of work. We were blessed with having some incredibly talented friends. People like guitar legends Kid Ramos, Kirk Fletcher, Enrico Crivellaro, Junior Watson. Then some excellent drummers like Ed Mann and Dave Kida and a whole bunch of other super talented players. Together, we put out a CD of Jeff's songs on our own label, Fathead Records, in 1997. It was called It Takes One To Know One. Jeff never wanted to do it. I really had to sell him on the idea and drag him through the process. He didn't think anyone would be interested in hearing his songs. I disagreed. Jeff was always writing, putting together lyrics and music that amazed me and anyone who heard them. I insisted that his songs should be recorded. I loved singing them. He had been writing since high school, but before the CD, the only thing he did with his tunes was put them on cassette tapes and give them to very appreciative friends. He wasn't the least bit driven or ambitious, but I kept pushing for us to put out a record. We'd go round and round about it constantly.

We gotta make a record, I'd say. Come on.

We have no money to make a record, he'd tell me.

We'll figure it out, I'd shoot back.

How, he'd say?

It took a year, but we finally got it done. The release turned out to be a door opener for both of us. Fathead will loom large later in my story, so I may as well pause here for a second and explain how we came up with the name. When Jeff was recording those cassette tapes for friends, he created a company he called Tight Shoes Music. When I asked what it meant, he said, you know the old saying, tight shoes, thin wallet, fat head.

That's it, I told him. Let's call our label Fathead Records. He wasn't as excited about the name as I was, but he went along.

Jeff and I started getting more work and recognition, me as a singer, him as a musician, singer-songwriter. Radio play, reviews of the CD in magazines, and a number of gigs in Europe came our way by virtue of putting out that record, and we were having a blast. But eventually, after a good run together in the band, Jeff was getting more and more unhappy. He came to me one day and said he wanted a wife, not a business partner.

There wasn't much I could say in response. I knew he felt that way. He actually said it the first year we were married and began performing together. This time he was adamant. It pissed me off. I would later come to understand he was right, but it took me a long time to get there. I was stubborn about it, to be sure. We sounded so good together. I am a workaholic. When I am in a groove, busy and things are going well, I want to keep working. I didn't want to change anything, It turned out he was right. Pulling apart professionally allowed him to pursue his own thing; the same was true for me.

The decision proved to be good for the marriage, too. At least for a while. But the music business is notoriously hard on relationships, especially when you're both in it. We were going in different directions. Eventually, in 2010 Jeff said he wanted to separate and "see how things go."

I had been fighting that idea for five years, suggesting we go to couples counseling, which we did three different times. We took vacations together. We talked things out. We took the steps couples try when they have problems and one person wants to salvage things more than the other. Nothing stuck. Things would get better between us for a time, then the gulf would be growing again. It was a painful time.

Ultimately, Jeff got what he wanted. He filed for divorce and as difficult as our split was, I can't say I have very many regrets. There was no doubt in my mind that I had met and married the love of my life, even though our marriage was over. We had 17 good, if imperfect, years. At least I thought so. Loving him and being loved that deeply, for that long, helped heal me in ways I never knew were possible. It was nothing I ever expected for myself. Hindsight, of course, allows you to see things more clearly than when you were in the midst of them. I recognize now that the progress we made together personally and musically helped give me enough confidence as an artist to finally begin to pursue what I wanted to do next in my career and in my life.

Twenty-Two - Crossroads

Blues Leaf was a small label out of the shore town of Deal, N.J. I had already done three releases with them but working with those guys felt a little bit like dealing with Tony Soprano and I needed a change.

In the summer of 2002, I had the extremely good fortune of meeting Colin Linden, and it was not long before my career did take a big turn in a positive direction. Colin is an accomplished Canadian roots artist, producer, songwriter and slide guitar player extraordinaire. We were introduced at North Country Fair, a Canadian Folk Festival that resembles a mini-Woodstock. We clicked personally and musically. Colin would wind up co-producing my next two CDs on a label called Northern Blues Music.

Colin has produced CDs for people like Bruce Cockburn and Colin James. He played with Emmylou Harris, Bob Dylan, Robert Plant, Allison Krauss, Lucinda Williams and a lot more heavyweights. His songs have been covered by The Band, The Blind Boys of Alabama, Keb' Mo'. The fact that he seemed to love my singing and began talking me up to a Canadian record company was another pivotal opening for me. Our work together was a hugely positive step for my career and finally helped me get where I wanted to be—recognized. That meant more bookings and gigs, which is what I was after. Before I started recording with Colin, nobody in Memphis was aware of me. That changed in a big way when I started collaborating with him.

Not long after we met, Colin and I put together a tight little ensemble band for a record together that included top-flight players like Richard Bell, who played keyboard for the late, great Janis Joplin, and Stephen Hodges, an amazing drummer who played with me for many years as well as with Smashing Pumpkins, The Fabulous Thunderbirds, Mavis Staples and the incomparable Tom Waits. Stephen has been my good friend for as long as I have been in L.A. My then-husband Jeff, played guitars and bass. We included several of Jeff's compositions, including the eerie title song, Bury Him at the Crossroads, about suicide and crows that I mentioned earlier. I dedicated the record to my dad, who, as the notes on the CD said, "I hold . . . liable for turnin' me into a musician by singin' to me at night. Oh, he loved him some Hank Williams, Tex Ritter and Buck Owens every Sunday morning without fail, louder than Jesus." That CD will always hold an extra-special place in my heart. I love how it turned out. It also brought my first nomination from The Blues Foundation for Best Contemporary Female Artist in 2004. I didn't win that year, but the positive notoriety was a major blessing.

The next CD that Colin produced with me was Do I Move You? I got nominated again, this time winning Best Contemporary Female Blues Artist. I have to tell you, being recognized by The Blues Foundation, my peers and blues fans made me feel like a million bucks—cash. It also seemed to finally tip the scales for me with Bruce Iglauer and Alligator Records, the label that has long included some of the top blues artists in the world.

Another big plus from working with Colin and Northern Blues was the fact that the two releases I did for the label brought me even wider recognition internationally. That occurred in large part because my contract called for hiring a top-notch publicist and radio people to help make things happen and get the CD noticed. It was the first time for me that I didn't have to pay out of my own pocket for a publicist or handle publicity as a one-woman maniac machine. That made me happy.

Northern wound up hiring my dear friend, the publicist Michael McCloon, to work my releases. That was a super sweet deal for me. I had the opportunity to work with the same known and solid personnel—and best news of all, someone else wrote the checks!

We also brought in a fantastic photographer named Jeff Dunas, who I knew from the scene in L.A. and who had been a good friend of mine for years. His work is gorgeous, and he graciously agreed to shoot the first album cover on Northern Blues, Bury Him at the Crossroads. When it came to release my second CD with

Northern, it made sense to see if Jeff was available again and to my delight, he was. That release was called Do I Move You, a sexy Nina Simone song that I loved.

We shot the cover photo for that release at Dunas' Hollywood photo studio. There is something deeply soulful about Jeff Dunas and his work, so much so that it makes me want to open up in a way that I have not been able to with other photographers. Or with very many other people, to tell the truth. Letting my defenses slip with him does not make me unique because when you look at his work, you see the same kind of response in the faces of all his subjects. And many of those subjects have much greater reason to protect their privacy than I do. All the same, Angelina Jolie, Brad Pitt, Sir Anthony Hopkins—the list of people he has photographed is massive. They all open themselves up widely to the photographer's lens in a way that results in deeply moving images. It's true art and I am in awe of his technique and his skill.

For the Do I Move You cover, he had the idea of me lying on the floor of the studio, in front of an antique mirror, with Jeff shooting my reflection. As we were getting ready to go, I was lying face down doing a yoga pose to stretch my aching back and looked up at him. This wasn't the pose I was anticipating. I was trying to take away some of the throbbing from my back, but next thing I knew I heard the shutter clicking rapid fire. That was the shot that made the cover. To my mind, it was about as close to perfect as you can get.

When we sent the image off to Fred Litwan at Northern Blues, Litwan almost choked in his phone call to me to sound the alarm. He was uncomfortable with the cleavage and convinced if we went with Jeff's image, he would have every feminist in Canada at his throat. He pleaded with me not to use the shot, but I disagreed strongly. Since the early 1970s I have considered myself a hardcore, bra-burning feminist. I am not afraid of my body, not afraid of sex or my sexuality and my power as a woman. I was uptight about these things when I was younger—what woman isn't? —But by the time I was out there performing, I had finally begun to be comfortable enough with my body and my sexuality more than I ever had been. I was not in the mood to revert back because of some fear and shame-based ideas about a woman's sexual power or our bodies. Strong, independent women are my core demographic and had been for a long time. We had a series of heated arguments, Fred and I, but the sexy photo Jeff Dunas snapped when I didn't expect him to made it on to the cover of Do I Move You. I was happy to have prevailed. It was my fucking CD, wasn't it? At least that is how I saw it.

Fred was right in one respect. There was some pushback about the cover shot, but most of what we heard was positive. Women at my shows came up to me and said things like, "Good for you. Right on. You go girl. Gorgeous. Love that cover. Love you for shooting it. Love you for not being afraid." I never doubted I made the right decision. It felt pretty damn good to hear all those women sticking up for me.

This CD also marked the first time I won a Blues Music Award for Contemporary Female Blues Artist of the Year. That blew my mind. I didn't think for a second there was a chance in hell for me to actually win. I was a decided underdog, to be sure. Shemekia Copeland was a shoo-in, or so I believed. She is not only the daughter of legendary blues guitarist Johnny Copeland, she had been the gifted, reigning Contemporary Female Blues Artist for several years running. She was also the darling of Alligator Records, which everybody knows is the premier blues label in the world. Alligator has the biggest hammer in the business when it comes to blues. It's the label most serious blues artists want to be with. I know it was where I wanted to be. I just assumed Alligator's muscle and Shemekia's talent, track record and star power would be too much to overcome.

When the master of ceremonies at the awards show announced "And the winner is...," I didn't hear any of it. My brain was somewhere else. Roger Naber, the impresario who puts on blues cruises to a variety of exotic locations, yelled and slapped my arm, barking at me to get up there and claim my award. The crowd was on its feet, screaming. I stared at Roger with a blank look on face. He shouted at me again. "You won! You won! Get up there."

I leapt to me feet, hurried to the stairs at stage left, traversed two steps in my micro mini skirt and stiletto heels and what did I do in my moment of a lifetime? I fell forward and hit the stage like a load of bricks tossed to the ground. Stunned, I managed to get back on my feet and stumble to the podium. It was scary and hilarious at the same time. I did not land softly; my arm and ankle immediately throbbed with pain. I mumbled something to the audience about being Mrs. Magoo, please forgive my clumsiness. I then gave the most incoherent acceptance speech a person could possibly deliver, the pain in my limbs growing as I stood there and put weight on my damaged ankle.

It was a wild night. I won, nearly maimed myself, acted like a fool at the podium and then had to perform two songs to boot. My band was on its toes, though, ready and able as always. With the rush of winning and all that happened, we cut loose.

We played Prisoner of Your Good Love and You Were Never Mine from our new Do I Move You CD. The crowd was solidly in our corner; the place went nuts. We got a long standing ovation. I was a wobbly, emotional and physical mess.

I left the stage with every fiber of my body vibrating. I felt like I had been zapped full force with a taser. People swarmed around me backstage, offering pats on the back and congratulations. All of the sudden, there was Bruce Iglauer, the president of Alligator Records who had written me edgy, encouraging, but also critical letters after listening to tapes I had sent him over the years. Suddenly, he wanted to be my best friend.

"We need to talk," he commanded. "I would be happy to talk," I told him, trying to ignore the ache in my ankle. I was leaving early the next morning to get back on the road with our tour. We had shows in Texas the next night. There was no time to take a meeting with anyone. I could barely put two words together at that point anyway.

What I really needed more than anything was to limp over to the bathroom and pee. As I made my way to the lobby, I bumped into Taj Mahal, who had been holding court with some friends and admirers. He stopped me in my tracks to say congratulations.

"Do you realize what you have done?" he asked with intensity. "That was an incredible performance! They love you! They all love you, the young ones, the older ones, the black ones and the white ones! Do you realize what you have done? I really dig what you're doing. It's very important for us all! Keep doing it. Never stop. We need you."

Are you fucking kidding me? In my shock and gratitude, I said thank you about a million times before somehow excusing myself to go to the ladies room. I locked myself in one of the stalls and began to sob like a baby. I could not comprehend what had happened. I'd won best female artist of the year and one of my blues heroes, Taj Mahal, had said he loved me. He said I was doing important work. If I'd died then and there, I would have been a happy, satisfied woman.

Now, on top of all of that, Alligator finally wanted to talk to me. It was all too much for me to take in.

My preoccupation with Alligator as a possible recording home had actually started many years earlier. It was fueled in part by a conversation about record companies that I'd had with recording artist John Hammond Jr.in the early eighties. Alligator was already on my mind when John told me if I could go into a record store anywhere in the world and find a label's records, that was a good record company. At the time we spoke, that could be said of two blues labels. Alligator, out of Chicago, and Rounder from Cambridge, Mass. Alligator was the biggest and better known, with the most street cred. The label was started by Bruce Iglauer in 1971 when another record company he worked for wouldn't record his favorite act, Hound Dog Taylor and the House Rockers. Forty-eight years later, Alligator is still going strong. In a business that has been remarkably unpredictable and economically unstable for a long time, Alligator's success and staying power speaks volumes about Bruce and his business acumen.

I had been sending demos to Iglauer for years. After waiting six months or longer, I would get a thanks-but-no-thanks letter from him, with some qualified words of encouragement sprinkled in. I was happy to get a response, but it was never the answer I wanted.

"There was a lot to like here; you're quite a good singer with a lot of personality," he wrote in April 1993. I don't remember how many months it was after I sent him a few songs on tape, but it seemed to take forever for him to get back to me. That's how it went. He apologized for taking so long to write back; he was engaged enough to respond which many do not, and he always seemed unable to resist a few blows upside the head for good measure.

"I'm not sure it's clear what your style is," the letter from 1993 went on. "You hit a lot of bases. I heard Bonnie (Raitt), Rory Block, some swing and folk people. But I enjoyed it overall."

In another barbed response to some tapes I sent, he wrote: "As I remembered, you have a lot of talent—a good voice, nice presence. I find some of your vocals a bit mannered, as though you were trying to be someone else rather than singing your own style. In fact, the tapes make me wonder more what your style is. Sorry, I have to be honest. I think you've got something, but to my ear, you're finding your own direction. I'll be glad to keep listening. By the way, your piano player is definitely struggling on some of these songs."

It was no surprise that Bruce had a reputation for being harsh. But looking back on it, I have to admit some of his critique was on point. Something was keeping me from putting everything I had into my performances. He heard that. His letters irritated the hell out of me, but I tried to rationalize them by reminding myself that Bruce was not particularly well-liked by many musicians who'd had dealings with him. His reputation for being hard-headed, and certain that he knows more about the music business and music history than most people, preceded him. He may be right. But from where I sat, it appeared Bruce also seems determined to create conflict where there was none. He has butted heads over the years with many artists I admire. More than anything, I took his early rejections as a challenge. They pissed me off, but they also fueled me. Alligator's rejections had provided another motivation for me to push on when I needed it.

Now, with the multiple Blues Music Awards nominations and an actual win, I was genuinely starting to believe I could carve out a living with my singing.

There is a saying I have always been fond of, and it is this: "Persistence alone is omnipotent." Sometimes I see myself as living proof that it's true. My persistence was paying off. Several months after talking to Iglauer backstage in Memphis, Alligator made me an offer I did not refuse.

I was thrilled, but Jeff had a different take. "You made a deal with the devil," he scolded me. Maybe so, I told him, but the devil might have just met his match. 'No doubt," Jeff said with a knowing laugh. I was pretty pleased after having pursued Alligator so long ago.

The contract was what we called a one-plus-one deal. It called for a loan to make my first Alligator CD. Depending how sales went, there was an option for a second release. That's how a lot of record deals are structured. They are essentially a loan with a detailed set of obligations to be fulfilled by both parties. When things go well, artist and record company benefit. The artist and label release the recording, the artist goes on tour, traveling from hell to breakfast selling the goods to pay back the record company loan, pennies at a time. You hope like hell you are in a profit margin at some point.

The music industry today, at least for independent artists, means the artist is a store on wheels. The artists often times are the largest distributor of their own product, though many fail to realize this. With very rare exception, sales are not made, radio charts are not hit and reputations are not built unless you are out there day and night on tour promoting yourself and your goods. Music streaming has made all of this at least twice as hard.

The cost of touring, just like overhead for any small business, is severely challenging. You have to cover gasoline, vehicle maintenance, payroll, planes, trains and automobiles, commissions, you name it. And you pay the band to boot. It can seem as if the bleeding never ends. It all goes into the "cost of goods." You may be an artist, but you are operating a business.

These are the realities most people don't like to think about when you are buying what seems like a higher-priced ticket to see a favorite artist or their merchandise at the show. But the overhead is built into the price of admission. It has to be. When you buy a ticket to see an artist or shell out cash for a CD or T-shirt, you are investing in their company, dollar by dollar. Signing with Alligator meant I was going to have to bring a producer to the table who would be able to navigate through Bruce's agenda. There was only one guy who I felt certain fit that bill and could handle Bruce's personality and style of doing business. That was my longtime, ultra-talented friend, Dave Darling. Great name, I know. Just as great a talent and human being, too. He is basically an all-purpose musical genius who has produced countless records for artists like Glen Campbell, Tom Waits, the Stray Cats, Brian Setzer, Def Leppard, etc. His list of credits goes on and on. When I reached out to him, Dave was already a successful producer and songwriter. He didn't need Bruce and he didn't need Alligator. Convincing him to come on board the project was a coup for me. I hoped it would be fun and a rewarding challenge for Dave, too. I knew for sure it meant I had a much better chance of coming out of the studio with music I could be reasonably happy with and my audience would dig it, too. As things turned out, despite my concern about navigating office politics, it all worked out far better than I had imagined.

That didn't mean we didn't have to negotiate some rough pushback from Bruce. We got through it with some bruises and a few scratch marks, but we got it done. This was my eighth release under my name, my first for Alligator. It's called What Love Will Do; the title cut was my favorite Little Milton song. We got some fantastic press and radio play, along with a huge audience and fan response. It sure felt like winning to me.

Twenty-Three - Connection

Being able to sing for a living is a huge gift, but I have come to understand that it's not the real job. My real job is to reach out and connect with people, to share some of what I have been through in my life and have the kind of heart-to-heart connection with another person that lifts up both of us. Music is simply the vehicle that allows me to do that. A mind-blowing trip I took a few years ago drove home what I'm talking about.

Shortly after that first CD on Alligator came out in 2008, I was invited to appear as a headlining act for something called Bluzapalooza. It was the first-ever blues concert tour to perform for American troops in Iraq, in an active war zone. The trip was a grind, filled hands down with the hardest gigs I ever played. All the same, I would not have missed it for anything.

Two of my band members—Zach, the lead guitarist, and Gary, my bassist and road manager—were in the desert with me performing, hanging out, eating in mess halls, taking it all in, eyeballing pallets stacked with everything imaginable, all stamped Halliburton. We were gone just ten days but it felt much longer, especially since it was just about impossible to sleep the entire time.

We were about seven days into the tour, when we found ourselves on an airstrip. Everyone on the tour was out getting pictures with smart bombs, helicopters and guns. I felt disconnected from the group by that time, emotionally spent from the travel and the stress of being in a war zone. I was ready for the trip to be over, desperate to get back home to Los Angeles. My brain was fried. I wasn't eating much. I was barely sleeping. My inner demons were wide awake and busy inside my brain. As it turned out, we were never in the Green Zone – a supposedly safe zone - as we were told we would be. Pretty much every minute of the trip was intense and unsettling.

Bombs went off, Soldiers yelled at us "Where is your flak? Put your flak on! Put your flak on now!" We raced into shelters. It wasn't constant, but it was enough to rattle me. I didn't realize it until later, but my PTSD was in full play. I was starting to lose it and there was no closet to hide in. There was never a moment on the trip, day or night, when I didn't think something terrible could happen at any moment.

Let me explain a few things about Post Traumatic Stress Disorder. It is a highly sophisticated and wildly complex coping system of the brain. In my experience, it is a self-protective mechanism to keep from going totally mad. I know that seems like a contradiction, because it can cause what appears to be insane and unbalanced behavior. But it's a response to very real past trauma. Memory of the experiences lives in the part of the brain that absorbs severe trauma. Sometimes, every detail remains: sights, sounds, smells, emotions, everything. They are centered at the base of the brain, in the region scientists refer to as the "wolf brain" or the "lizard brain." It's all about total instinct. It's the same part of the brain where "fight or flight" resides.

We all know, sadly, that PTSD is very common in combat veterans. But Foster youth suffer PTSD at twice the rate of combat vets. The truth is that shocking numbers of people suffer with this monster. Left unchecked, PTSD can be a living hell for a sufferer, with no notice or warning whatsoever. Given the right trigger or stimulation, you essentially are hurtled back in time, living and suffering the memories of whatever traumas you endured; your mind is taken over by severe and debilitating anxiety. Sometimes it is like outright insanity.

It can be so bad that it becomes impossible to discern past from present. It's as if you are reliving the original trauma all over again. This is not some sign of mental weakness or imagination. It is physical and chemical memory flooding back in a torrent that can leave a person debilitated or completely disoriented.

This is why a combat veteran can snap and become violent back at home with what appears to be no warning. It's why a veteran or someone who had been abused as a youngster will find his life intolerable and kill himself. It's why I ended up hiding in closets shaking and sobbing well into my 40s. Once established, PTSD creates so much anxiety and sheer terror that the reality of a person's everyday life can be overwhelmed and overridden. It's fucking awful, believe me.

When I was standing around an airstrip in Baghdad with nothing to do but fret and watch time tick by, it was game-on for me. I felt an overwhelming urge to tell everyone I was with to go fuck off. I wanted to lecture them about how wrong the war was, that our troops should not be there, and on and on. I was losing my ability to separate truth from fear and fiction, struggling to keep my mouth shut, when I saw a young soldier with his gun, kind of standing guard all by himself. I stood there for what seemed like a long time, trying to make a decision. I wanted to run off into the desert, but my feet wouldn't move. Something kept me planted there in that moment. I remember thinking to myself, Magness, get the fuck away from these people before you do something stupid. I finally took a few steps away from the group of people I was with and walked toward that soldier. I started to speak to him, figuring if I engaged with someone else, maybe I'd get outside my head long enough to stop feeling like I was about to explode with rage.

When I said hello and asked how he was doing, this young soldier refused to make eye contact with me. He stared straight ahead, just spitting out terse one of two-word answers. Yes ma'am. No ma 'am. Fine ma'am. I was an intruder and felt like one.

"Where you from?" I persisted.

"Kentucky ma'am."

"Really. Whereabouts?"

"In the hills ma'am."

He was just being a soldier, I thought. Short answers, revealing next to nothing.

Very slowly, after five or ten minutes of me pestering him, he started to open up.

"How many times have you been here?" I asked.

It was his third or fourth tour, I remember him telling me.

"How's that going for you? Are you going home soon?"

"Yes ma'am. I'm being discharged."

"Is that a good thing?"

"No ma'am. It is not."

Something must have switched in his head, because the young man began to unload his history to me like it was no big thing to share intimate details of his life with a perfect stranger, a nosy one at that.

He told me that he came from total dirt-poor family in the hills of Kentucky. His mother had abandoned him and his siblings when they were kids. He was raised by a single father. He joined the military to get a pilot's license because he married young and wanted to provide for his wife and family when he got home. He figured a pilot's license was the ticket to do that. His dream was to become a commercial pilot. He'd make good money, enough to support a family, which is what he wanted.

There were a lot of young kids like him over there, people not sure what to do with their lives, so they signed up to fight a war they thought was noble, a war they thought would keep our country safe.

He did become a pilot in the military, and now he was about to go home. But the pilot license that would be his salvation was gone. He said the military yanked it because he had PTSD. A bad case of it. He required medication. He said they had him so heavily doped up he would never be able to fly a plane out in the civilian world.

I listened to every word. I felt as if the hair on my body was suddenly standing up. My skin was covered in goose bumps. A revelation hit me full force. This was why I had come all this way. I was on this trip so I could talk to this young man, on this airstrip, in the middle of fucking nowhere outside the Green Zone in Iraq. I was there so I could have an honest conversation with this scared kid. He was the reason for the whole fucking trip. Never mind my own political leanings, which are pretty hard left. None of that mattered.

"Honey," I said, looking him square in the eye and placing my hand on his chest. He was a big guy, and I immediately got the vibe that this was not cool. I had touched a soldier on duty. He looked down at me like he couldn't believe what happened, so I pulled away my hand and kept talking.

"Honey," I said, "it's okay. It is okay. And let me tell you something." I went on to let this kid know I also had PTSD. He shot me a hard look, like he couldn't believe it.

"I've had it my whole life, and what I want to tell you is that it doesn't have that kind of hold on my days and nights anymore. It no longer defines me. It no longer owns me."

He said he had it so bad he never sleeps. He was always edgy. His nerves were shot. I knew I was there to give him something to hold on to.

"Really?" he said.

"Yes. Really. I've had to work incredibly hard, but I know firsthand that this doesn't have to define you for the rest of your life. I've gotten through it. Most days and most nights. You can get through this, too."

Then I gave him a compressed version of my story. Told him about Foster Care, about living on the streets. Both parents committing suicide. My first suicide attempt at 4. Molested at 6. I just went boom, boom, boom with my story to this scared, sweet young man.

We were connected. There was no mistaking it. For the next three days, I couldn't get rid of him. It was funny and it was beautiful. The kid shadowed me everywhere I went. Smiling whenever I looked his way. It was very sweet. I heard later that he got out in one piece, and for that brief moment in time, we had a genuine connection. The experience lifted me up. I hope it helped him, too. I like to think it did, at least a tiny bit. That young man needed something. I did, too. In that strange place and in a difficult time when I felt my grip on reality slipping away, we were there for each other. To me, that's how spirit works. You get outside of yourself and connect with someone who needs a hand to hold or someone just to talk to and be heard. It is an experience I will always remember.

Twenty-Four - In the Trenches

For What Love Will Do, my first recording for Alligator, we rounded up the best musicians we could find, including my then-husband, Jeff, who played guitar, bass, tenor and baritone sax. As always, Zach Zunis was with me on guitar. So was my longtime bass player, good friend and now Road Manager, Gary Davenport, otherwise known as Scruff. For the producer, I was able to enlist my old friend, and musical genius, Dave Darling. Dave loves the same old-time blues I do, what I call the crusty old dead-guy stuff I grew up on. He is well-versed in it, just as he is with soul and funk. Perhaps most importantly, I've known Dave for a long time. We're comfortable with each other. I trust and respect him. I knew he felt the same way about me. That's crucial for anyone, but especially when you're a woman singing the blues and you don't want to deal with the male-dominant recording studio politics you get with a lot of producers. I don't do well with "my way or the highway" ass-holes. When I'm making a record, I want a relationship of mutual trust and respect. That's what I have with him. I'm grateful to be working with him.

It took about a year to record What Love Will Do, and we were fortunate enough to get a lot of great reviews for the finished product. One review characterized the CD as a personal breakthrough, which was fine by me.

"After over a decade of hard labor in the blues trenches, Janiva Magness finally gets a shot at the brass ring with her debut Alligator release," wrote Hal Horowitz, a well-known Georgia-based music writer. In 2009, Hal won The Blues Foundation's Keeping the Blues Alive award for journalism. "Six increasingly accomplished albums provided the studio experience in crafting her music for maximum dynamics, and the results show on this rollicking set of blues and R&B . . . It's a great place to start enjoying a veteran performer who burns through these songs like she's got everything to prove."

I had been in the trenches a lot longer than a decade, but I hadn't stopped feeling like I had something to prove. Mostly to myself. I had to convince myself that I really was an artist with some of the talent and all the persistence and toughness it took to be successful. I wanted to prove to Iglauer and Alligator Records that they were right to sign me and maybe should have done it long ago. And to the music industry itself, I wanted to prove that I had what it took to be a top-tier artist who could deliver the goods and reach people if I had the right team and got the right opportunities.

I covered artists on the recording from Little Milton to Marvin Gaye, Tina Turner and Annie Lennox. I also included two strong songs written by Jeff, including the somber and hopeful last tune, Sometimes You Got to Gamble. Played over a mournful gospel piano. It seemed to sum up how I felt about life a lot of the time.

"Everybody dreaming about something they can't touch . . . Everybody need a little good luck, oh when bad luck is all you got".

We put a ton of hard work into that CD, but I felt pretty lucky to be working with the super team, studio and label. Our efforts paid off, and I was feeling more confident.

For one thing, I had become more comfortable pouring my feelings and vulnerability into my music, just as I had seen artists like Etta James and Otis Rush do so many years earlier. I had begun to understand there was no reason to hold anything back. I think that had a lot to do with Iglauer offering me the contract at Alligator. I was starting to put my own stamp on the songs. I wasn't afraid to put all my emotional energy into them. You might be able to hear some of the influences from the greats like Etta and Koko Taylor, which is a solid and respected tradition for the blues. But I was becoming myself in more ways than ever, both in my music and in my life. All the recovery work I was doing had a lot to do with it, but my confidence as an artist was probably what allowed me to put more of myself out there. I was putting more of my emotions and personal signature on the material and in my live shows.

Confidence is key, of course, in just about anything you try to do in life. There were days when I still felt shaky about things, but I finally had some solid self-assurance. I know that might sound funny that I was now in my forties and just starting to get truly comfortable on and off stage. A little late, don't ya think? But as they say in recovery, it takes what it takes and you're ready when you're ready. Period.

I was also speaking around the country more on behalf of at-risk youth and Foster Care in the twin roles of spokesperson for the National Foster Care Campaign and Ambassador for Foster Care Alumni USA. That program helped save my life; giving back and doing some good by drawing attention to young people who needed help was extremely gratifying. I could feel myself getting stronger the more I told the truth about my life and what I'd been through.

When I talked about Foster Care and saw a light of recognition go on in another person's eyes who had been through it, I felt the connection. A kid still in the struggle moves me like few things do. I see myself in her face, in her fear and in her sense of uncertainty. I understand how a helping hand can turn a kid around or at least make her feel like she matters. That's a big fucking thing for me. I feel blessed to be able to travel the country, tell my story and connect with people in that meaningful way.

We called the first Alligator CD What Love Will Do, after Little Milton Campbell's song, because I felt both the music and my life at that point spoke to the power of love. It was a perfect fit. If I am covering someone else's song, it has to resonate with me; that one sure did.

Getting signed by Alligator had been a silent dream of mine for so long. Now here I was with my first Alligator release bringing in strong reviews. The band and I were touring non-stop. Momentum from the buzz around What Love Will Do and our work on the road helped land me my first nomination for the biggest prize of all in blues, the B.B. King Entertainer of the Year at the Blues Music Awards in 2009. It had been nearly a decade since I'd had to unload trucks, stock shelves and frozen food at the local food co-op, or drive some guy around in a limo so I could eat and pay the rent. I was no longer frightened to go all-in with my singing. I was all in and then some.

That doesn't mean I was home free without a care. It never will be that way for me, and that's perfectly okay. Depression and disappointment were still a familiar fit for me. The Magness Curse is damn near impossible for me to shake. But — and allow me to knock on wood here just to make sure — I was busy already collecting material for my next CD, and it was no accident that I chose to cover a classic Nina Simone song from 1965.

Feeling Good was co-written by the actor Anthony Newley for his Broadway musical, The Roar of the Greasepaint, The Smell of the Crowd. It is a classic underdog's story of hanging in there and overcoming adversity. Now it felt like my own personal theme song when I put it on my record. I love singing it. On stage, I usually do the first verse a cappella before the band kicks in, and the audience tends to be rapt with attention.

Birds flying high you know how I feel. Sun up in the sky, you know how I feel. Breeze drifting on by you know how I feel. It's a new dawn, it's a new day, it's a new life. For me . . . and I'm feeling good.

The energy in that song washes over me like a soothing, warm wave. And it helped carry me all the way to that wondrous night in Memphis in May 2009 with B.B. King and Bonnie Raitt. But in some completely unpredictable and unexpected plot twist, something happened just before I left my hotel for The Blues Foundation's awards ceremony that rocked my world. Rocked it even more than winning Entertainer of the Year.

Twenty-Five - Blast From the Past

One of the songs I co-wrote on my Stronger For It CD is called Whistling in the Dark. And whistling in the dark is exactly what I did that night in Memphis in 2009 when B.B. King called my name to the stage to hand me the Entertainer of the Year award. It also pretty much captures how I have gotten through countless struggles and mistakes I've made in life. It could be a theme song for my entire life. Just as the refrain says, "I'll just keep pretending and whistling in the dark." Sometimes the only way I can put one foot in front of the other and keep carrying on is to put the bad shit out of my mind and act as if none of it ever happened.

Back at the hotel in Memphis a few hours before the awards show, my daughter, Pearl, and I were excitedly primping for the big night. We were doing our hair, getting dressed, painting on makeup. Just two gals having a ball, grooving to one of my favorite Memphis soul singers from the 1970s, Ann Peebles. In the middle of it all, I looked at my phone and noticed I had a new Facebook message. When I saw who it was from, I had to look at the name twice because I could not believe my eyes.

The text on my phone read, "Janiva, is this you? I can't believe I finally found you. I had no idea you were so famous. Please call me as soon as you can. I miss you so much. Love Sam."

Holy hell. Sam and I had not talked in more than thirty-five years. Not since we'd had a terrible fight early one morning and she screamed she never wanted to see me again.

I'd spent years dragging myself over cut glass about Artese's drowning, pushing down the shame and pain of what happened with as much drugs and alcohol as I could get my hands on, trying to kill myself more times than I can count. Now, on what would become the most triumphant night of my career as a blues woman, those awful memories came rushing through the flood gates and threatened to engulf me.

Without breathing a word to Pearl, I stared at the message again to make sure I wasn't hallucinating. I knew instantly that what that message signified was too big and messy to even consider dealing with just then. The memories and emotions attached to a simple little "hello" from a dear old friend were too much to comprehend, so I literally started to whistle. It was a dark little joke between me, myself and I, but if I was going to make it to the awards dinner in one piece, I had to put that shit as far out of mind as possible. I did my act of pretending everything was fine, so for the next little piece of time, it was. I was good at this, owing to years of practice under tough circumstances.

During the awards show, when the band and I were introduced to perform along with other nominees, no one in the packed house could have suspected how shaken up I was feeling. We played Little Milton's That's What Love Will Make You Do, a classic blues number about a love affair turned sour. It was spooky how spot on some of the lyrics were about how I felt hearing from Sam after so many years of silence between us.

When I hear your name, I start to shake inside, yes I do.

No shit. I gave the song and the audience all I had, but it was nearly impossible to keep my mind off Sam. Just seeing her name after what seemed like a lifetime of no contact brought back so many horrible memories, that God-forsaken house in St. Louis where my mother and Artese died most prominently. What the hell did Sam want with me after so many years? Did I really want to find out? The honest answer was hell no. That was not a door I wanted to open. It scared me to death.

It was impossible to have Sam's name cross through my brain at all without being transported back to 1970, that awful year when I was 13. The year my mother took her life and then Artese drowned in our backyard pool. At that same fucking house. The tragedies, just five months apart, were stacked one upon the other, with no room to breathe. To say I was angry and unbalanced is putting it mildly. I was consumed with guilt for not looking into the garage the night my mother killed herself, despite my premonition that something was wrong. My last words to her — "Go to hell!" — played again and again in my head. More guilt piled on over my negligence that cost Artese his young life. Yet Sam and I had never spoken about it. Not a single word, just as my father and I had never said a single word about my mother's death. These were cruel silences, tormenting me for decades, and now there was a loud and sudden pounding on the door.

When Sam's Facebook message appeared on my phone, it was impossible for me not to flash back to those dark times. When I say the flood gates opened, I'm not kidding, and that was some seriously dirty water pouring through.

The first place I traveled in my head after Sam said hello was 1979, years after Artese and my mother died. I was living on the edge of White Bear Lake, a St. Paul suburb, at a place we had called Dresser's Farm. It was a real shithole. But rent was cheap, and things were lively with huge blowout parties. There were demolition derby contests like you'd see in some B movie, where guys raced and wrecked their cars. I had two jobs for part of the time I was there, driving a school bus in the morning and working alongside Sam at night as a cocktail waitress at a bowling alley turned into a rock and roll bar. It was called the Sunset Lounge, and the place was always jammed.

One night at the Sunset, Sam asked me why the hell I was living at Dressers. There was no heat, the place was filthy. Come stay with me, she said. I started renting a room in her basement apartment in White Bear Lake.

Sam had a baby girl by then and had broken up with the little girl's father, so it was just Sam and her daughter living there. Neither of us did anything terribly productive while we were roommates. We just worked at the bar, marking time. The musicians she knew got us into shows around town when we weren't working; we'd go backstage and party with the bands. Both of us were pretty depressed, getting loaded a lot, just going through the motions of living.

After what happened to Artese, it was hard for me to believe she was letting me live with her again—and her little girl, no less. That was Sam. If she thought I was responsible for taking Artese from her, she never showed a trace of anger or resentment about it. Even as I tortured myself non-stop. I did it like a Magness. Silently, alone, but I did it. It was easy, since I was one hundred percent convinced that I was responsible. Then one morning, our silence on the subject ended when Sam's pain came pouring out in torrents.

On the surface, the fight began over a guy named Sonny, a drug dealer, Sam had a crush on. Sonny came to the Sunset a lot. He liked me, but I was not about to get involved with him. He kept coming on to me, flattering me with kindness and attention, deadly lures for me back then. So I finally brought up his name with Sam;

she assured me she didn't care if I went out with him. Sonny and I soon took off, disappearing for four days of drugs and sex. When I finally showed up loaded one early morning, Sam had a worried look on her face, but I could tell she was more angry than worried. I was pretty sure I smelled alcohol on her breath.

"Where the hell have you been?" she screamed. "Why didn't you call me? I have been worried sick about you." Her concern seemed genuine, though it was hard for me to believe that anyone truly cared about my well-being. It never occurred to me that someone actually might.

Without warning, she let loose a barrage of words I had expected to hear from her right after Artese died nine years earlier, words I will remember until the day I die.

"Get the fuck out of my life. You killed my baby. I never want to see you again. Get the fuck out of here. Go, God damn it. Go."

Sam dumped my clothes onto the ugly brown lawn, which had a dusting of frost that had fallen during the night. Her explosion leveled me. I believed every syllable that came out of her mouth. I couldn't have felt worse had I been buried alive. I knew without question I would never see her again as long as I lived. I let her yell for a few minutes longer and after she was finished, I knew what I had to do. It was time for me to disappear from her life. Forever. That and pray.

So that's what I did. I split and never looked back. And I prayed for Sam every single day of my life. I never stopped. I prayed for her, for my brother Jimmie, for Artese. I prayed for them when I was drunk, when I was stoned and when I was sober. I prayed on my knees, in the shower, in my car. I did it because it was the only thing I knew how to do. I never stopped feeling love for Sam, but I was compelled to respect how she felt. The only thing I knew to do for certain was to stay away from her. I did not want to do anything to remind her of the loss she'd endured because of me, so I just got down on my knees and asked God to look after her and protect her. I never sought God's forgiveness for my role in the death of her child or for anything else terrible that I had done in my life. I didn't seek forgiveness for myself because I was convinced I was not worthy of His grace or forgiveness. But I prayed for Sam like I was trying to set a world record.

In Memphis, Sam had left her phone number in the Facebook message, and right after the awards ceremony I began to think about calling her. I'd speculate how a call might unfold and then just as quickly, I pushed the idea out of my mind and kept whistling in the dark. The last thing I wanted to be was face to face with her. The day after the B.M.A.'s, we were on tour again, so it was easy to avoid confronting the idea. I didn't have a moment to spare. I was busy with travel and shows, but I was also lying to myself. I knew I was running away, hiding. It was impossible to wrap my head around the conversation we might have. I had no clue how to even face her.

Finally, several weeks after she asked me to, I dialed Sam's number because I knew I had to. I owed her that much. My imagination ran wild. I was petrified at what she would say.

When we finally connected, I was at the airport in Louisville, Kentucky, heading to a speaking engagement for Foster Care. It was a good thing I was flying in a day early for the speech because I would need to time to get my head together after we finally talked. When I heard her voice for the first time in more than three decades, I couldn't believe it: Her soft, soothing tone was exactly how I remembered it. She still sounded like the sweet-natured best friend I had loved like a sister yet hurt so profoundly.

I could tell she was happy to talk with me, but I held back. There was something I needed to say to her, but I had no idea how.

We talked about other topics so long I missed my flight to Louisville. I am a pretty well-organized person. I don't miss flights or appointments. Being on time is important to me but that day in the airport, I lost all sense of time.

Over the next few weeks, we had several more phone conversations, reminiscing about Jimmie and my mother, people from the old days, how life was going for each of us now. We made meaningful, albeit small talk, but I was growing more anxious about what I knew was coming. Finally, one afternoon when I was talking to her from my home in Los Angeles, I was out of time and I knew it. I had to bring up Artese.

My voice was a thin whisper. "Sam, is it okay if we talk about Artese for a minute?"

"Of course, honey," she answered. I remember swallowing hard, silently asking God to provide the words because suddenly I had none. Sam waited for me to speak, but I was stuck. All I heard was my heart slamming against my chest. This was a conversation I imagined so many times before. A conversation I was desperate to have, but I could not speak.

"Sam," I finally sputtered, "I need to tell you . . . I realized I have never told you how sorry I was about the baby. I know it was my fault. I've always known it. I walked away from him when he needed me. When you needed me. Sam, I am so sorry about Artese."

My voice cracked. I began to sob, and tried to catch my breath. "I . . . am . . . so. . . very. . . sorry." Each word seemed to take a minute to draw out.

It goes without saying that I could never begin to touch or make up for the loss she suffered, but I wanted her to know I had been praying diligently for her, the baby and for Jimmie all these years.

"I didn't know what else to do, Sam, besides pray and stay away. I shouldn't have walked away from him and turned my back on that sweet little boy, but I did."

I was crying Niagara Falls, my body heaving in pain.

Then Sam blew me away once more. Oh no, honey, she said with a calm certainty and strength in her voice. There was something I didn't understand, she told me, something I needed to realize.

My eyes were flooded with tears. I could not see straight. What could be left to understand? I understood clearly what happened on that dreadful Sunday. I couldn't imagine what was coming next.

Softly, in a soothing voice, Sam reminded me that she had loved my brother with all her heart. But as a Catholic, she said she never would have left him. She would have never divorced him in the natural course of things.

"You know Jimmie was trying to kill me," she said. "He eventually would have succeeded because I couldn't leave him. He probably would have killed the baby, too."

Her words triggered another flashback. In an instant, I was in that house again, witnessing the vicious beatings Jimmie had inflicted on her when he was using. Sam and the baby were screaming. I could hear their shrieks and didn't know how to make them stop. I heard the thick thud of Jimmie pounding on her like raw meat. He wouldn't let up. I saw all that sick Magness rage exploding from my brother's fists, I felt it each time he kicked her with his heavy work boots. I saw Sam absorbing his drunken blows, his powerful, enraged kicks to her petite feminine frame. I saw her lying unconscious in pools of her own blood on the floor of the baby's nursery.

I was living those nightmare moments again. I jumped on my brother's back, furiously trying to pull him off her, screaming for him to stop, cursing him, hitting him with my fists. I was back in that fucking house in Kirkwood, Mo., immersed in hell, horrified by his brutality. I was plotting to get my dad's shotgun from the closet so I could blow my brother's head off. It was the only way for Sam to survive. I failed to save my mother when I should have. I would save Sam, no matter what it took. I was dead serious about it.

I told Sam that I knew Jimmie would have killed her. I kept saying over and over into the phone, "I know, I know, I know. It's the truth, no question about it."

God has reasons for everything, she went on. All of it. Even if we didn't understand. It didn't matter what I believed, she said. Or anyone else. This was her truth. This was what she knew to be real.

"When the baby died," she went on, "that was my out. I could finally break free of your brother. I realized that maybe Artese was put here just for that short period of time so that I would leave Jimmie. That's how I came to look at the whole terrible ordeal. So it really is ok."

Sam said the time had come for me to stop beating myself up. I no longer needed to punish myself. She wasn't angry. She loved and forgave me.

"It's been too long, sweetie," she said tenderly. "It's been way too long. Besides, I know that the baby is with your mother. He is with Billie. I loved your mother so much. I know he is OK. He has been with Billie since the moment he left us. In fact, I think she took him from that wretched place to spare him the pain that was destroying all of us one by one. So he is fine. I am fine. We are fine. You need to move on from this, honey."

I understand that people with a deep belief in spiritual practices or in God often don't see death on this earth as the final act. It's something bigger for them, part of some grand plan I won't pretend to understand. But what Sam said to me was unfathomable.

I never thought I'd saved anybody. Far from it. I knew I didn't kill Artese. I loved him and would never have intentionally harmed him. But it was my fault he drowned. That was the ugly truth. For years, I dealt with it the only way I knew how — drinking, drugging, acting out, punishing myself, trying to forget. It's like people in recovery sometimes say: If you want to know why you drink and get high, quit drinking and getting high. You'll know real quick what you are pouring "alcohol" over.

And now this. In one single moment, Sam changed the world for me. If this was how she framed what happened to Artese after all this time, all I can say is bless her impossibly large and graceful heart. If that's what it took to make her own life bearable, who was I to question her? I had no right to question her. None.

I was consumed with the impossible, far too overwhelmed to comprehend it at the time but Sam showed me in that miraculous act of grace something I had been stumbling around and searching for my whole life. She presented me with the true miracle and total power of genuine forgiveness. She gave to me what I would never have had the ability to ask for. She gave me something I certainly did not deserve.

I understand today that Saint Francis was right when he said, "It is in pardoning that we are pardoned." It really is better to forgive than be forgiven. This is a healing act second to none. I certainly had never been able to forgive myself. To carry the burden seemed right and just to me.

But Sam's love and grace forced me to reconsider my position. She'd forgiven me for the worst transgression of my life. The single most reckless and destructive thing I have ever done, irreparable harm inflicted by me on her and her baby. One of the worst things that ever happened in her life, and she had not simply pardoned me. You can do that with someone and never want to see them again. Sam wanted me in her life. That's why she tracked me down and sent that message. She wanted to restore our connection, to be sisters again. I was blown away by her action like nothing before or since. If I went to the beach and saw God's hand come down and split the fucking sea in two, it would pale in comparison.

I have worked this over in my brain until my head hurts, but years after it happened, I still can't fully comprehend what Sam did or how she reconciled things. To me, this was a miracle, another example of true divine grace. The dictionary definition of grace as unwarranted, unmerited, divine goodness. I take that to mean it is nothing you can earn and it is nothing you deserve. It is a gift from heaven. All I could do was accept and embrace it. That and work like hell to keep my heart open and forgive. Forgive my mother and father. Forgive my siblings. Forgive God, the Universe, everyone and everything in it. Forgive myself.

I had spent years doing a ton of incredibly difficult therapy and recovery work of trying to forgive. In a crazy way, being a drunk and an addict in recovery were a blessing because it enabled me to do that work. With help from an exceptional therapist and friends in drug and alcohol recovery programs, I no longer walk around with rage at people who have let me down or caused me harm. This change is extraordinarily liberating, and it has freed me of so much self-destructive baggage. Doing this work has made my life better and it has made my music better. My heart is far more open and less clogged up with ugly, negative energy.

Now, in the weeks and months after those first tearful conversations with Sam, very slowly I began to feel as if I might finally begin to embrace forgiveness not just for others, but maybe, just maybe there would be a pardon of some kind for me.

Through Sam's grace, something big shifted inside me, even while she was still talking. Something inside my soul broke off, causing my armor to fracture and crack. My own internal landscape was changed forever because of her. In a profound and amazing way.

It's not as if the wound I have carried so many years is ever going to disappear. That scar will always be on me. I can't whitewash it. There's no way to have it surgically removed. I can't hit auto correct and erase it. There is no going to the best Beverly Hills surgeon and say work your magic, erase this so it doesn't show. I can't hide it like my mom covered up the rope burn on my neck when I was four. I have had to find a way to live with this scar, moving forward instead of living with it and staying stuck in place. I was frozen with it in place for so many years. Now that was changing too. The ice was actually starting to melt.

I can say now that I have come to accept what happened in my backyard swimming pool so many years ago. What I do today is try to see it in a different light. That still requires work. It doesn't come easy or naturally for me, but I could never rewrite my history in a way that would allow me to ease my burden or soothe my heart. I cannot deceive myself that way. But can I actually forgive myself? At least now I can get closer to the idea thanks to Sam. For her, this was not an issue. Writing these words is difficult for me. I am crying as I type and I know I will cry again when I read them. But Sam's grace and love changed that pain. Softened it in a way. I am still uncertain that I deserve to feel better about any of it, but I cannot dismiss or disrespect what she said. I am compelled to honor this sweet woman and my brother. I remain eternally grateful to her for this.

I now know I was never a bad person. I did do some very bad things. I behaved in horrible and irresponsible ways. That's an understatement. But I am not rotten, as I once believed with total certainty.

Talking with Sam over the phone was hard enough, but she insisted she wanted to see me. Just thinking about that made me nervous all over again. I desperately wanted to believe we could be close again. That things between us really had come full circle now that we were both leading healthier lives and had finally talked about what had happened. I wanted so much to see her face, hug her tight and feel my arms around her, but thinking about being in the same room with Sam unraveled me. We'd had our talk. I was finally able to tell her how I felt about things. Wasn't that enough?

I told her I would be in touch when we booked a date close to where she lived. A few months later, a blues festival in Billings came up on the calendar. I knew what I had to do, jumping to accept the gig even though it didn't even allow me to break even - I would lose money. A Billings show would allow Sam and me to connect with the least amount of trouble and travel for her. She wanted to see me. At that point, if Sam asked me to scale Pike's Peak, I would have strapped on a backpack and started to climb, rope or no rope. It didn't matter.

On Thursday, August 12, 2011, more than two years after she tracked me down in Memphis, the band and I flew from Los Angeles to Billings. We were touring constantly. The road wears you out faster than just about anything I know and we were all emotionally and physically tapped out. On the night before the show, I got to our hotel in downtown Billings, feeling as nervous as a criminal with the law closing in.

During one of our phone calls, Sam suggested we take a drive into the rugged, rocky country outside of town because she wanted to show me the beautiful landscape. It would be a great way to talk and catch up.

The idea filled me with dread. Sure, I convinced myself, she will get me out of the car to marvel at some vista and she'll nudge me off the edge of a cliff. I would be dead. That would be that. It wasn't as if she wouldn't be justified. I can't say for sure I would have resisted if she did try to push me over. I didn't really believe things would play out that way when we met, but that's where my Magness mind went. Fear and shame were parked in my brain right next to the wonder of having heard from her after so many years. And her kindness. My mind went to the dark side countless times before we met. I had no idea what to expect or how either of us would react to seeing one another in the flesh. Playing big venues with thousands of people in the audience no longer makes me nervous. Meeting this petite, ginger-haired woman from my past scared the shit out of me.

The summer had taken a toll already. Completely exhausted from all the touring and traveling, and my brother Jimmie had died several months earlier. I took a few days off from the road to view his body with the family and to attend his funeral. Right after the funeral, Carson tried to kill himself and was in a psychiatric hospital in diapers and four-point restraints. I had been doing what I could from the road to help my sister get Carson the care he needed, but it was horribly stressful and sad. At the same time, my brother Joe was tending to his ailing wife, who was sick again with cancer. My family was imploding. Yet again. Now I was about to meet Sam in the flesh. I didn't know if I could handle one more thing on top of everything coming my way.

I am a strong woman. I have proven this to myself time and again over the years. But even before Sam tracked me down that summer, I could have been blown over by the first gust of wind that hit me. My long marriage to Jeff Turmes was ending. Good friends said they had not seen me so emotionally raw in years. The guys in the band were worried. They stuck extra close, never letting me out of their sight. My defenses were eviscerated. Even though he had been sick for so long from the ravages of a lifetime of drugs and alcohol, Jimmie's death took a lot of life out of me. I wanted to run and forget I ever agreed to meet Sam, but thankfully, backing out was not an option.

I was at the Clarion Hotel in downtown Billings when my cell phone rang. It was Sam, telling me she was in the hotel, too, stuck in an elevator that wouldn't move, wondering how to find me. I was unpacking my suitcase in my room and told her I would meet her in the lobby. We were still on our phones when I got down to the first floor.

I hit the "up" button on the elevator next to mine, figuring I would stop and peer out at each floor and find her that way. The elevator came. I moved forward to step in. There was a tiny woman inside talking on her phone. I kept speaking into mine for a second, waiting for her to notice it was me standing there.

"Don't worry," I said as she looked up at me and grinned. "I'm here." Leaning forward, Sam reached out her arms, pulling me close. Her embrace melted me the instant I felt her touch.

We were both showing the years, but she looked wonderful, with a big, satisfied smile on her face. We held on tightly to each other. We both began to laugh and cry at the same time. A wave of relief coursed through my body. I was unable to catch my breath, but at the same time it felt soooooo good.

I had the Billings show the next night. I try not to talk when I'm touring to preserve my voice. But I could care less. There was so much to catch up on.

Sam and I talked and talked and talked. Then we talked some more. We never took that ride out to the country. We went instead to a mall and shopped. Girlfriend stuff. I loved being with her again. She kept telling me over and over she couldn't believe she got her baby sister back. "You are the only living witness to that part of my life," she told me with a gleam in her eye.

Her husband knows some of her past, but not the whole picture. Her daughter knows some, but not very much. Sam told me that she kept parts of those stories to herself, just as I never told my daughter the full version story of my role in Artese's death. It wouldn't serve any productive purpose in those relationships to tell everything, but I guess this book changes that.

"You're the only person who knows," Sam told me. "The only one I can talk to about it."

Sam, like me, has reinvented herself. We both have lives today that bear no resemblance to our self-destructive, reckless pasts. She and her husband are successful and comfortable. Sam has lived in Wyoming since going there for a friend's wedding years ago, falling in love with the open spaces, the rugged, independent way of life and a handsome cowboy. She is active and prominent in Wyoming politics. Just a few months before we met in Billings, she was the subject of glowing newspaper reports after being elected secretary of the Wyoming Republican Party executive board. It is one of the most politically powerful positions in the state. Our politics could not be more different. Who cares?

We talk now and when we do, we are like gabby teenage girls unaware of the world beyond us. We've gotten together a number of times since Billings. When I was on the plane to go back home after our first visit together, she sent me a text message that she already missed me and couldn't wait until the next time we would see each other. She came to several of my shows after Billings, watching me sing while standing close to the stage with a beautiful smile on her face.

I know today that if you stick around long enough, no matter how desperate things may get, life has a funny way of coming around full circle. In time, you can be ok and find healing – you can even find redemption. In God's time, not ours, but it can happen. My heart breaks when I reflect on how my parents could not manage to stick around to have that kind of experience. They missed out on so much. But it's true, even if I don't understand how it works. I could never have known or imagined how all the pieces would fit together. Or that so much forgiveness, joy and healing could occur. But I am still here. Still standing. Somehow, I have been allowed to stay around long enough to see all of this and more take place.

Twenty-Six - Detroit

Reconnecting with Sam was not the only emotional event for me during that summer of 2011. I mentioned Jimmie's death already. Now, about the same time Sam and I began communicating again, I miraculously found myself in the middle of downtown Detroit on a gorgeous, 80-degree day, feeling my father's presence in a way that I had not done in many years.

I had been flown into town by the state of Michigan so I could serve as keynote speaker for Family Reunification Day. Detroit press and TV cameras were there. My eyes kept welling up with tears. At the same time, I was grinning like a chimp and my heart swelled as eleven local families were being honored for completing the hoop jumps and hard work of all the court-ordered steps to piece their families back together and regain custody of their children.

Every little girl wants her father's approval. I know it's always been that way for me. When I walked up the steps of the white and black marble Coleman A. Young Municipal Center in Detroit, just a few blocks from the First Precinct station house where my father spent fifteen years as a patrolman, Dad was finally pleased with me. I could feel it; I could hear him speaking to me, I could see his prideful smile. We were connected in a way that I always yearned for. Finally, he was proud of his baby girl. And once again, my life had come full circle.

By the time my dad took his life in 1973, he couldn't have been blamed for believing his youngest daughter would never amount to anything. He left this earth before I could give him a reason to think anything else. By no stretch of the imagination, was I a good daughter. From the time I ran away with the drug dealer who lived across the street from me when I was just 13, I was nothing but trouble.

Somehow, against all odds, I came through it. I have become a good and decent human being. I have made something of my life.

Now I was a stone's throw from where my father walked the beat with his billy club at his side and Bill Magness, patrolman for the First Precinct. Protector of the City of Detroit as a policeman, work he deeply loved. You did good, Dad, I said to myself. I was proud of him, too. Proud to be his daughter after all we went through. That was not a state of mind I ever expected to feel about him. At the same time, I felt his pride in me. It was palpable, as if he was standing beside me telling me so. His little arrogant shit of a daughter had finally grown up. She was being held in high esteem by the city he loved, by people he would have respected and liked. By a justice of the state supreme court, among other people, in the center of the city he worked so hard to keep safe.

My relationship with my father was always complicated. When he was alive, I spent so much time hating him for how he treated my mom and the family. For his explosive temper and the violent outbursts and the beatings he inflicted on Jimmie and me. At times, Dad had a true streak of cruelty in him. All the same, I felt abandoned and deeply wounded when he took his life. Even though he and my mother died in ways that were eerily similar, losing him hit me much differently than losing my mom did. Her death left no room for hope of forgiveness. No light could ever penetrate what that loss felt like to me for many years to come, no matter how hard I tried to make it so.

But the gift my father gave me, that simple phone conversation we had a few months before he died, that changed the whole loss experience for me. Where we cut through all the crap and spoke from the heart, we were open enough to say, "I love you."

Don't misunderstand me. This was a crucial element in my overall healing and emotional and spiritual recovery. When we were finally able to connect in a way that was honest and loving, my father's steel armor melted away. So did mine. What I always thought was impossible had indeed occurred. The light came into our relationship after there was only darkness and pain for so long. Our short conversation took place in that ray of light. There was an exchange of love, respect, understanding and humor. That beautiful moment was his final gift to me. It changed my head and changed my heart.

I didn't begin to understand it until many years later, but my father, with that brief and tearful call, probably became the first person in my life to show me the meaning of forgiveness. Maybe it was easiest with him because I always knew he loved me. Despite all the bad stuff between us, it was something he had demonstrated throughout my childhood.

I think often about how the only photos of me being held as a little girl were of me in my dad's arms. There is not one photo of me and my mom like that. Bless her soul, the poor thing was burned out by the time she had me, so there was nothing much left for her to share. Whenever I think about her and question those distant memories, I remember there are no photos and know that is irrefutable evidence that my recollection of things is on the mark.

To this day, for a bunch of reasons, I still sometimes struggle with depression. But now, when my brain goes to dark places, I often turn it to thoughts of my dad. When I feel most lost, I conjure up his image in my mind, wishing he were still here to tell me what I should do. Just thinking of the exchange makes me feel better. What I would not give to hear him say, "It's going to be Okay, kid." What I wouldn't give to hear him tell me, "Let me handle it," because he would, taking away my anguish and worries. I still miss him terribly.

I knew the reunification ceremony in Detroit would be emotional. Anything like that involving kids, especially those at-risk like I was for so long, gets to me. This ceremony was a thousand times more intense because it was held in Detroit, where so much of my dad's life was lived. It took all my strength to maintain my composure. I felt as if I would break down at any moment. I leaned on my father's love, imagining his deep, baritone voice, imagining him smiling and laughing with joy at what his baby girl was doing on this warm afternoon in downtown Detroit.

In my remarks, I talked about how one loving Foster mom — Carrie — and an empathetic seventh-grade English teacher were there for me when no one seemed to care. Now it was my chance to lend a hand to others in distress, my turn to help people realize that standing up for a child at risk is not only worth the effort, it can change a lifetime.

"I'm doing good Dad, don't you think?" I thought to myself. "Your little girl ain't such a train wreck after all. She made something of herself, wouldn't you say, Dad?"

There was no noise in my head about the lousy hand I was dealt. Nothing about being born into a screwed-up family. Not a whisper about abuse, pain, suicide. No reminders of bad choices or my self-destructive past. I was in the joyful moment, happy to be alive. Grateful my life had a purpose. Grateful it had this purpose, standing up and being there for kids who are desperate to have someone in their corner. There was no need to whistle in the dark on this particular day. The sun was shining, I saw clearly, and like the kids say, it was all good.

I have said in a lot of media interviews over the years that my fate no longer defines me, and I think I said it during an interview or two that day in Detroit. It's not my destiny. There is a difference between the two. Fate is what we are handed. Destiny is what we make of it. Life requires hard work. It's about choices and the decisions we make along the way.

"Be part of someone's quantum leap," I told the crowd. "We need more good people coming up to the line. Fostering isn't right for everyone, but it's right for a whole lot of people." My heart raced. I am always nervous speaking in public. It's not like singing, where I am comfortable after so many years performing. On this day, my dad was there to help me through it. I needed him and he came through. I heard him. I felt his presence beside me.

"Good going," I heard him say as if he was sitting in the chair occupied by the state Supreme Court judge. "You've been through a lot. You never gave up. I'm so proud of you kid."

Thanks, Dad. That's right. I never gave up. In spite of everything, I got that from you.

Twenty-Seven - Stronger For It

In the spring and summer of 2012, I was busy touring on the strength of the great reviews and buzz that followed the release of Stronger For It, my 10th CD and my third release for Alligator. I was extra nervous about that one, more than I had been for anything I'd done in years. Under the best of circumstances, making a record for me is like being naked in public, under the lights with cameras running. And that's the best of circumstances! Making a record is a vulnerable and intense process. Sometimes I can still hear that old creep boyfriend of mine who said I couldn't sing, telling me I sounded like a cat in heat.

Also, with Stronger For It, I finally took the deep plunge and co-wrote three of the songs with my brilliant producer, Dave Darling, a friend of twenty-plus years. Writing my own songs required a different level of willingness to be vulnerable and exposed than anything I had experienced to before. It was also my first record not involving my then soon-to-be ex-husband (he had written or played on all the others). The whole undertaking felt more dangerous and uncertain to me. At the same time, there was an exhilaration and freshness to the process that I had not felt in years. Like life, conflicting emotions and feelings swirled around me when I was hunkered down in the studio making that record. But it was a hundred percent raw honesty. Maybe that explains why it came out as well as it did.

The process wasn't easier thanks to another big fight with Alligator boss Iglauer over the CD title and artwork. He insisted on calling the record Battle Scars. I wasn't going for that; it sounded way too harsh for me. It smacked of something you'd see on the Jerry Springer show.

I understood where Bruce was coming from. Some of the staff at Alligator were on the same page as him. They knew what was going on in my life. I had been scarred by too many recent battles and losses. My marriage of seventeen years had ended. Eight people I loved very much, including my dear Foster mom, Carrie, and my brother, Jimmie, were dead and recently buried. The band and I had been touring our asses off during it all; I was drained and exhausted. But the title still struck me as too extreme. I wanted something less in your face. Bruce was dug in, insisting he knew best. He told me again and again the media would love it. He kept bringing up a CD by Otis Taylor called Respect the Dead, but I really didn't give a shit. It wasn't happening. I dig and respect Otis Taylor, but just because something worked for him didn't mean a thing to me. I was just as dug in as Bruce. Since it was my record, and I would have to be the one to live with media and fan reaction as well as my own peace of mind when I laid my head on the pillow each night, the argument was over as far as I was concerned. As a matter of fact, there was no argument. I wasn't going to be the title. Period.

In the middle of all this back-and-forth with Bruce and the staff, I was sitting inside my touring van in a mall parking lot one afternoon when the Alligator crew and I were on a conference call to talk through all the final and critical details that go into putting out a CD. I had gone to the mall for, what else, a new pair of shoes and a few other last-minute items I needed before traveling with the band. The photo for the CD had been beautifully shot again by Jeff Dunas. We had a print deadline of the following morning. There was a strong sense of pressure on the call as final decisions needed to be made and they needed to be done now, once and for all. Any bickering had to stop.

Finally, a member of the Alligator staff broke the deadlock when he blurted out, "Why don't you call the record Stronger For It"? Boom. All the talking stopped. The phone went quiet. I began to tear up and cry. I had no doubt that was the perfect title for this piece of work.

Bruce, who was also on the line, wanted to know why I didn't say anything when the new title was proposed. "Because I'm crying," I sobbed into the phone, which was getting wet from my tears. "It's the perfect title." Everyone agreed. Months of heated argument ended on a dime. I was Stronger For It, beat up and wounded, but somehow stronger nonetheless. What is it the ancient Greeks said? That which doesn't kill you makes you stronger? At least I think it was the Greeks, but who knows? It could have been Oprah. All I know is that shit is true as the day is long. I was delighted we found the perfect title for the CD.

Unfortunately, the sense of relief was short-lived. A few days later, Bruce and I were arguing again. He insisted that if I didn't cave in on his choice of artwork and images, he'd be done with me. I could buy the Master Recordings from him, take my record and go home.

Suddenly I channeled my dad again, just as I did in Phoenix when the Mojomatics were booked to back Otis Rush without me. I was in no mood to be told what to do. I called Bruce's bluff. As far as I was concerned, he had just opened the door to contract negotiation with his statement, which any good litigator will tell you. I'm no lawyer, but I do know how to negotiate. I told him I would call back in a couple of days. I knew I needed a moment to find the money required to call his bluff.

Two days later, I got him on the phone and said, okay, I will buy you out. I'll buy the master recordings and as far as I was concerned, we'd be done. I don't think he expected me to go balls to the wall like that. He said he had made that comment in the heat of an argument. I didn't budge. I told him I would write him a check then and there for $15,000 as a down payment. Then I would roll on down the road, all my business with Alligator over.

I was unsure how he'd react to that option, but I was more than ready to do it. I called his hand, but I was not bluffing. Now he dug in deeper, only this time he said there was no way he would allow that to happen. He said he didn't mean it when he said he'd sell me the masters. He just wanted to show me how strongly he felt about what he wanted.

I have to admit that in one view, much of what Bruce asks for is not that unusual. Just as it's not that unusual for the artist to end up less than happy with the record company boss. It goes with the territory, sorry to say. I learned long ago from the Bill Magness school of salesmanship that's it's more productive to be congenial in business. But I also learned that doesn't mean you roll over when someone is being manipulative or combative. It took a long time, but I have learned how to stand firm when I need to. That's something that can be hard for people accustomed to getting their way. It's hard for me too. It's not something I enjoy. But a girl has to do what a girl has to do, right? Bruce and I actually got along relatively well much of the time, as long as it wasn't time to make the record. That's when there would be sharp differences between us. He was used to being the boss across the board I suppose that is why he runs his own company. I never operate well under those conditions. You have to compromise in business and in life, but you don't compromise your principles or your artistic integrity. The writing was on the wall as far as I was concerned. I had just finalized my divorce with my husband. Now I was going to get divorced from my record company and I saw it coming. There was no other way.

I have no such problems with my producer. I am incredibly lucky to have Dave in my corner. He helps me stay brave enough to take the kinds of risks necessary to make a great record. He is also a hundred percent honest with me, and it never comes from a place of trying to prove who's in control. The line in the sand for me is that I never want to make the same record twice; Dave is indispensable in that formula. He pushes me, driving me to be a better artist. To take risks and share even more of myself with the music. He has also helped me acknowledge that I am really an artist. There has always been a part of me that is waiting for the official guy with the badge and the megaphone to appear and shout: "Step away from this life. That woman is an imposter! There has been a big mistake here, folks."

While we were making Stronger For It in late 2011, I spent a lot of time weeping. So many deaths and losses were piling up. In addition to Carrie and my brother, I also had to bury Katie, my sweet little kitty, ten days before Christmas. I was emotionally raw, thanking God for the music even more than usual because it allowed me to pour the emotion into my writing and performing. I try hard to never take any of my frustrations out on my band mates. I'm not that kind of person and they are great human beings. I'd beat myself up before venting my frustrations on anyone else. But I did spend my emotional currency up on stage. People have told me my performances were more raw than ever. I know I felt more vulnerable. My feelings were more exposed than they had been in a long time. Having to perform during that time offered me a much-needed emotional healing and a way to keep my head together when I really needed something to lean into.

Stronger For It debuted at Number One on the Billboard Blues charts, resulting in wider recognition than any of my earlier CDs and a lot more work and prizes, including Song of the Year at the 2013 Blues Music Awards for I Won't Cry. I also went home with the hardware for Contemporary Blues Female Artist of the Year. That felt pretty fucking good, I must say. And that was followed up with Living Blues Magazine, which was actually started in part by Iglauer and six others in 1970, and is the oldest blues publication in America, naming me female Blues Artist of the Year in its Readers Poll. At that point, I was the second white woman and third white person to walk off with the Best Artist prize from Living Blues. I am still amazed by everything that happened around that CD.

It was also gratifying to know that my fans, radio and the media all responded so favorably to the songs I co-wrote. That was such a relief to me, and it's given me some confidence to do more writing. The reaction was especially favorable to I Won't Cry and Whistlin' In The Dark. Another favorite for a lot of folks was There It Is, a funny tune about killing a man. (I know, who can't see the humor in that scenario, right, ladies?) There is an endless tradition of blues songs where women meet their demise. Women are being done away with left and right in the blues. Dave and I came up with an alternative, one for the gals I like our take on this traditional blues form and so do my fans, I am happy to say. It's always a fun one to sing on stage. The ladies love it.

When I won "Best Contemporary Female Blues Artist" in 2013 in Memphis, it was my fourth time winning that prize, an incredible honor. And when Dave and I won Song of the Year for I Won't Cry, that was sweet icing on the cake. I took that as a very loud and resounding yes from the universe telling me to keep writing songs!

I'm not bragging when I say Stronger For It felt like a personal triumph on so many levels. I was pleased, proud and feeling pretty good, even if the experience of writing some of my own songs was at times gut-wrenching and painful.

After Dave and I walked off the stage on May 6, 2013 in Memphis with our awards, we were basking in the good feeling backstage. I was feeling happily stunned with our success, but he just stood there grinning at me like a happy chimp, twirling a toothpick in his mouth. Then he looked at me and said, "You know what's next... right?" I said, "We go eat?" He said "Nope... next record...all originals." Then I swear, he cackled like the devil. I yelled at him to stop torturing me! We laughed about as hard as I have laughed in years. It all felt fantastic.

Within a few weeks, Dave and I began talking seriously about the next CD, what it should be like and how to go about putting it together. Pretty soon, we were writing together again. The idea of doing all originals scared the crap out of me. It took a lot of emotional energy for me to co-write the handful of originals on Stronger For It. But that's how the game is played. You always have to strive for something better, something that pushes and challenges you as an artist. That's how I've always approached being in the studio; that's the way Dave operates, too. You never want to do the same thing twice. You have to stretch yourself and hope to hell there's an audience for it. That your audience grows instead of shrinks because you left behind some of your most ardent fans. That can happen quite easily, before you know it. I honestly didn't think I had it in me to come up with a whole record of original songs. I felt I said all I had to say on Stronger For It. But one of the joys — or terrors, depending on my mood — of working with Dave is that he always pushes me, in a loving and supportive way, to do more. To get better. To reach down deeper and pull out something I didn't know I had inside me. Terrified though I was, it didn't take long to realize Dave was right. Doing more of my own songs was the next logical step for me to take as an artist. What the hell, I told myself. I trusted Dave explicitly. With him in my corner producing and co-writing, I would probably survive.

But first there was something else I had to endure and it scared me more than the idea of going back into the studio with all original songs. This was something that could very well cost me my career and maybe even my life.

Twenty-Eight - Fathead

My back had been giving me problems for a long time, probably due to all the car accidents I had been in over the years, particularly the one in Tucson that totaled my car. Add all the wear and tear I have put my body through touring, singing and stomping around the stage in high heels, and I was in a lot of pain. I do yoga almost every day, which helps keep me limber and strong, but the constant ache in my back and neck was getting progressively worse. It was time to face the facts and do something about it. The way I was going, performing would be out of the question in a few years if I didn't get this fixed. Plus, my doctors told me that my spine and neck were so beat up that if I was in even a minor car accident — a real risk, considering all the time I spend in my van driving to gigs — I could be paralyzed for life. That got my attention.

On December 13, 2012, about nine months after Stronger For It was released, I underwent a very delicate neck and spinal surgery that lasted more than five hours. The surgery was especially frightening for me because the surgeon had to cut into my throat for access to my spine. That's right, my throat. It still creeps me out to say it. One wrong move, and my voice could be gone forever. This was far riskier than I'd imagined or prepared for. So much was going on at the time. We were touring to promote the CD. My dissatisfaction with doing business with Bruce was at the breaking point. I wanted to expand my audience and record some new music, more songs I wrote myself, and Bruce wasn't keen on the idea. I did not want to go under the knife and be confined to bed for six weeks while I was recuperating. Plus, I was also very scared about being inactive while I was mending — scared especially about getting strung out on pain medication, which is exactly what happened. Somehow, with help from friends and family, I made it through hideous withdrawals and a grueling rehabilitation regimen that had me immobile, on my back, my swollen neck in a brace and unable to eat solid food, for six weeks. I now have $93,000 worth of titanium screws and pins in my neck. There are little metal cages inside parts of my neck now that stabilize it. Miraculously, I am mostly pain-free today, able to move around on stage as much as I want. The best part of having done the surgery and gotten it behind me is that I know I am singing better than ever before.

Dave and I had been talking about broadening my audience and doing more roots or Americana than straight blues even as we were recording Stronger For It. When I started to feel better, we talked some more.

Branching out like that was not something I could see doing for Alligator. Bruce and I would never see eye to eye about it. The older I get and the further I have gotten into owning the idea of actually being a legitimate artist, the less energy I have for certain kinds of fighting. Especially the kind required to defend myself creatively. I'm not interested in having to justify or sell my creative self. It's not arrogance that makes me say that. It's my age and the simple fact that I'm exhausted. Doing what I do takes so much out of me. I need to save my energy for the music, not the bullshit with the record company or anyone else.

The road, the touring, the bad hotels, the emotional capital you have to spend to really put all your heart and soul into the work takes a toll. Singing on stage up to two hundred nights in a given year is exhausting. It's not working in a coal mine. There are harder ways to make a living. I am blessed to be doing what I love. But that doesn't make it any less of a struggle. My energy needs to go into the work. That's demanding enough. There's no time to fight with people who insist they want me to do things their way. Hard work and a fair amount of success equals I get to walk away if you don't respect me. Or if something doesn't feel true to me. I think I've earned that.

I came across a quote a while back from an author named Sherry Argov. She wrote a book called, Why Men Love Bitches: From Doormat to Dreamgirl. I love the title and the quote. "Truly powerful people don't explain why they want respect. They simply don't engage someone who doesn't give it to them." I've seen the line with the word "people" replaced by "women;" at this point in my life, I try to subscribe to that theory a hundred percent of the time.

I knew what I had to do with Bruce and Alligator. Despite our conflicts, it was a great six years for me and the label. I feel good about our body of work—three strong

CDs my fans seemed to really dig. The relationship and the work we produced were a great boost to my career and my level of recognition. I can only say that the staff at Alligator is a solid team of professionals and they are wonderful to work with.

Still by 2014, it became clear to me that it was time to move on after Dave and I had four songs shaped up well enough to send along to Bruce and his reaction to the material was considerably less than happy. In fact, it was the opposite. He hated the songs and made fun of them. I might have predicted it, but I'd wanted to give him a chance before making my final decision. Among other things, he said "the songs might be good, but they would never be on an Alligator recording." If I'd had any doubts about moving on, here was my answer. The moment was here to jump. I hoped there would be something solid to land on when I took the leap.

It's not like the decision caused a fast-moving crisis. Dave and I had already discussed the "what if?" scenario quite a bit. I'd had a lot of time to think about it as I was lying in my bed recuperating through the holidays in 2012 and early 2013. Once I was feeling healthy and strong again, we wrote and wrote and wrote - Dave and I, along with some incredibly intuitive songwriter friends Carl Sealove and Gary Davenport, my dear friend and longtime bass player, plus Lauren Bliss and Andrew Lowden from Australia. Fairly early on, we started to formulate a backup plan in case Alligator passed on its option for my next release.

I never felt more engaged and alive. I had my health back; working on the CD was just what I needed. It was a rush and a release to be set free to follow my heart and instincts. I knew it was the right thing to do, stretching into the songwriting even more. I was clear that meant my relationship with Alligator had run its course. I was going, but I was not exactly sure to what or where.

Years earlier, in 1997, my ex-husband Jeff and I had started the label Fathead as a way to release his music. We'd put out the all-original release It Takes One To Know One. But I eventually signed with Blues Leaf, Jeff eventually went on to release more of his original music on Fathead.

During our negotiations in the divorce, I got the rights to the label. So when things went down with Alligator, I already had a label and a business license in hand. There was just one tiny detail that had to be worked out. I had no money to fund a record.

So Dave and I unleashed our Plan B. We finished writing and compiling the material. We came up with the next best move for Fathead Records, putting together a lean, ace team of seasoned music business professionals to help us record, put out and promote a CD.

The first to come on board was Niels Schroeter as our general manager. He has more than a quarter century of experience in the music business. Plus, he's a great guy. We then set our sights on publicity and radio, enlisting Cary Baker from Conqueroo, a highly regarded boutique music publicity firm that gets results. We added Leslie Rouffee and Frank Roszak, two smart radio public relations experts who know how to get your music airtime on Americana and blues stations respectively. We added John Oszajca, a super-talented Los Angeles singer-songwriter who is also a social media marketing genius. Done, done and done! We had our team; it was a group I would gladly go into battle with anytime, anywhere.

Things came together in a strange and beautiful way. Everyone was on board and knew the risks involved. Such as: We might not be able to raise the money to finish the job, and we might not get any media recognition for the CD if we did get it done. Everyone dug in a little deeper because we were underdogs. As things turned out, this was the perfect combination to get the attention we needed for the music.

We were financially challenged, to say the least, but with Niels and Dave at the helm, I was in with two very creative, experienced and insightful people; I felt confident we would find a way.

I was lucky enough to have other angels appear when I needed them most. Being an established artist has its ups and downs. One of the ups is that you get to meet some remarkable people. Some fans cross the line and you see them so often at shows and get to know them so well, they become true and personal friends. Such has been the case with three dear souls named Barbara, Amanda and Raymond. They are known to many in the blues world simply as "The Hammermans." They are longtime blues fans, supporters of artists and philanthropists. They were excited when I told them about the move I made to re-launch Fathead and record my own record, offering to do whatever they could to support my leap into the unknown.

We knew we could work at Dave's personal studio in his home and elsewhere, but the initial funding to get things moving came from the grace of dear friends. Barbara and Amanda came down for the photo shoot and to be part of the recording dates when we laid down the bones of the record.

We filmed the recording sessions, which gave us some great candid material to use in social media clips we could use to tease out the CD in messages to my fans and to build a sense of expectation around the new record. We were going full tilt seven days a week. It was exhausting, but the most alive and excited I have ever felt doing a record.

Letting out timed video clips of the new material was just what the doctor ordered when it came to creating buzz and raising cash. We began the fundraising with a premium item—a limited edition box set of the new record with assorted goodies inside—to help motivate support for the release. This engaged my fan base in a way that blew my mind. I always knew my fans were devoted, but I wasn't sure about how to bring them into the process and get them fully engaged until John Oszajca formulated a grassroots marketing plan that made it happen.

We started with a blog post from me that we titled "Woman Bites Dog." It was a comment I had made to John when I was leaving Alligator and he grabbed on to it, finding a way to use it in our marketing.

"For the last few months, it's been impossible to sleep more than five hours a night," I wrote in my blog post. "My ulcer is talking to me again. I just finished writing the songs and recording my 11th CD with my stellar band, collaborator and producer, but I am stressed at an entirely new level . . . Instead of working with the known, the solid team at Alligator and benefitting from its accomplished marketing, financing and publicity network, I went with the unknown. Me."

I wrote in the blog how Alligator had once been my Holy Grail. Now that I had split from the label I had always revered, my anxiety was in the next room doing pushups, getting stronger by the day.

"What if my fans and critics don't like the new direction?" I wrote on the blog. I suppose I was pining for some reassurance, but there was nothing put-on about it. I felt this way every second I was awake working on that CD.

"What if it actually sucks? I'm not a 20-something artist who can roll with a break in my career momentum. That can be deadly to a musical career. I feel confident and hopeful people will like it, but I'd be lying if I said my mind didn't go to those scary, negative places. It certainly does. I learned long ago, after much pain and heartbreak, that I have to be true to what's in my own heart, no matter how awkward or frightening it may seem. It took me a long time and a very crooked journey to understand that."

I was pouring out my soul, sharing my deepest fears and most precious dreams, so I kept going.

"Gratitude is probably the overwhelming emotion in my life these days, but I'm not kidding when I tell you that even with decades of working on myself (therapy, yoga and meditation), going as far out on the tightrope as I am with this new CD . . . I'm still scared to death of making a bad move and tumbling to the ground. A wise person once described faith this way: When you come to the edge of light and everything you know and are about to step off into the darkness of the unknown, faith is knowing one of two things will happen. There will be something to stand on or you will be taught to fly. God, I sure hope so. I do believe it. And I know one thing for sure: No matter what happens, these songs had to be written, this record had to be made and I had to do it this way. I had to be free, artistically and spiritually. It really is my declaration of independence. And just like I sing on the last track, I'm still standing and my heart's still beating. That's the solid truth no matter what comes next."

For a new record, the first week of sales means everything. Especially for a new record on a young label. How a new CD does in those first crucial days tells the entire industry if the project has legs or not. If things go well and there are sales and a good buzz, you get radio play, media and booked gigs. That's the simple and crazy truth of the business, so I appealed to my fans — damn near begged them — to pre-order the CD right now.

"All pre-orders will be counted towards the first week of sales," I wrote in my pitch, "and you'll totally be a part of showing the industry that's it's not all about the big guns. But rather that the small, independent and STUBBORN guns can pack a huge wallop. I love that . . . don't you?"

I did love it. It was a thrill to take the world on in this way. My fans, bless their hearts, came through as I hoped they would. John said he has never seen a fan base engage the way my fans jumped on board. The sheer number of people who answered my call to support me and the record — and do it so quickly, when it mattered the most — was one of the most remarkable things that has ever happened to me. Like I said, gratitude is the overwhelming emotion for me these days.

What began as a modest grassroots campaign took off like wildfire after a drought. First the blog post, then the box set premium and the tracking session video clips. We sold out the first pressing on pre-order sales before the release date. It was crazy; I kept telling myself and others, "Go Team Fathead!"

Pre-orders went so well we had to scramble to get another order from the manufacturer before the actual release date of June 23, 2014. It was a definite headache, but a good one to have, to be sure. We managed to pull it together thanks to Niels and Dave stepping up and pulling favors with the manufacturer. I breathed such a sigh of relief you could have heard it in the next county, I was sure.

John kept having me shoot home movies and posting them on the blog site he had set up, which was tied to my multiple Facebook page feeds and my website. We were getting the word out pretty effectively and all I was doing was telling the truth. The truth was, I was working harder than I ever had and I was sweating bullets over it. I am not exaggerating when I say that working eighteen to twenty hours a day was not unusual. I did it virtually every day for months. I was so wiped out, I started hallucinating, and this time it wasn't from LSD. It's not the textbook way to make a record or how I would recommend doing it, but at the same time I felt deeply happy because everyone on our team was so committed. We were all into it a hundred and fifty percent, as if our lives depended on it. That made me feel like I could conquer the world, or at least like I would survive the experience and come out the other end with a solid product and good results.

I was inspired by warm wishes of support from fans, friends and family. They were all cheering me on. There's nothing better than that. I was flooded with emails and Facebook messages wishing me well, telling me to hang in there, people saying they were so proud I was taking the plunge and doing it my way. I'm not sure I could have made it through the entire insane process without all that love and support. My fans were like the cavalry to me, a safety net that caught me and kept me going when I was so tired I could barely put one foot in front of the other. It was like electricity, supplying the energy we needed to keep things going. To keep us going. What a beautiful trip this was turning out to be.

In the end, our plan worked. We came out in the top five albums on the Billboard Blues charts, number one song on the Living Blues Radio charts and in the top twenty albums on the Americana charts. Five of my songs showed up high on the various charts as well. We had the number one blues song, I Need A Man, on radio all summer long. Oh yeah, then we got three Blues Music Award nominations for the album. Amazing! Original struck a chord with a large number of people.

For that, I will always be grateful. It was hard for me to not feel vindicated with regard to Alligator. I had no regrets over moving on from the comfort and security of the label, despite all the stress and midnight sweats that had come with the decision.

In a strange and beautiful way that filled me with some quiet tears on more than one occasion as I worked through all this, I could feel my father's support. I felt him being proud and happy that I was forging out on my own, that I showed 'em I could do it and do it well. With integrity and commitment to my music, the way I wanted to do it. He'd think it was the Magness way and who was I to argue? It got me through the nights I was cross-eyed writing blog posts and filming thirty-seven takes of me at my desk with my I-phone. It felt like something I had no choice over. Who I was and all I had been through took me to this place. There was no other way for me to keep moving forward as an artist. It felt like I was being taken on a trip and guided through it in spite of my deep-seated fears and uncertainty. I thank God and everyone who helped and supported me for allowing it to happen.

When it was finally time to release the CD, I wanted to do it at a place where I could feel supported, where the audience would actually be able to listen. We also wanted a place with a friendly enough vibe that media would enjoy the experience, too. One of the best venues in the L.A. area that fits that bill is McCabe's Guitar Shop in Santa Monica. It's famous, more than fifty years old, a throwback to the days when you could walk into a guitar shop and get help from someone who really knew their shit and took a personal interest in trying to help you. Sadly, that has become a rarity in music retail stores—the ones left that is. McCabe's offers classes on almost all manner of guitar playing, singing, performance workshops, harmonica, you name it. And it has a world-famous concert hall in the back that is a perfect setting for listening to new music. Bookings are difficult to get, since A-list songwriters and multiple genre artists play there. Jackson Browne and Townes Van Zandt have graced the stage at McCabe's. So have Bruce Springsteen, Joni Mitchell, John Hiatt and Emmylou Harris. The place is musical royalty. If you walk through the upstairs hallway, you'll understand why. There are photos from intimate moments in concerts by Bonnie Raitt, Roosevelt Sykes, John Hammond, Jackson Browne, Mose Allison, Ginger Baker, The Bangles, Beck, Stephen Bishop, Karla Bonoff, Laura Nyro, Jeff Buckley, Taj Mahal, Bettye Carter, Roseanne Cash, The Chambers Brothers, Blind Boys of Alabama, Clifton Chenier, Vic Chestnutt, Guy Clark, Vassar Clements, Jackie DeShannon, Willie Dixon, John Lee Hooker and more. You get the picture. The place is to quality singer-songwriter artists what the Hall of Fame in Cooperstown, New York is to baseball. A shrine, hallowed ground to be sure.

McCabe's also has deep meaning to me on a personal level. I had not only heard about the shows for years, a lot of L.A. firsts happened there for me. McCabe's was the first place I went to when I relocated to Southern California from Phoenix in 1986. I went there because I knew I would meet some of my pack at McCabe's, people who were like me. I was right. I made friends and eventually had band members who also worked at the store over the years. Dana Ferris and Fran Banish both became dear friends and were guitarists in my first L.A. band. They worked there. McCabe's was also the first store in Los Angeles to sell my music. I was lucky enough to perform there a number of times over the years. It is a place that means a hell of a lot to me.

Unfortunately, it was also a place I tended to avoid in the few years leading up to release of the new CD. I stopped in from time to time to see old friends, but my soon-to-be ex-husband and his new girlfriend worked there, so it was uncomfortable for me. Still, it seemed like the only place to launch my new CD. Screw it, I said, putting all the discomfort aside and asking my agency to book the CD release there. They did, and we sold out!

 It was an amazing night for me and the band. People seemed to be locked into the performance and the songs; we sold a lot of CDs. I was glad I did the release there, but I was also uncomfortable. Too many intertwined relationships became impossible to ignore.

The experience reminded me that when a marriage breaks up, there are losses at many levels. Friends and associates choose sides. It's human nature to do so. You split them up like you split your personal belongings. I jokingly told friends, "He got the Volvo, I'm keeping Paris." I was only half kidding, because that's how it seemed to go. It made me sad to realize I'd lost McCabe's, too, in the split, at least for the foreseeable future. I have always loved that place and the people in it, but being there was too hard. After the show that night, I took a few moments alone in the dressing room, crying and saying goodbye to McCabe's Guitar Shop and my attachment to its funky beauty and authenticity. It might be different in the future, but for now my heart was heavy over the close of another chapter that meant a lot to me. What I didn't know at the time was that my heart would soon be filled with something else I never expected.

Twenty-Nine - Answered Prayer

In the summer of 2014, I was working at my customarily frantic pace. The band and I were on tour in the Midwest, and a month or so earlier, I'd received another message on Facebook that wound up changing my life. Funny how that works: You're locked into your routine, running hard to keep up and all of the sudden a thunderbolt will come down and shake things up. It happened to me when Sam reached out and we were able to reconcile after all those years and bad memories. Now it happened again when I looked at my computer and saw some nice comments from a fan. I'm lucky that kind of thing happens a lot. I usually read what people say, get a little good feeling from their kind words and get back to the grind. But something about this message was different. When he asked me to be his friend, I checked him out a little, thanks to the power of the Internet. He seemed cool. Besides, he was incorrigibly handsome. We had several mutual friends to boot. I considered his friend request and figured, why not?

A little while after that initial encounter, a post of his came into my feed about a subject with which I was all too familiar. It was clear he had lost someone very dear to him and was grieving. I wrote some words about the grieving process in an effort to provide a little comfort to a fellow sufferer; we began communicating in private online. I was right. The son of his girlfriend had passed unexpectedly the year or so before, and the anniversary of his death was approaching. We began writing to each other, mostly on Facebook, and found out we had a lot in common. Turns out he was an up-and-coming blues harmonica player from Great Britain who fell in love with the music after listening to a Lightnin' Hopkins cassette. He taught himself to play by ear and went on to perform with some of the top blues artists in England, so of course I found him interesting. On his website, he listed his favorite quote as a line from martial artist Bruce Lee that said, "Don't think. Feel." Hell, I could probably learn something from this guy, I thought to myself. His name was T.J. Norton and we connected pretty quickly - which was a shock for two extremely hard-working individuals without a lot of time for much more than work. Plus, we're both guarded and private, our presence on Facebook and social media notwithstanding. I don't think either of us expected anything deep to develop between us. There wasn't time, for one thing.

He came to Los Angeles to visit in November 2014. I returned the favor and traveled to the U.K. for the Christmas holidays. It wasn't long before we both knew this was serious. And when I say things moved quickly, I mean quickly. He came back to the States in April 2015. On June 7, 2015, we were married in a small ceremony performed by a woman we both knew through Facebook and from her love of the music. Since she was also an ordained minister, it was perfect. We were married in Topanga at the Inn of the Seventh Ray, which was the closest place to an English shire I could find in the City of Angels. The entire experience was a whirlwind and a dream all at once.

Now that we are together, I cannot imagine being without him. It seems remarkable to have found someone who was such a perfect fit for a partner in my life. He is an extremely strong and compassionate man. I am insanely grateful for his presence. We have found a deep and profound love. It is a miracle for sure.

As I've said earlier in this story, living happily has always been a challenge for me. The truth is, the biggest part of that challenge is, well, you guessed it . . . the biggest part of that challenge is yours truly. Keeping myself from giving up on life. Getting out of my own way. And that has required a level of perseverance it's taken most of my life to appreciate and understand. Why I hung in there when my parents could not. It's a riddle I have turned around in therapy, in recovery, and in my life for decades. And I am here to tell you, that shit can be exhausting. But I consider it a gift today.

I think often of that time more than twenty-five years ago, my friend Lila summed me up so well (I'm gonna repeat this), "We know you're tough. We know we can tie your hands and your feet and gag you and you will scale that brick wall with your teeth. Not a problem. You got that. We know that. Nobody's worried about that. But let's untie your hands and your feet. Let's take that gag off. Let's give you a really good life and then let's see what you got. Let's see how you handle that. Let's see what you're made of then honey, when life gets good."

Lila was a lot older than me and a lot wiser. She laughed in my face after sharing her sage observation. It was the most joyous, loving laughter you could imagine. The same kind of laughter you would expect from a Buddha or some wise old oracle who knew much more than you could ever wrap your little fear-based brain around. She quickly became a trusted friend and spiritual advisor for me, but what she said way back in 1992 scared the crap out of me. Mostly because I could not imagine my life actually getting good. She was right. I had no idea what that might look like. It felt like a foreign concept to me. Because, in fact, it was.

It's taken me a lifetime to trust. To learn how to accept the universe saying "yes" without totally fucking things up. Sad truth is that I was most comfortable when things were fucked up, in a mess, when I was moving on to the next calamity or tragedy because that was familiar landscape. I recognized the geography, needing no map or GPS to navigate through it. Being happy and contented, that's like the idea of walking on the moon. Totally alien space with no landmarks or anything familiar to use as a guidepost.

Over the years, I had many occasions to be happy and say "yes" to glad tidings from life, even with all the crazy shit that happened. Some of those opportunities didn't happen by accident. I worked hard for them. But they have all been gifts, even those that came with blood, sweat and tears. Especially those, perhaps.

But can I accept joy? Can I accept success as an artist? Success as a human being? Can I believe any of it to be real and not some cruel illusion only to be snatched back because, well, because the truth is I don't think I am worthy of any of it? I think I can. It's taken so long but I am much better equipped today than I ever was to handle happiness, joy, success as a human being, success in my profession and positive recognition in both areas of my life.

Sadly, my friend Lila passed away in 2008 from ovarian cancer, but I can still hear her words ringing in my ears as I write this. I can conjure up her wonderful laugh and the sparkle in her blue eyes. Let's see what you're made of now, tough girlie. Well, my friend, it took me a lifetime but I am finally starting to figure it out. I am finally starting to believe that feeling joyful, happy and fulfilled are not only possible, they are becoming a comfortable fit. It blows my mind after all these years to even be able to write that, let alone truly believe it.

Lila helped me understand that despite all the adversity I experienced in my life, despite the bad start that came from being born into a deeply dysfunctional family, my fate does not have to be my destiny. When it comes to examining my life, I understand today that I can be both prisoner and jailer if I am not careful. We all can. I have the keys to the cell. It's my choice whether to lock myself in or open the door and go free. I can raise a flag and ask for help when I need it and get on with my life, but I have to be willing. To me, asking for help and admitting I can't do things alone are a sign of strength, not weakness as we are conditioned to believe. This may all sound overly simplistic, but it's come to be the truth for me. And there was nothing simple about it. It required a ton of personal work and hard self-examination to get there. Work, help from other kind souls like Lila, and the grace of the universe. All I can say at this point is thank you very much.

I have lived most of my life not just turning my back on beauty, joy, happiness or love when they showed up, but rather flying into magnificent and destructive tailspins. Why? Probably because I know so much about fighting, adversity, struggling and just plain duking it out with life. I have a PhD in pain. It's been my stock and trade. Barn's burnt down, hallelujah, now I can see the moon. Today if the barn happens to catch fire and burn, I jump up, douse the flames and say holy shit, I'm going to have to rebuild that motherfucker. I would love to have some help, which—when I am open to it—always seems to miraculously appear. That's pretty cool, if you ask me.

But I can't lie. My life is not all peace and roses. I still have to fend off the old me enough of the time that I feel worn out and wonder how the hell can I continue to push forward. But these days, I recognize that state of mind when it starts to appear; I have ways to push out the fear, depression and anxiety. Most of the time. Sometimes they move down the road quickly and I am back in the game. Sometimes they linger and I am at sea, trying to stay afloat. But I know relief is there. I find dry land and go on about my business.

I came across a quote online from a child development researcher and author by the name of L.R. Knost that sums things up pretty well for me. "Life is amazing," she wrote. "And then it's awful. And then it's amazing again. And in between the amazing and the awful, it's ordinary and mundane and routine. Breathe in the amazing, hold on through the awful, and relax and exhale during the ordinary. That's just living heartbreaking, soul-healing, amazing, awful, ordinary life. And it's breathtakingly beautiful." No shit.

Thirty - Original the Musical

One night after a show during our tour for the Original CD, some fans came up to talk, as they always do. I was standing behind the merchandise table, hawking CDs and T-shirts, handing out literature about Foster Care. My energy is always low after a performance, but fans like to come up and say hello and we sell most of my records at the shows, so as much as I would like to go get something to eat and get back to the hotel and rest, I hang around for a good hour or two and connect with as many people as possible.

The folks who came up to me this night — I can't even remember what city we were in — said they were from Minnesota, and as it turned out, we had some common history. Some familiar stomping grounds and old places. They were nice people, and as our conversation progressed, they told me they used to be in theatre and now had a production company of sorts in Los Angeles. One of them, Rachel Nee Hall, told me she could not get the songs from Original out of her head. She read about me online and checked out my bio on my website, telling me it all added up to an epiphany of sorts for her. She was convinced she needed to write a musical based on my life story. My music would form the backbone of it, especially the new material from Original.

All I could do was burst into laughter when she told me this. I thought the idea was hilarious. When my goofy giggling finally subsided, I looked back at her and her partner, Jeff Richards, and they stared back in total seriousness. They also seemed slightly embarrassed at my response. It was probably not what they were expecting. They came to the show to run the idea past me and I was cracking up about it.

They asked if we could get together sometime to discuss the idea. We met a few weeks later in L.A. and after hearing them out, I had to say I was intrigued. Why not, I said. Let's give it shot.

We would work together on Original, the Musical, and see if the universe would play along.

I didn't know much about productions like this, but with help from Rachel and Jeff, I learned quickly. Putting together a show like the one they envisioned typically takes much longer than any of us had time for, but we worked our asses off and launched a preview in August 2015.

The show is about eighty minutes long. It features an actress who plays me as a young girl, up to the age of fourteen, then an older version of me from the time I was about twenty into my early forties. The real-life Janiva appears at the very end. The whole thing is surreal to me, but I have to say the show is pretty damn good.

It is a multi-media production, with music, a live band and some footage from old home movies I had. We also include current footage of me answering questions in an interview with a college student. As I answer the questions, stories are more or less re-enacted on stage by the cast.

I have learned that when you do these kind of things and are seeking investors, you need to show enough potential to make them want to back you, but without producing a complete show just yet. You want the potential investors to understand that without their help, you won't get the production where it needs to be to find success. We have nineteen songs in the show, either co-written by me or that I have recorded in the past.

It was a ton of work pulling together producers, cast, crew and enough financial backing to run fifteen rehearsals, two previews and a sold-out premier at an intimate little theatre in North Hollywood. The audience seemed to love it, and we were soon holding discussions with a potential financial backer and lawyers so we could stage an ongoing production. Talks are still underway.

I'll tell you this: It's one thing to admit your own past. That's unsettling enough. It's another experience altogether to actually write the crap down and tell the whole sordid tale to other people. That's hard one on one. To do it and then watch it played out on stage, complete with a soundtrack of my music and the dialogue of things I actually said and did, many of them not pretty or noble, well, that took more out of me than I realized when Rachel and Jeff stopped by to say hello and pitch the idea after my show on that fateful night.

My therapist, Naomi, would likely say she could have predicted that my reaction to this out-of-nowhere experience would be a combination of surprise, disbelief, joy, absolute anxiety, PTSD flashbacks and depression. Great, right? Sounds like a backbreaker, so of course I say let's charge full fucking speed ahead and do it.

Watching two actresses do a really good job portraying me, and the rest of the cast as well — navigating, narrating and acting out periods of my own life— was simultaneously beautiful, sad and shocking for me. In other words, the whole undertaking is a mixed blessing. The universe was saying yes to me again, but it was saying something else as well: Janiva Magness, if you want to play along, be prepared to have your guts turned inside out and be exhausted and worn out in ways you've never known before. Okay, I answered back, bring it on.

I do have a lot of pride. I persist. It's what I do. Without vanity, I can say that I understand today that it's important for me to tell the truth about my life. To own it because it's mine and because I want to be an example for others who struggle. That's why I am writing this book. It's why I said yes to the musical. Both may advance my career, which would be cool. But my primary motivation in sharing my story has always been to help others get through pain long enough for their lives to come full circle as mine has done. Like it is said, you have to stick around long enough for the miracle. If I can do it, other people can do it, too. This is called holding the light, and I feel compelled to do it. It's the only way I can make sense out of all the crap I went through. Otherwise, it has no meaning except that it almost killed me and the suffering would have been in vain. I know today it was not in vain. I know today that there was a reason for all of it. I am committed to that reason.

I was grateful beyond words for the theatre promoters' interest in me, but I was also angry. Not at them, but participating in this project was hard. It threw me off my schedule and my game. Just as writing this book has done.

Working on the musical left no time for anything else. My life was suddenly completely out of balance. My inner dialogue got dark and negative real fast. I couldn't help it. There was no time for the yoga or meditation I need to stay grounded. This went on for weeks. I was feeling more and more pressure, more and more that my life was once again out of control. That is a familiar feeling and I am no longer comfortable with it.

At the same time, I felt excited. The cast and crew were beginning to dig into the roles of my family members and other important people in the story. I kept it to myself as best I could, but as the project progressed and took shape, it was harder and harder for me to go to rehearsals. All my grand mistakes were being played out in front of me. In front of other people I barely knew.

One night, about ten days before the premier, I fell into a severe PTSD episode. It was the first in many years, but it grabbed hold of me full on. It was impossible to discern past from the present. I felt lost and afraid, as I did when I was a small child. It was a terrible episode. It seemed as if I might be losing my mind and believe me, I know what that feels like. I trembled and sobbed uncontrollably one night on the bathroom floor of my apartment. I could not articulate why because nothing made sense to me. I was unable to eat or sleep. I was stuck somewhere in my traumatic past despite everything good that was happening in my life. My mind went to a dark, self-destructive place, and it felt out of my control.

Gently and slowly, my husband was able to coax me back to bed after the bathroom crying fit, holding me in my inconsolable state of mind until I finally passed out. When I woke up the next day, I still felt frightened and more than a little ashamed from my loss of control. This was a side of me my new husband had not seen before; I wasn't sure how he would react. But he met this crazed woman with a gentleness and understanding exactly as I needed. He didn't judge me for it and I began asking myself, who is this man? How could it be that I married someone who would actually get this? Someone who was such a good fit for me, in good times or bad. I started to think more clearly and rationally. I thanked God for my good fortune.

This is sometimes the thing that can bring people with PTSD back to the now. The experience of today. The reality of the lives we have here and now. That is critical with those of us who are haunted with this issue, and believe me, it feels like a haunting when I am in the middle of a PTSD episode. Thankfully, it happens a lot less frequently than it did back in the day.

If working on the musical and trying to finish this memoir were not enough, I was also starting the process that goes into putting out my next CD. It felt like mad pressure, but I was getting through it with a lot of help from some kind and loving souls.

You know how your eyes hurt when you've been in the dark and the lights suddenly go on? It's too bright, but you still have to look. That's how I felt as work on the musical and book reached critical mass. My eyes were open as wide as they could be, and it began to hit me yet again that I'd endured a lot to get to this point in my life. I scratched my head over how I came through it all and somehow landed on my feet. It would probably be easier to just go with the flow and stop all the self-questioning, but I am always looking for a better understanding of things. I am still looking, I suppose, for an explanation. How is it that I survived? Not only survived, but I am fully engaged in a beautiful life. How the hell did I get from there to here?

As I said toward the start of this story, I have to tie a lot of it back to my paternal grandfather, that stubborn S.O.B., C.A. Magness. I have not heard anyone who knew him say a kind word about the man. He was consistently described as ornery and mean, his legacy living on through the generations of Magness kin who seemed to always be out of sorts with life and those around them. He made the lives of many of his children and grandchildren miserable. He's doing it still from the grave.

But like so much in life, something else was afoot. There was another story. It came through to me as I worked on the musical and this book.

We know how the light gets in, right? It seeps in through the cracks. All it needs sometimes is a tiny pinhole or fissure and pop. There is suddenly a ray of light that was not there before. Suddenly, you can see, and everything in front of you takes on a different shape. I feel certain now that the reason I had been able to survive all that adversity was because of that precise genetic template of C.A. Magness. His absolute unwillingness—his downright genetic inability—to give up is buried inside me. I tried so many times to give up and quit, but something kept me alive. It has been the sheer arrogance of his bloodline. Once a decision had been made, the power of his DNA took over and forced survival through any and all circumstances. By any means necessary. This makes perfect sense to me. I know the ability to survive is in me and the choices I make. But I owe that motherfucker a debt of gratitude. Ain't it funny how life works out? Sometimes the things you think you hate the most are the same things that can keep you alive.

My dad said many times that the truth will set you free. I never paid much attention to the idea when I was younger, but he was sure right. First you have to find it, then you have to find a way to accept and deal with it. It's never been easy for me, but over time the truth has actually set me free in ways I could not imagine. To me, that is a genuine and sanctified miracle.

Thirty-One - Love Wins

Iunderstand balance. I know it's something to strive for. It can always spell trouble for me to get too far out of whack between work and the rest of life. But balance has never been something I could master. Since you've followed my story up to now, that'll be obvious. I tend to stay over-committed and busier than a person in her right mind should be. But it is one of the things that keeps me sane. I get over-tired. I might get sick because I run until I am worn down. My immune system crashes, and my body eventually does, too. But for my own mental stability, I need to stay busy and keep moving. I don't do well when I'm static or inactive for too long. That's when the KFUK radio in my head switches on loud, and tries to take over. I'm still working on it, but rest and relaxation don't come naturally for me. So what did I do? With everything else going on in my life—being newly married, well into the six-year process that is this memoir, which gave birth to a musical ...I decided, okay, not enough going on. It's time to get into the studio again and work on the new CD. What can I say? I am chronically human, forever a work in progress.

So there I was, with Dave Darling and the band working on a record we titled Love Wins Again. Feels right, don't you think? There is a lot that's different with this project, though. In a good way.

I am now connected with Blue Elan' Records, a relatively new, small label started by a good man who has been a highly successful attorney and a music fan all his life. Kirk Pasich has represented some of the biggest names in rock, pop, jazz and R&B for more than thirty years. He started the label because he wanted to put out music he loved in a way that is more respectful to the artists. Novel concept, right?

He put a contract on the table that I did not want to refuse. It includes a multi-record deal for my own label, Fathead, and I get to maintain the artistic autonomy I often had to fight for elsewhere. Kirk trusts me to come up with work that's faithful to my art and that my fans will enjoy. That level of trust and respect are too rare in the business of music. I was happy to have signed with Blue Elan'. Not only do I retain autonomy with my own label and the power that comes with it, I also have access to a strong support system, and a better budget for recording and publicity. I have more of that with Blue Elan' than I have ever had with any label, and I'm committed to bust my behind to make it work.

This is another huge blessing, but none of it ever gets easy. I suppose it shouldn't be. I call it Artist Tax. I get it, but sometimes when I lay my head down on my pillow at night, I have to confess I dream a little about what it would be like if this artists life were not such a challenge. Working on another release and writing songs once again stretched my brain and soul beyond their limits. Part of me wanted to crawl back into the closet and hide while all this was going on. Back by the long coats where no one could find me. But I just couldn't, there was too much to get done.

For the most part, the songs on Love Wins Again are about joy, love and redemption. Nothing about suicide, killing a man or getting buried out at the crossroads. The universe delivered another big fat yes. But now, with love, redemption and good things abundant, I was about to send new music out into the world with a great record deal. Someone like me could get pretty fucking nervous, right?

My brain did try to go there. I heard myself thinking more than once in the process of making Love Wins Again, "This shit is too happy. Too much fucking happy… you're gonna fuck this one up big time, Magness." But more than just the song lyrics were different this time around. For whatever reason, I was able to laugh at myself about it. It didn't stop me or lead me down the rabbit hole. It didn't make me feel the urge to blow everything up and go into a tailspin. I found time to meditate, I felt the love and joy in my life, and I answered back. Clearing my throat and taking a breath, I said out loud: "Okay, Janiva. Or whoever you are. Thanks so much for sharing. Now, I have to ask you to leave me the fuck alone because I have work to do."

That's often the trick for me these days. To act as if. Stay busy. Whistle in the dark. Show up for work. Even if I look like shit, dressed in sweats with my face swollen like a goldfish from the tears, I show up. I show up for work. More importantly, I show up for life. There's no hiding in the closet anymore or behind the bed. I find a way to pause multiple times every day to remain thankful and keep saying yes to the grace I am given. Now I actually can tell the dark voices in my head to shut up. Get lost, I'm too busy to go there. There isn't time because, like I said, I've got work to do.

Postscript
Walkin' In the Sun

I was always a lonely kid. I turned into a lonely adolescent, a deeply troubled teenager and an angry young woman with a lot of justifiable demons. I know I held onto those feelings longer than I should have, maybe. But they were familiar to me. And in hindsight, I realize that they gave shape to my life. I could cling to them and know somehow that I was alive. Just like an old friend who was a bad influence, I recognized them and somehow took comfort in their familiarity.

Violence, bullying, incest, addiction and alcoholism, rape, clinical depression, parental suicide. Add it all up. By the time I was a 14-year-old run-away, I was in many ways both hypnotized by the past and prisoner to it.

I suppose it would have been a miracle if I was not captive to it. Foster care, three psychiatric hospitalizations, countless suicide attempts of my own beginning at age 4, nine high schools—at least I think it was nine—pregnant and orphaned at 16. One year later giving up a baby for adoption when she'd been on this earth for just four months. My personal downward spiral into a bottle, pills, powder and eventually intravenous drug use. Not the greatest odds to get from there to here.

But somehow, without complete understanding of how, I have come out the other side. I forged a way into a future. Like the old gospel song, How I Got Over, by Clara Ward: My soul looks back and wonders how I got over. I'm here somehow. By the grace of God who I do not understand, I am still here. Those four words ring in my mind, like an old bell in a church tower or the refrain of that powerful song. I. Am. Still. Here.

When I sat down to finish this book finally and write this postscript, my intention was to be current and talk about the life I have today and the incredible experience of looking over my shoulder to see the wake of my journey and all that has transpired while I've been untangling the string. But life just does what life does sometimes and we have no choice but to ride it out.

As I tried to finish this job, my brother, Joe, died in January of 2017. He was 64. A life of opiate addiction finally claimed him. My other brother, Carson, the baby in the family, died eight months later on August 1, 2018. He was 54. Chalk it up to his long addiction to meth. My older brother, Jimmie, was already gone a few years earlier from his own drug overdose. So hard to witness it all, the destruction of the family from within -- untreated mental illness and addiction. It goes on for the Magness family like it goes on for so many stricken families everywhere. You can see it coming at you like a high-speed train with a mad conductor and still can't stop it. For me, that's the definition of true powerlessness.

So, there it is. I've laid it all out in a line as straight as I could. I ask myself "Now what, Magness?" The way I look at it today, I have one healthy choice: to try and accept and love others unconditionally. To try and love them exactly as they are today. Easier said than done of course. But I am trying.

My sister and I are now the last two family members standing, and that's both sad and interesting to me how we came through while our parents and brothers could not.

I know I am in debt in more ways than I can count. To the music, and my fans for sure. A long list of folks who have held my heart in so many ways and have given me countless reasons to stay strong and carry on. And I am indebted to the Magness gene pool, however flawed. It brought down the rest of my family but somehow it gave me an inexplicable source of inner strength that keeps me moving even when I would just rather stop and let the screen go blank. The self-will to move through whatever my demons or life have in store for me. That has as much to do with my survival as it does having actually thrived. Miraculous as it may be, I have found a way to build a life against all odds. A beautiful, blessed and imperfect life that most days I actually want. That's nothing but grace to me.

Gloria Steinem said, *"The final stage of healing is using what happens to you to help other people."*

Yeah, what Gloria said. I want to do the work, let more light in and hope to help someone else in the process.

As it turns out, I have become a singer and songwriter of some note, with 14 albums to my name and #15 in the works. A respected and highly awarded artist and woman in the business of Blues and American roots music, including a 2017 Grammy nomination. I have traveled world-wide to perform music and it has been incredible. I stand as an ambassador and spokeswoman for our most vulnerable and at-risk-youth in Foster Care. I am blessed with a strong and consistent spiritual practice and 28 years of sobriety. I am gratefully well partnered and happily married. I actually have people in my life I trust. It's a short list, but hey, I can see actual names on it. And I often trust and sometimes love myself, which has always been the steepest hill for me to climb. I can even accept that I am a sensitive, loving, soulful, creative, quirky, successful and imperfect human woman and that ain't a bad thing to be.

I ain't braggin'. It is simply a testament to the massive change that has occurred within my heart and mind. There is one definition of a miracle I am particularly fond of: *A surprising and welcome event that is not explicable by natural or scientific laws and is therefore considered to be the work of a divine agency.* Writing this memoir has made me sort of wonder. What the hell, maybe I am a bona fide miracle?!

What's really funny to me is that my life continues to get better in the most strange and remarkable ways. That is my story today. And that's what I call walkin' in the sun!

Love, Janiva

The Debt...

I have tremendous gratitude for my friends, music fans and everyone who supported my music and helped me stand against the tide.

Thank you Gary Delsohn, for the book you pulled through me. This memoir would literally not exist without your patience, compassion, understanding and just plain mad skills as a writer, interpreter and exceptional craftsman. Your contribution made it possible for this memoir to become a reality, and for my story to be articulated in a way that is actually understandable for the reader, instead of a bunch of unbelievable memories in a jumbled blob. And finally, thank you for always respecting my view and my voice, never attempting to portray me as someone I am not.

I have immeasurable gratitude to the following list of people without whom this story - which is my story, would have never been told ...bless your patient and steadfast souls. Thank you for helping me stand in the light... T.J. Norton, Gary Delsohn, Naomi Siegal, Deborah Block, Val Sagrillo, Geri Hockhalter, Carrie Staeheli, Alice & Glenn Culhane, Peggy & Frank Ulasek, Clara Lieberman, Gary Davenport, Dave & Brie Darling, Eric Steiner, Virginia Pryor, Ant Morgan, Dan Navarro, Michael McClune, Beverly Macy, Julie Jenkins, Sara D. Firehorse and of course The Garbage Man.

Weeds Like Us

Chapter 15 – Alive For A Reason
Crossroad – Robert Johnson

Chapter 16 – Bleak City
I Ain't Drunk – Albert Collins

Chapter 17 – City of Angels
Bring It On Home – Sonny Boy
Williamson

Chapter 18 – Tate
You Sound Pretty Good – Janiva Magness

Chapter 19 – God's Time
Fixin' To Die Blues – Bukka White

Chapter 20 – Insurance Scam
Bitter Pill – Janiva Magness

Chapter 21 – Billie's Blues
When You Were My King – Janiva
Magness

Chapter 22 – Crossroads
Make It Rain – Janiva Magness

Chapter 23 – Connection
Trouble In Mind – Richard M. Jones

Chapter 24 – In The Trenches
Sometimes You Got To Gamble –
Janiva Magness

Chapter 25 – Blast From the Past
Hard Times – Ray Charles

Chapter 26 – Detroit
I'll Be Seeing You – Billie Holiday

Chapter 27 – Stronger For It
Everything Gonna Be Alright – Janiva
Magness

Chapter 28 – Fathead
If It Be Your Will – Leonard Cohen

Chapter 29 – Answered Prayer
I Need a Man – Janiva Magness

Chapter 30 – Original the Musical
Standing – Janiva Magness

Chapter 31 – Love Wins
Love Wins Again – Janiva Magness

Discography

Janiva Magness (2019) – *Change In The Weather:*
Janiva Magness Sings John Fogerty
Produced by Dave Darling – Blue Elan / Fathead Records

Janiva Magness (2018) – *Love Is An Army*
Produced by Dave Darling – Blue Elan / Fathead Records

Janiva Magness (2017) – *Blue Again EP*
Produced by Dave Darling – Blue Elan / Fathead Records

Janiva Magness (2016) – *Love Wins Again*
Produced by Dave Darling – Blue Elan / Fathead Records

Janiva Magness (2014) – *Original*
Produced by Dave Darling – Fathead Records

Janiva Magness (2012) – *Stronger for It*
Produced by Dave Darling – Alligator Records

Janiva Magness (2010) – *The Devil is an Angel Too*
Produced by Dave Darling – Alligator Records

Janiva Magness (2008) – *What Love Will Do*
Produced by Dave Darling – Alligator Records

Janiva Magness (2006) – *Do I Move You?*
Produced by Colin Linden, Janiva Magness – Northern Blues Records

Janiva Magness (2004) – *Bury Him at the Crossroads*
Produced by Colin Linden, Janiva Magness – Northern Blues Records

Janiva Magness (2003) – *Use What You Got*
Produced by Janiva Magness – Blues Leaf Records

Janiva Magness Band (2001) – *Blues Ain't Pretty*
Produced by Janiva Magness – Blues Leaf Records

Janiva Magness Band (1999) – *My Bad Luck Soul*
Produced by Janiva Magness – Blues Leaf Records

Janiva Magness & Jeff Turmes (1997) – *It Takes One to Know One*
Produced by Janiva Magness, Jeff Turmes – Fathead Records

Janiva Magness (1991) – *More Than Live*
Produced by Janiva Magness – Tige / Fathead Records

Appears On

Jack Tempchin (2017) – Peaceful Easy Feeling
Produced by Joel Piper – Blue Élan Records

Jeff Turmes (2010) – *Five Horses, Four Riders*
Produced by Jeff Turmes – Fathead Records

John "Juke" Logan (2007) – *The Chill*
Produced by John "Juke" Logan – Sky Ranch Records

Jeff Turmes (2006) – *The Distance You Can Travel*
Produced by Jeff Turmes – Fathead Records

Brian Setzer (2005) – *Dig That Crazy Christmas*
Produced by Dave Darling – Surf Dog Records

Kirk Fletcher (2004) – *Shades of Blue*
Produced by Randy Chortkoff – Crosscut Records

Jeff Turmes (2002) – *Every Day's My Lucky Day*
Produced by Jeff Turmes – Fathead Records

Kid Ramos (2000) – *West Coast House Party*

Produced by Kid Ramos – Evidence Records
R.L. Burnside (2000) – *Wish I Was In Heaven Sittin' Down*
Produced by Andy Kaulkin, Antony Genn, Brad Cook, Bruce Watson, Iki Levy,
John Porter, Matt Johnson – Fat Possum Records

Doug MacLeod (2000) – *Who's Truth, Who's Lies*
Produced by Joe Harley – Audioquest Records

The Blue Hawaiians (1999) – *Savage Night*
Produced by Brad Benedict, Michal Frondelli – Coolsville Records

Kid Ramos (1999) – *Kid Ramos*
Produced by Kid Ramos – Evidence Records

Catfish Hodge (1996) – *Adventures At Catfish Pond*
Produced by Bob "Catfish" Hodge, Ira Ingber, Martin Kibbee, Leib Ostrow – Little People / Sony Records

Kid Ramos (1995) – *Two Hands One Heart*
Produced by Dave Ramos, Jerry Hall, Richard Duran – Black Top Records

The Freewheelers (1995) – *Waitin' For George*
Produced by George Drakoulias – American Records

Neal Casal (1995) – *Fade Away Diamond Time*
Produced by Jim Scott – Zoo / BMG Records

Tommy Wiggins (1980) – *This is Fun, Expensive Fun*
Produced by Tommy Wiggins – Chilidog Records

Made in the USA
Monee, IL
02 December 2019